New South Wales

LITTLE HILLS PRESS

Text: Chris Baker, March 2003

Maps by MAPgraphics © Little Hills Press

Cover Design by Michael Brown
Edited and designed by Michael Brown

Printed in Singapore

New South Wales
Short Stay Guide
ISBN 1 86315 213X

Little Hills Press
Sydney, Australia
www.littlehills.com
lhills@bigpond.net.au
or info@littlehills.com

Little Hills Press is a proud supporter of the See Australia National Tourism Initiative. See Australia is a Federal and State Government and Industry funded initiative launched in November 2000. Its purpose is to ensure Australians rediscover the importance of holidays (in particular Australian holidays) in maintaining a balanced life and to recharge the batteries in order to cope with the pace of life in the 21st century.

See Australia acknowledges and thanks its industry sponsors. Premium sponsors: Accor Asia Pacific (Hotel and Resorts Category), Mastercard International (Preferred Credit Card). Partners: AAA Tourism, Avis, Captain Cook Cruises, Hertz, lastminute.com, Qantas and travel.com.au

Please visit www.seeaustralia.com.au, the portal to all Australian travel and tourism information and product.

The use of See Australia's name and logo in this publication has been authorised by See Australia on the basis that the publisher has acknowledged and agreed to recognise See Australia's sponsors (above) without fee and and that those sponsors will not be disadvantaged commercially by the manner of the use of placement of See Australia's name, style or logo in this publication. See Australia does not expressly or impliedly endorse the products and services featured in this publication nor is it expressly or impliedly responsible for any representation made in this publication. To the extent permitted by the law, See Australia is not liable for any injury, damage or loss arising from the use or unavailability of any services or products featured in this publication or any representation made or not made in this publication.

DISCLAIMER

Whilst all care has been taken by the publisher and authors to ensure that the information is accurate and up to date, the publisher does not take responsibility for the information published herein or the consequences of its use. The recommendations are those of the writing team, and as things get better or worse, with places closing and others opening, some elements in the book may be inaccurate when you arrive. Please inform us of any discrepancies so that we can update subsequent editions.

Contents

Acknowledgements

Thanks

A special thanks to the helpful staff at the following Tourism outlets for assisting with the production of this book:

Ballina Visitor Information, Byron Bay Visitor Information, Coffs Harbour-Tourism Holiday Coast, Eurobodalla Visitor Information, Great Lakes Visitor Centre, Newcastle Tourism, Port Macquarie Visitor Information, Port Stephens Visitor Information, Sapphire Coast Tourism, Shoalhaven Visitor Information, Wagga Wagga Visitor Information Centre,

Maps

Maps supplied courtesy of MapGraphics

Photography

We are very grateful to Tourism New South Wales for allowing us access to their libray of excellent photographs.

Photographs courtesy of Tourism New South Wales on pages, 5, 6, 7, 9, 19, 21, 23, 24, 25, 26, 27, 29, 31, 33, 35, 36, 43, 45, 47, 51, 52-53,55, 59, 65, 67, 69, 71, 73, 75, 77, 79, 81, 84, 85, 88, 89, 91, 93, 95, 97, 101, 103, 107, 109, 113, 115, 119, 123, 124, 125, 129, 131, 132, 136, 137, 139, 143, 145, 147, 150, 151, 155, 158, 163, 164, 165, 167, 169, 171, 173, 175, 176, 177, 181, 183, 187, 190, 191, 193, 197, 199, 201, 205, 207, 209, 212, 215, 218, and 224.

Photographs courtesy of Little Hills Press on pages, 17, 22, 39, 57, 63, 154, 200.

Photographs courtesy of Leonardo on pages, 13, 14, 15.

How to Use This Book

Symbols

Throughout the text you will find that symbols have been used to denote the information that follows, whether it be an admission price, opening time, phone number or web address. This will aid you in locating the specific details you desire more quickly.

Here is a list of the symbols used with an explanation of each:

- indicates a phone number
- indicates a price
- indicates opening times
- indicates a web site
- indicates an email address

Goods and Services Tax

The prices quoted in this book include Australia's 10% GST. It should also be kept in mind that many products are exempt from the tax, including basic food items.

Accommodation and Eating Out

The Accommodation and Eating Out sections contain by no means an exhaustive list of what Australia has to offer. We have tried to cater for a range of tastes and provide suggestions for your selection. They are designed to give you a basis for comparison and to act at the very least as a starting point for the planning of your holiday. All budgets from lavish to limited have been considered and included.

With regard to eating out, remember that there are always cheaper meals available at fast food outlets and in the food courts of most shopping complexes; we have focused on listing only popular and recommendable restaurants. Again, the GST is excluded from any prices listed. For ease of reference, these pages have been coloured differently:

Accommodation pages are yellow and

Eating Out pages are purple

Layout

The chapters of this book are laid out by region, with the major population centres listed first. Information on chosen locations can be accessed easily, regardless of which direction you are heading, or what part of Queensland you cover.

From regional characteristics, how to get there, where to stay, and what to see, we have approached in detail every way a visitor might occupy his or her touring time, with the intention of helping to make the most of that limited time. The headings are clear for ease of use, and our comprehensive Index and Appendices will assist you in locating your area of interest.

We hope your stay in New South Wales is both memorable and enjoyable.

Moonan Flat
Upper Bowman
Taree
Manning Point
Barrington
Tinonee
Old Bar
Barrington Tops
1556 m
Gloucester
Lake Glenbawn
Krambach
Faulkland
BARRINGTON TOPS NATIONAL PARK
Stratford
Nabiac
Hallidays Point
Craven
Tuncurry
Forster
Salisbury
Wards River
Coolongolook
Muswellbrook
Lostock
Bandon Grove
Wootton
15km
Lake Liddell
Allynbrook
Stroud Road
151
Blueys Beach
Ravensworth
Gresford
Dungog
Bulahdelah
47
Hwy
Myall Lake
Booral
Jerrys Plains
Wallarobba
MYALL LAKES NATIONAL PARK
Singleton
Hunter
Hwy
Thorley
Paterson
Karuah
43
Greta
Grahamstown Res
Port Stephens
Broke
MAITLAND
Nelson Bay
20
Raymond Terrace
28
Cessnock
Bellbird
Kurri Kurri
Paxton
NEWCASTLE
NORTH
Pacific
Rathmines
YENGO
PARK
85
Wangi
0
25
50 km
Swansea
Lake Macquarie
Mannering Park
Gwandalan
Budgewoi
Toukley
Wyong
Noraville
Wisemans Ferry
The Entrance
Tuggerah Lake
Bateau Bay
Long Jetty
Gosford
Terrigal
Hawkesbury
Avoca Beach
Woy Woy
Broken Bay
Kuring-Gai Chase NP
Berowra
88
Terrey Hills
SYDNEY
Botany Bay
Colo Heights
Wisemans Ferry
Gosford
Terrigal
Hawkesbury
Woy Woy
Avoca Beach
Bilpin
Patonga
North Richmond
Wilberforce
Broken Bay
Mount Victoria
Richmond
Nepean
Blackheath
Windsor
Berowra
Galston
Terrey Hills
Katoomba
Springwood
Riverstone
Leura
Glenbrook
Emu Plains
78
Western
Parramatta
BLUE MOUNTAINS NATIONAL PARK
Mulgoa
Prospect Reservoir
23
Port Jackson
Hwy
SYDNEY
Warragamba
Bringelly
Lake Burragorang
Narellan
Liverpool
Botany Bay
Camden
The Oaks
Campbelltown
Port Hacking

Sydney

Population over 3,900,000
Sydney is the capital city of the State of New South Wales, the birthplace of the Nation of Australia, and the largest city in the country.

It is located on the south-east coast of Australia, latitude 33' 53" south, longitude 151' 13" east, on the shores of Sydney Harbour, arguably the most beautiful harbour in the world. It is always busy with ferries, hydrofoils, charter cruisers and pleasure craft. Circular Quay, between the Harbour Bridge and the Opera House, is the ferry terminal, known locally simply as 'The Quay'. The area is always crowded with people arriving or departing on ferries, a variety of buskers, and culture buffs strolling towards the Opera House.

Australia's oldest city, Sydney began as a penal settlement clustered around what is now Circular Quay. The present city sprawls about 55km east-west from the Pacific Coast to the Great Dividing Range, and roughly 70km north-south.

The distance along the actual coastline, allowing for all the bays, is 350km, and in fact there are so many bays and beaches that even Sydneysiders who have lived here all their lives don't know every one by name, and probably haven't visited more than half of them. The ocean beaches have beautiful white sand and rolling surf.

Life in this cosmopolitan city is geared to outdoor activities, taking advantage of the long hours of sunshine and the moderate climate.

Climate

Sydney has a temperate climate, and the average temperatures are: January max 26C - min 19C; July max 17C - min 8C.
The Seasons are:

Summer - December through February
Autumn - March through May
Winter - June through August

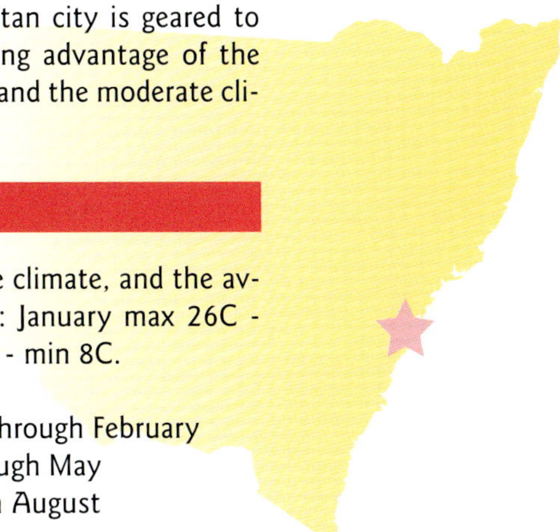

Sydney

Spring - September through November.

The average annual rainfall is 1216mm, with the heaviest falls in the period from February to July. Sydney does not experience snow and only rarely sleet, and quite often the temperature on a winter's day is higher than that of London or San Francisco in the middle of their summers.

Lightweight clothing is necessary for the summer months, and medium to heavy for the winter months. A raincoat, or at least an umbrella, should be included in your suitcase whatever the season.

How to Get There

By Air

Airlines in Australia

Sydney is the major gateway to Australia from overseas, and all overseas airlines servicing Australia fly into Kingsford-Smith International Airport.

Qantas, ✆13 13 13, is the major internal Australian airline, and there are a number of smaller ones servicing the country towns and some interstate destinations, such as Kendell Airlines and Hazelton, to name a few. Virgin Blue, ✆13 6789, are the latest carriers flying to major centres.

Airport Facilities

Kingsford-Smith is situated in the suburb of Mascot, 10km from the city centre. The Domestic Terminals are 3km to the east, and taxis and express buses connect them with the International Terminal. The large green and gold Airport Express bus runs every 10 minutes, 7 days a week and costs ✪$3 adults, $1.50 children and $7 for families.

The Airport Express also operate services between the Airport and City (route 300), Kings Cross (route 350), and Darling Harbour & Glebe (route 352), from all passenger terminals to Central Railway and return.

Bus Route 300 travels between the Airport and Circular Quay, stopping at specially-identified places along George Street, and in Eddy Avenue near Central Railway. Bus Route 350 travels between the Airport and Elizabeth Bay, passing through Kings Cross. Buses run every ten minutes to and from Central Railway Station and every twenty minutes to the city and Kings Cross. No reservations are needed. Services run every day between, 6am and 11pm, ✆9667 3221 or ✆9667 0663. Fares are ✪$7 one way, $12 return, $4 for children under 12.

Other Sydney Buses routes that travel via the airport are Route 100 (Dee Why-Airport, every 30 minutes Mon-Fri), Route 305 (Railway Square-Airport, every 30 minutes Mon-Fri) and Route 400 (Bondi Junction-Airport-Burwood, every 20 minutes Mon-Fri, every 30 minutes Sat-Sun).

Taxis are readily available at the airport for transfer to the city, and the fare is at least ✪$25.

CityRail established a link between Sydney Airport and Central Station. It provides an efficient alternative method of transportation to the city. The line comprises four stops, running northwards from the International terminal to the Domestic terminal, then to Mascot and Green Square before joining the City Circle. Travelling southwards it connects with Wolli Creek. A single ticket to Central costs ✪$15 one-way from the domestic terminal and $20 from the international terminal. Trains operate at fifteen minute intervals between the four stations.

Sydney Airport has all the facilities expected of an international airport - money changing, information, hotel bookings, car hire, shops, cafes, bars, restrooms/showers.

International Airline Offices

Following is a selection of airline reservation and flight confirmation telephone numbers.

Qantas - ✆13 1313.
Air New Zealand - ✆13 2476.
Canadian Airlines - ✆1300 655 767.
British Airways - ✆8904 8800.

Cathay Pacific - ✆13 1747.
Singapore Airlines - ✆13 1011.
United Airlines - ✆13 1777.
For further details of airline companies, refer to the *Internet Information* section at the back of the book.

By Bus

Following is a list of some of the bus companies that travel to/from Sydney and other cities and town in Australia. Many also offer day tours and package deals for touring the entire country.

Greyhound Pioneer, McCafferty's - ✆13 2030 (see also *Internet Information*).
AAT Kings - ✆ 9347 2760.
Firefly Express - ✆9211 1644.
Murrays - ✆13 22 59.
This company has an express service to Canberra priced at $35 one-way

By Rail

The State Rail Authority's Countrylink branch, ✆13 22 32, has XPT services between Sydney and Brisbane, Melbourne and Murwillumbah. The XPTs are fast, smooth and comfortable with air-conditioning, aircraft style seats and big panoramic windows.

There are overnight and daylight interstate services from/to Melbourne, frequent services to Canberra, an overnight service from/to Brisbane, and a motorail service from/to Murwillumbah with bus connection to the Gold Coast and Brisbane.

A ***Countrylink East Coast Discovery Pass*** may be a viable option if you plan to make rail your primary means of transport on your east coast holiday. This ticket offers travel one-way with unlimited stop-overs in a six month period from: ✪Brisbane to Cairns ($160); Sydney to Brisbane/Gold Coast ($94); Sydney to Cairns ($248); Melbourne to Sydney ($94); Melbourne to Brisbane/Gold Coast ($176); Melbourne to Cairns ($330). Note that the above rates apply for travel in the opposite direction.

Other extended travel passes are available, see www.countrylink.nsw.gov.au

By Road

From *Melbourne*, via the Hume Highway (867km), via the Princes Highway (1032km).

From *Brisbane*, via the Pacific Highway (975km), or via the New England and Cunningham Highways (1008km).

From *Adelaide*, via Sturt Highway (1427km), or via Princes Highway (1936km).

From *Darwin*, via Tennant Creek, Mt Isa, Toowoomba, then the New England Highway (4262km).

From *Perth*, via Great Eastern Highway, Eyre Highway, Sturt Hwy, Hume Hwy (3128km).

Visitor Information

The ***Travellers Information Service*** at the Airport can make accommodation bookings, and also has a telephone information service that operates seven days a week between 8am and 6pm, 9669 5111.

First stop in Sydney for all visitors should be ***Tourism NSW***, 11-31 York Street, 13 20 77. The office is open Mon-Fri 9am-5pm, and has numerous brochures, maps, etc, and a large and very helpful staff. Pick up copies of all the current city information guides and you will have plenty of reading material, and good tips on what to see and where to go.

The AMP Sydney Tower Visitors Information and Booking Service is located at the top of the tower, 9223 0933. It is open seven days 9.30am-9.30pm (Sat till 11.30pm), and is a minefield of information for those people brave enough to take the lift to the top.

The ***Sydney Convention and Visitors Bureau*** has an information kiosk in Martin Place that is open Mon-Fri 9am- 5pm, 9235 2424.

The ***Sydney Visitor Information Centre***, 106 George Street, The Rocks, is open seven days, 9am-5pm, 9255 1788. The website is www.tourism.nsw.gov.au

There are three recommended websites that will give you additional information about Sydney's highlights, from obscure clubs and pubs to major attractions and current events.

- www.sydneyvisitorcentre.com
- sydney.citysearch.com.au
- sydney.sidewalk.com.au
- www.cityofsydney.nsw.gov.au

Independent Traveller Information

The ***Youth Hostels Association Membership & Travel Centre*** is at 422 Kent Street, 9261 1111.

For information and travel advice, there is a Backpacker Travel Centre in Shop P33, Imperial Arcade, Pitt Street Mall, 9231 3699.

The website for the Youth Hostels Association Australia is www. yha.com.au and their email is yha @nswyha.com.au

Accommodation

ANA Hotel

Sydney has a wide range of accommodation, from luxurious 5-star hotels such as the *ANA* and *Park Hyatt*, to small budget-priced establishments offering the basics. Something to keep in mind though: even if you opt for the lower-priced accommodation, you are still going to pay a significant amount for the quality you receive, as is common in major cities. Caravan parks, for example, are rare, and the closest you will find is in North Ryde, about half-an-hour's drive from the city centre. Simply put, if you wish to stay in the heart of Sydney you are going to have to pay for it - there are very few short-cuts.

If you are after something a little different, *Staying in Sydney* by Sam Lynch provides comprehensive details of those 'tucked-away' establishments in Sydney which offer a unique alternative to mainstream chains and well-known accommodation venues. Rates are listed and assessed by the author so that you have a good idea of the places with facilities, service-levels and an ambience to match their price tag. The information gives a valuable insight into this niche market.

Following is a selection of standard accommodation, with prices including the 10% GST, representing a double room per night, which should be used as a guide only. Establishments are listed initially by rating, and secondly from most expensive to least expensive (in terms of their base rate). Considering that prices increase frequently and without notice, this will at least give you the best foundation for comparison. The telephone area code is 02.

City Accommodation

Hotels

5-Star

Even if you can't afford to stay in the places listed below, they *are* local icons in themselves, so if you find the time, have a quiet drink in the lounge or stroll through the foyer. The cocktail lounge of the *ANA* is recommended in particular for its panoramic views of Sydney from a stunning height; although standard cocktails cost no less than $16.

ANA Harbour Grand Hotel, 176 Cumberland Street, The Rocks, ✆9250 6000. 40 suites, 570 rooms, restaurants, cocktail lounges, heated pool, spa, sauna, gym - ✪$430-680.

Accommodation

Sheraton on the Park

Hotel Inter-Continental

Park Hyatt Sydney, 7 Hickson Road, The Rocks, ✆9241 1234. 36 suites, 158 rooms, licensed restaurants (including the *harbour**kitchen** &bar)*, Club Bar, rooftop heated swimming pool, spa, sauna, gym - ✪$600-5000.

Sir Stamford at Circular Quay, 93 Macquarie Street, ✆9252 4600. 13 suites, 106 rooms, licensed restaurants, cocktail lounge, heated swimming pool, sauna, gym - ✪$515-2000.

Hotel Inter-Continental Sydney, 117 Macquarie Street, ✆9696 9000. 29 suites, 498 rooms, licensed restaurants, cocktail lounges, heated pool, sauna, gym - ✪$460-560.

Sheraton on the Park, 161 Elizabeth Street, ✆9286 6000. 48 suites, 558 rooms, licensed restaurants (*Botanica Brasserie* and *Gekko*), cocktail lounges, indoor heated swimming pool, sauna, gym - ✪$370-450.

Four Points Hotel Sheraton Sydney, 161 Sussex Street, ✆9299 1231. 47 suites, 645 rooms, licensed restaurants, cocktail bars, *Dundee Arms* pub, gym - ✪$315-340.

Quay West Sydney, 98 Gloucester Street, ✆9240 6000. 132 suites, restaurant, heated indoor pool, spa, sauna, gym - ✪$380-1650.

Accommodation

The Observatory Hotel
89-113 Kent Street, ✆9256 2222. 21 suites, 100 rooms, licensed restaurants, cocktail lounges, heated swimming pool, spa, sauna, gym - ✪$420-670.
"The Observatory is as good an example of a complete luxury hotel as can be found in Sydney. Located on the western edge of the Rocks area, the Observatory Hotel caters to every whim and caprice of its guests.
...The basement houses a fully equipped health centre including a pool with the most astonishing reproduction of the night sky. All the constellations are depicted by using optic fibres in its roof.
The Observatory is essentially an opulently luxurious hotel of the first order, every detail of which has been meticulously planned and cared for, without giving any impression of rigidity."

From *Staying in Sydney* by Sam Lynch

4-Star

The establishments below are centrally located and convenient for self-guided walking tours of the city.

All Seasons Premier Menzies Hotel Sydney, 14 Carrington Street, ✆9299 1000. 8 suites, 446 rooms, licensed restaurants, cocktail bars, heated indoor pool, spa, sauna, gym - ✪$200-350.

The Wentworth, 61 Phillip Street, ✆9230 0700. 29 suites, 384 rooms, licensed restaurants, cocktail lounges, gym, heated pool, sauna - ✪$300-720.

Old Sydney Holiday Inn, 55 George Street, The Rocks, ✆9252 0524. 174 rooms, licensed restaurant, cocktail lounge, swimming pool, spa, sauna - ✪$255.

3-Star

The hotels listed below tend not to bear the frills and indulgences of the places mentioned above, but do provide you with good, clean accommodation, the occassional perk, and prices that are perhaps more reasonable for most travellers.

Harbour Rocks Hotel, 34-52 Harrington Street, The Rocks, ✆9251 8944. 54 rooms, 1 unique suite, licensed restaurant, cocktail bar - ✪$220.

Sydney Vista Hotel, 7 York St, ✆9274 1222. 120 units, 8 suites, pool - ✪$160-270.

Hyde Park Inn, 271 Elizabeth Street, ✆9264 6001. 6 suites, 85 units, licensed restaurant (closed Sun), cocktail lounge - ✪$160.

Park Regis Hotel Sydney, cnr Castlereagh & Park Streets, ✆9267 6511. 120 units, 8 suites, swimming pool - ✪$170.

Castlereagh Inn, 169 Castlereagh Street, ✆9284 1000. 2 suites, 83 rooms, licensed restaurants - ✪$145-170.

Lower Rating

The Lord Nelson Brewery Hotel, cnr Kent & Argyle Streets, The Rocks, ✆9251 4044. 9 rooms (no private facilities), licensed restaurant - ✪$120-180 including breakfast.

The Wynyard Hotel, cnr Clarence and Erskine Streets, ✆9299 1330. 14 rooms, restaurant open Mon-Fri - ✪$105.

Accommodation

Sydney

The Mercantile Hotel
25 George Street, ✆9247 3570. 19 rooms, 4 higher-standard rooms, spa bath - ✪$100-130.
"The Mercantile is an Irish theme pub that makes itself the centre of St Patrick's Day celebrations in Sydney and is generally a very popular night spot with tourists and locals alike. Being in the Rocks, the Mercantile is close to every amenity you could want, including shops, restaurants, the harbour, attractions and night life.
...Guests should be aware that the Mercantile's bar and night life and live entertainment all contribute to a delightfully rowdy atmosphere, so those seeking an early night with a book in bed should go elsewhere."
From *Staying in Sydney* by Sam Lynch

Y on the Park
5-11 Wentworth Avenue, ✆9264 2451. 122 rooms - ✪$135.

Serviced Apartments

The places below are recommended for those who wish to opt for the extra space of an apartment-style room, and prefer a sense of self-sufficiency, even though the rooms are serviced in a fashion similar to hotels.

High Rating

Saville 2 Bond Street, cnr George & Bond Streets, ✆9250 9555. 180 units, gym, heated pool, spa - ✪$245-1000.
The Waldorf Apartment Hotel, 57 Liverpool Street, ✆9261 5355. 60 units, swimming pool, spa, sauna - ✪$195-470.
Carrington Sydney City Centre Apartments, 57 York St, ✆9290 1577. 20 units - ✪$220-275.
The York Apartment Hotel, 5 York Street, ✆9210 5000. 134 units, 101 suites, licensed restaurant, heated swimming pool, spa, sauna - ✪$260-400 (suites $380-610).
The Stafford, 75 Harrington Street, The Rocks, ✆9251 6711. 40 units, 21 suites, swimming pool, spa, sauna, gym - ✪$240.
Metro Suites on King, 27-29 King St, ✆9290 9200. 17 units, pool - ✪$160-180.

Lower Rating

The Savoy Apartments, cnr King & Kent Streets, ✆9267 9211. 72 units - ✪$170.
Metro Suites on Sussex, Beehive Tower, 132 Sussex Street, ✆9290 9200. 32 units - ✪$135-185.

Inner-Suburban Accommodation

The suburbs listed here are within a 10km radius of the CBD. Staying in one of these adjacent areas will give you a feel for Sydney different to what you would experience in its centre. The fringe suburbs have their own independent ambience - from beach life to night life - which may appeal to the visitor who has already seen it all and is searching for an alternative.

Bondi Beach (8km east of the city)

High Rating

Swiss-Grand Hotel Bondi Beach, cnr Campbell Parade & Beach Road, ✆9365 5666. 203 suites, licensed restaurant, heated swimming pool, spa, sauna, gym - ✪$230-720.
City Beach Motor Inn, 99 Curlewis Street, ✆9365 3100. 25 units, swimming pool - ✪$140-200.
Bondi Hotel, 178 Campbell Parade, ✆9130 3271. 50 rooms - ✪$95.

Lower Rating

Bondi Beachside Inn, 152 Campbell Parade, ✆9130 5311. 67 units, licensed restaurant - ✪$100-120.
Beach Road Hotel, 71 Beach Road, ✆9130 7247. 22 rooms, restaurant - ✪$90.
The Alice Motel, 30 Fletcher Street, ✆9130 5231. 31 units, swimming pool - ✪$100-120.

Accommodation

Coogee Beach

Coogee (8km east of the city)

High Rating

Crowne Plaza Coogee Beach, 242 Arden Street, ©9315 7600. 207 rooms, licensed restaurant, heated swimming pool, gym, tennis - ✪$200-240.

Coogee Sands Apartments, 161 Dolphin Street, ©9665 8588. 81 units - ✪$155-220.

Coogee Bay Boutique Hotel, 9 Vicar Street, ©9665 0000. 52 rooms - ✪$90-210.

Double Bay (4km east of the city)

High Rating

The Ritz-Carlton, 33 Cross Street, ©9362 4455. 15 suites, 140 rooms, licensed restaurant, swimming pool, gym - ✪$190-3000.

Savoy Double Bay Hotel, 41 Knox Street, ©9326 1411. 4 suites, 39 units - ✪$120-190.

Double Bay Bed & Breakfast, 63 Cross Street, ©9363 4776. 3 rooms - ✪$145-190.

Elizabeth Bay (3km east of the city)

High Rating

Sebel of Sydney, 23 Elizabeth Bay Road, ©9358 3244. 24 suites, 141 rooms, licensed restaurant, cocktail lounge, heated swimming pool, sauna, gym - ✪$280-340.

Gazebo Hotel, 2 Elizabeth Bay Road, ©9358 1999. 11 suites, 395 units, licensed restau-

Accommodation

Sydney

rant, cocktail lounge, heated swimming pool, sauna - ✪$125-255.

Seventeen at Elizabeth Bay Boutique Apartments, 17 Elizabeth Bay Road, ✆9358 8999. 35 units - ✪$180.

Lower Rating

Roslyn Gardens Motor Inn, 4 Roslyn Gardens, ✆9358 1944. 29 units - ✪$75-110.

Kings Cross (2km east of the city)

High Rating

Millenium Hotel Sydney, Top of William Street, ✆9356 1234. 390 rooms, licensed restaurants, swimming pool, gym - ✪$135 including breakfast.

The Crescent on Bayswater, 33 Bayswater Road, ✆9357 7266. 44 suites, 67 units, *Studebaker's Nightclub*, brasserie and bar, swimming pool, fitness centre - ✪$200 including breakfast.

The Crest Hotel, 111 Darlinghurst Road, ✆9358 2755. 226 rooms, licensed restaurant, cocktail bar, swimming pool, spa, sauna, gym - ✪$140 including breakfast.

Kingsview Motel, 30 Darlinghurst Road, ✆9358 5599. 67 units, unlicensed restaurant - ✪$75-110.

Lower Rating

Astoria Private Hotel, 9 Darlinghurst Road, ✆9356 3666. 30 rooms - ✪$95.

Cross Court Tourist Hotel, 203 Brougham Street, ✆9368 1822. 20 rooms, 2 suites - ✪$80.

North Sydney (4km north of the city)

High Rating

Rydges North Sydney, 54 McLaren Street, ✆9922 1311. 46 suites, 166 rooms, licensed restaurant, cocktail bar - ✪$160-200.

North Sydney Harbour View Hotel, 17 Blue Street, ✆9955 0499. 2 suites, 211 units, licensed restaurant, swimming pool - ✪$230.

Potts Point (3km east of the city)

High Rating

The Landmark Parkroyal Hotel, 81 Macleay Street, ✆9368 3000. 10 suites, 470 rooms, licensed restaurant, cocktail lounge, swimming pool - ✪$195.

The Grantham, 1 Grantham street, ✆9357 2377. 38 units, pool - ✪$120-180.

Macleay Serviced Apartments, 28 Macleay Street, ✆9357 7755. 80 apartments, pool - ✪$110-150.

Simpsons of Potts Point

8 Challis Avenue, ✆9356 2199. 14 rooms, ensuites - ✪$190.

The stately home which is now Simpsons was built as the residence of a prominent and wealthy parliamentarian in 1892. The current owners, Peter and Barbara Farris, have meticulously restored the building which gives the impression of being a vast, beautifully decorated home, rather than a small hotel.

The House is elegant without giving an impression of its age ... A comfortably furnished drawing room at the front of the house, and a lovely conservatory at the rear where breakfast is served all help to give it an atmosphere that lovers of history and historic houses will appreciate greatly.

Rooms are generally very spacious and are likewise decorated and furnished beautifully ... All rooms are air-conditioned individually, as well as being equipped with ceiling fans, direct dial phones, mini-bar, and clock radio. Challis Avenue is a relatively quiet street several blocks away from the noise and lights of Kings Cross, and the house itself is drawn well back from the road, ensuring quiet.

Simpsons is located at Potts Point north of Kings Cross station in a street close to the harbourside. Potts Point being elevated well above the level of the harbour, strolling about in the leafy street rewards you with magnificent views of the city and harbour. Potts Point is also home to a good many restaurants, and multitudes of coffee shops."

From *Staying in Sydney* by Sam Lynch

Accommodation

Rushcutters Bay (3km east of the city)

High Rating

The Bayside Hotel, 85 New South Head Road, ✆9327 8511. 99 rooms, licensed restaurant, cocktail lounge - ✪$140-160.

Budget Accommodation

Caravan Parks

These tend to be in the outer suburbs, but are generally good value for money.

The Grand Pines Tourist Park Ramsgate Beach, 289 The Grand Parade, Sans Souci, ✆2529 7329. (No pets allowed), 73 sites, unlicensed restaurant, barbecue - powered sites ✪$25-35 for two, park cabins $60-120 for two, on-site vans $50-60 for two.

Lakeside Caravan Park, Lake Park Road, Narrabeen, ✆9913 7845. (No pets allowed), 368 sites, playground, barbecue - powered sites ✪$20-22 for two, park cabins $70-135.

Lane Cove River Caravan Park, Plassey Road, North Ryde, ✆9888 9133. (No dogs or cats allowed), 216 sites, playground, pool - powered sites ✪$20 for two, park cabins $65-75 for two.

La Mancha Cara-Park, 901 Pacific Highway, Berowra, ✆9456 1766. (No pets allowed), 196 sites, sauna, squash, pool, playground - powered sites ✪$20-22 for two, park cabins $64-69 for two.

YHA Hostels

The following Sydney hostels are listed with prices for a double room per night.

Central Station, 11 Rawson Place (corner Pitt Street), ✆9281 9111 - ✪$35

Glebe Point, 262 Glebe Point Road, ✆9692 8418 - ✪$27.

Collaroy Beach, 4 Collaroy Street, ✆9981 1177 - ✪$26.

Pittwater, via Halls Wharf, Morning Bay via Church Point, (ferry from Church Point), ✆9999 2196 - ✪$21.

Local Transport

Sydney has an efficient public transport system, with buses, ferries and trains covering the city and the suburban areas. For information on all public transport contact the Infoline, ✆131 500, ✪6am-10pm, 7 days.

Sydney

Train

The railway network is the backbone of the Sydney transit system and is operated by State Rail. There are ten routes, each with a different colour code, and all services travel on part of the City Circle underground system.

The main station is ***Central (Railway Square)***. All country trains begin their journey from here. All suburban trains pass through Central and Town Hall stations, and you can change at either to link with the City Circle; to cross the Harbour Bridge; or to board the train for Bondi Junction, passing through Martin Place, Kings Cross and Edgecliff.

Central Station can be entered from Eddy Avenue, Elizabeth Street (best for suburban trains), or from the entrance road that runs off Pitt Street (best for country trains) to the left after crossing Hay Street if you are coming by car.

The stations in the City are:
Town Hall, Wynyard, Circular Quay, St James, Museum and Martin Place. These stations are all part of the underground network. The first five form the City Circle.
Tickets are purchased from a sales window before commencement of a journey, or you can use one of the machines on the city stations.

Bus

Details of the routes and schedules of Sydney Buses can be found by calling the Public Transport Infoline on ✆13 1500 or visiting the website at www.sydneybuses.nsw. gov.au

Sydney Buses services radiate from the city, ferry wharves and railway stations, and connect the Sydney central business district with the suburbs.

Generally speaking, buses from the Eastern Suburbs terminate at either Central Railway or Circular Quay; those from the North-western and Western Suburbs terminate at York Street (near the Queen Victoria Building) or Circular Quay; and North Shore and Northern Suburbs bus routes end at Wynyard Park, near Wynyard Station, or outside the Queen Victoria Building.

Bus no. 888 runs between Wynyard Station, in George Street, and the Art Gallery of New South Wales in east Circular Quay every 10 minutes, Mon-Fri.

The Sydney Explorer Bus

The red Sydney Explorer bus is a great way to get around the city. It travels a 35km (21 miles) circuit to 22 different stops from 9am-5.25pm, beginning at Circular Quay, every day except Christmas Day. You can get on anywhere along the route where there is a distinctive Sydney Explorer bus stop sign. Passengers can get off at any stop, stay as long as they like, then pick up the next bus that arrives. The buses run every 20 minutes, and the fares are $30 adults, $15 children under 16, $75 families.

If you miss the last Explorer bus, don't worry because your ticket is good on any State Transit bus running along the Explorer route until midnight.

1. Sydney Cove (Circular Quay)
2. Sydney Opera House
3. Royal Botanic Gardens/Museum of Sydney
4. State Library/The Mint
5. Mrs Macquarie's Chair
6. Art Gallery of NSW
7. Hard Rock Cafe
8. Kings Cross
9. Macleay Street
10. Elizabeth Bay House
11. Potts Point
12. Woolloomooloo Bay
13. Wynyard Station/Martin Place
14. Queen Victoria Building/Sydney Tower/ Planet Hollywood
15. Australian Museum
16. Central Station
17. Chinatown/Powerhouse Museum
18. Darling Harbour/Maritime Museum
19. Chinese Gardens/Powerhouse Museum
20. Sydney Aquarium

21. Campbell's Cove/Dawes Point
22. The Rocks Visitors Centre

Tickets can be purchased when boarding the bus, or beforehand from the NSW Travel Centre, 11-31 York Street; Australian Pacific Tours, 102 George Street, City; CountryLink Rail Travel Centres; 11 York Street, City; or from a local travel agent.

Bondi & Bay Explorer

Blue and white buses clearly marked Bondi & Bay Explorer operate on a 35km circular route from the city centre through the eastern harbour and bay-side areas.

They run at 30 minute intervals from 9am-4pm every day, departing from Circular Quay. The fares are ✪$30 adults, $15 children under 16, $75 families.

Bondi & Bay buses stop at the following destinations:

1. Circular Quay
2. Kings Cross
3. Top of the Cross
4. Rushcutters Bay
5. Double Bay
6. Rose Bay Ferry
7. Rose Bay Convent
8. Vaucluse Bay
9. Watsons Bay
10. The Gap Park
11. Bondi Beach
12. Bronte Beach
13. Coogee Beach
14. Royal Randwick Racecourse
15. SCG/Football Stadium/Paddington
16. Oxford Street
17. Hyde Park
18. Martin Place

If it suits your itinerary you can purchase twin tickets for both buses: ✪$50 adults, $25 children, $125 families.

Olympic Explorer

This service departs from the Homebush Bay Visitors Centre between 9.20am and 5pm daily, at 10-15 minute intervals. This is the most efficient way to explore the sporting

facilties, with ten stops along the route at which you can disembark, and join a later bus after viewing the attraction at your leisure. A ticket costs ✪$10 for adults and $5 for children, but the higher cost will come from making your way out to the Olympic site to take the tour. If you are in the city, the best choice is to take the RiverCat from Circular Quay and purchase an Olympic RiverCat Ticket for ✪$22 adults and $12 children - included in the price is access to the Olympic Explorer bus service.

Sydney

Ferry

Providing undoubtedly the most scenic way to travel, Sydney's ferries and RiverCats ply the magnificent harbour.

Full information on routes and schedules can be obtained by phoning ✆131 500 or visiting the same site as for Sydney Buses (*see above*).

Ferry services operate daily, 6am-11pm, from Circular Quay up-harbour to Balmain, Long Nose Point, Hunters Hill and Greenwich.

Across-harbour ferries travel to Kirribilli, Neutral Bay, Cremorne, Mosman and Taronga Zoo. Ferries and hydrofoils also service Manly.

The wharves at Circular Quay are well sign-posted to indicate which area they service, but on weekends there are changes, and it is best to check before putting your ticket into the automatic turnstiles. Tickets can be purchased from machines on each wharf, or from the kiosk underneath the Circular Quay Station. This kiosk also sells tickets to harbour cruises run by Sydney Ferries, which leave at 10am daily, 1pm Mon-Fri, Sat-Sun 1.30pm, and 8pm Mon-Sat; and river cruises which leave at 10am daily.

For information on times, connections and fares for all government and private bus, rail and ferry services in Sydney, contact the Infoline on ✆131 500 (daily 6am-10pm) - they can also advise on ***Sydney Discovery Tours*** tickets. Alternatively, visit the website listed above.

SydneyPass

If you are going to be in the city for at least a week, it will pay you to invest in a **SydneyPass**. It costs adults ✪$90 for 3 days, $120 for 5 days and $140 for 7 days. The Pass gives you unlimited use of the Sydney Explorer Bus, Manly ferries, harbour cruises run by Urban Transit, and all jetcat, ferry and bus services. These passes are available from the Travel Centre of NSW and State Transit ticket offices displaying the SydneyPass sign.

Water Taxi

Several companies operate on the harbour, including ***Taxis Afloat***, ✆9955 3222; ***Quay Water Taxis***, ✆9922 4252; and ***Water Taxis***, ✆9755 4660. They will take you from one landing point to any other landing point on the harbour, and also offer scenic cruises.

The Monorail

The monorail system runs anticlockwise and has seven stations - Harbourside (Darling Harbour), Convention Centre, Haymarket, Garden Plaza, World Square (Liverpool Street), Galeries Victoria (Pitt Street, near Park Street) and City Centre (Pitt Street, near Market Street).

It is the best way to get from the city centre to Darling Harbour, and if you are travelling to the city by car you can park in Pyrmont behind the Darling Harbour complex and take the monorail into the city.

The fare for the monorail is ✪$3.50 for everybody 6 and over, whether you travel one stop or the complete circuit. You are not permitted to stay aboard longer than one circuit.

An unlimited travel **Supervoucher Day Pass** can be obtained if you plan to use the monorail several times to make your way around the city (it also contains discount coupons

for nearby attractions). The ticket costs $8 per person (there is no adult/child distinction) and is valid until closing on the same day. The alternative is the **Supervoucher Family Pass**, which costs $24 for 2 adults and 2 children (or 1 adult and 3 children).

The monorail runs 7am-10pm Mon-Thu, Fri-Sat 7am-midnight and 8am-10pm on Sundays, ✆9552 2288 for further details. There is a website at www. metromonorail. com.au

Sydney Light Rail

This tram service begins at Central Station and takes you through Haymarket to Darling Harbour, up to Pyrmont, Star City, Fish Market, Wentworth Park, Glebe, Jubilee Park, Rozelle Bay and finally Lilyfield. It runs 24 hours a day and generally at 10 minute intervals. There are two zones for fares - Zone 1 (Central to Darling Harbour) and Zone 2 (Darling Harbour to Lilyfield). Fares per person are from $2.50 to $4.80. Children are half fare. A ticket for unlimited weekly trips costs $19 per person. This form of transport may prove useful as a quick and relatively cheap alternative for sightseeing. For further information, ✆9660 5288 or visit the web page at www.metro lightrail.com.au

Taxi

Sydney is well served by taxis, and charges are set by the Department of Motor Transport. The main cab companies are:
Taxis Combined Services, ✆8332 8888;
RSL Cabs, ✆13 22 11;
Legion Cabs, ✆13 14 51;
ABC Taxis, ✆13 25 22;
Specially outfitted cabs for people in wheelchairs are available, and must be booked in advance.

Taxis may be hailed in the street, hired at a taxi rank, or arranged over the phone for a pick-up, though there will be an extra fee. This service has vastly improved in recent years.

Taxi ranks in the city include Central Station, Circular Quay, Park Street opposite the Town Hall, and outside all the major hotels.

If you hire a taxi in the city to take you over the bridge, $3 will be added to the bill even though there is no toll for travel south to north. This extra fee is added because the taxi driver has to pay the toll to travel over the bridge when returning to the city, and may not get a fare going back that way. Be aware of this for other destinations whose routes involve toll roads.

If you are travelling to the airport from the northern side of the Harbour Bridge, it is safest to predict a $7 surcharge on your fare to cover all tolls and rates.

Car

Renting a car is relatively cheap if you are travelling in a group, but driving in the city is not really recommended. The one-way streets take a bit of getting used to, and parking is a problem. Street parking is extremely hard to find, and the parking station fees add considerably to the cost of your day out. However, for travelling in the suburbs and outlying areas, a car is definitely the way to go.

See overleaf for car rental companies which operate in Sydney.

Here are a few names of rental companies and their reservation phone numbers:
Avis, ✆13 63 33;
Budget, ✆13 27 27;
Europcar, ✆1300 131 390;
Hertz, ✆13 30 39;
Thrifty, ✆1300 367 227.
International and overseas drivers licences that are in English are accepted, and a deposit, or credit card details, are required before pick-up. Other car rental companies are found in the A-K Yellow Pages Telephone Directory.
The National Roads & Motorists Authority (NRMA) has reciprocal arrangements with overseas and interstate automobile associations. The head office is located at 151 Clarence Street, Sydney. The phone number for enquiries is ✆13 2132, and for road service, ✆13 1111.

Sydney Road Tolls

Both the Harbour Bridge (Bradfield Highway) and the Harbour Tunnel have a toll fee of ✪$3 for southbound cars. It should be mentioned that the Tunnel is not an alternative to the Bridge. It is for traffic heading for the airport and the eastern suburbs, and the Bridge is for traffic to the city and the Western Distributor (which will be extended with a cross-city tunnel over the coming decade).

The recently completed Eastern Distributor has cut travel time from the city to the airport dramatically, and for most tourists the ✪$3.50 toll (northbound) is worth paying to get to the hotel for a warm shower sooner.

If you are travelling out into the suburbs, the Motorways are the M4, (through mid-western Sydney out to Penrith) which costs ✪$2.20 both ways, and the M2 (to the Hills area in north mid-western Sydney) which will cost you ✪$3.30 east to west and ✪$1.70 from Seven Hills to Pennant Hills or $3.30 from Seven Hills right through to Lane Cove.

Eating Out

Sydney has a plethora of restaurants offering every type of cuisine imaginable. The harbour foreshores are liberally sprinkled with eating establishments, for there are not too many experiences that surpass, or for that matter match, a leisurely brunch on a sunny weekend with the harbour and all its craft as a backdrop.

Unfortunately, though, you often have to pay top prices for this indulgence. With so much competition, you would expect that prices would have to be kept to a minimum, but there are apparently enough people to ensure that each restaurant is well-patronised, and indeed bookings are essential when a water view is offered.

Restaurants are classified as **Licensed** or **BYO**.

Licensed means that the establishment has a licence to sell alcohol. **BYO** means 'bring your own' wine, etc, because the restaurant does not have a liquor licence.

Some restaurants, although licensed, allow patrons to supply their own wine (not beer or spirits), which is usually less expensive than paying the mark-up on the wines that the restaurant is legally allowed to add. In this case a **corkage fee** may be added, which will be per bottle or per person, but the end result is usually still less expensive.

Alcohol can be purchased from the bottle department of a hotel, or from one of the many bottle shops that abound in every suburb.

It is reasonable to say that the price of a bottle of wine in one of these shops would be less than half the price of the same wine in a restaurant.

Following is a list of recommended restaurants, rated:

Expensive (main course $23+),
Moderate (main course $15-$23)
Budget (main course under $15).

Not included here are the restaurants in the 5-star hotels, as everyone knows that they exist and are much the same the world over with regard to menus and prices.

Credit card abbreviations are:
Amex = American Express; BC = Bankcard; DC = Diners Club; MC = MasterCard; V = Visa.

One of Sydney's best, and most expensive, restaurants is ***Forty One***, Level 41 Chifley Tower, Chifley Square, ✆9221 2500. The view is magnificent, and complements rather than dominates the food. The cuisine is Modern Australian, and the presentation is first class. It is open for lunch Mon-Fri and for dinner Mon-Sat 6-10.30pm.

The Rockpool

Running a close second, though some might say that it is a dead heat, is ***The Rockpool***, 107 George Street, The Rocks, ✆9252 1888. The cuisine here is also Modern Australian, the presentation is excellent, and the prices are commensurate. Open for lunch Mon-Fri, dinner Mon-Sat.

Both the above are licensed and accept all credit cards.

Sydney

Eating Out

At the other end of the scale is a Sydney landmark that has been around a very long time: ***Harry's Cafe de Wheels***, Cowper Wharf Roadway, Woolloomooloo, ✆9357 3074. It is not a restaurant, not even a cafe, just a roadside stall - but everyone knows *Harry's*. Their delicious real Aussie meat pies, peas and more, are handed to you on a paper serviette. Eating a pie in this fashion requires complex synchronisation of hand and mouth - an ability with which most Sydneysiders are already born, or one they develop with rapid evolution at weekend football matches. So, when in Rome...

The City and The Rocks

Quay, Upper Level, Overseas Passenger Terminal, Circular Quay West, ✆9251 5600. Licensed, good harbour views, French/Australian cuisine, **expensive**, open Sun-Fri noon-3pm and nightly 7pm-10pm, Amex, BC, DC, MC, V.
Doyle's at The Quay, Lower Level, Overseas Passenger Terminal, Circular Quay West, ✆9252 3400. Licensed, good harbour views, outside tables, seafood, **expensive**, open Mon-Sun 11.30am-2.45pm and Mon-Sat 5.30pm-9.30pm, Sun 5.30-9pm, BC, DC, MC, V.
Bennelong, Sydney Opera House, Circular Quay, ✆9250 7548. Licensed, good harbour views, Modern Australian cuisine, **expensive**, open Mon-Sat dinner from 5.30pm-11.30pm, Amex, BC, DC, MC, V.
Rossini Rosticceria, Shop W5, Circular Quay, ✆9247 8026. Licensed, good views, outside tables, Italian, cafeteria style, **budget**, open daily 7pm-10.30am, 11am-4pm, 5-10.30pm, no credit cards accepted.

Eating Out

Sydney

MCA Fish Cafe, Museum of Contemporary Art, Quayside, Circular Quay, ©9241 4253. Licensed, good harbour views, outdoor tables, seafood, **moderate**, open Mon-Fri 12pm-4pm, Sat-Sun 9am-4pm, Amex, BC, MC, V.
Imperial Peking Harbourside, 15 Circular Quay West, The Rocks, ©9247 7073. Licensed, good views, outdoor tables, Chinese cuisine, **moderate**, open daily noon-3pm, Sun-Thurs 6pm-11pm and Fri-Sat 6pm-midnight, Amex, BC, DC, MC, V.
Sailors Thai, 106 George Street, The Rocks, ©9251 2466. Licensed, Thai cuisine, **budget**, open daily noon-2pm and 6pm-10am, Amex, BC, DC, MC, V.
The Summit, Level 47, Australia Square, 264 George Street, City, ©9247 9777. Licensed, revolving restaurant, incredible views of the city its and outreaches, Modern Australian cuisine, **expensive**, open daily 6pm-10pm and Sun-Fri noon-3pm, Amex, BC, DC, MC, V.
Casa Asturiana, 77 Liverpool Street, City, ©9264 1010. Licensed, Mediterranean cuisine, **budget**, open daily from 6pm and Tue-Fri noon-3pm, Amex, DC, MC, V.
Paragon Cafe, 1st Floor, Paragon Hotel, Circular Quay, ©9241 3888. Licensed, Modern cuisine, **moderate**, open Mon-Fri noon-3pm and Mon-Sat 6.30pm-10pm, Amex, BC, MC, V.
Merrony's, 2 Albert Street, Circular Quay, ©9247 9323. Licensed, Australian/French, **moderate**, open Mon-Fri noon-2.30pm, Mon-Sat 5.45-11pm, Amex, BC, DC, MC, V.
Caminetto, 13-17 Playfair Street, The Rocks, ©9247 5787. Licensed, Italian cuisine, **moderate**, open Fri-Sat 10am- midnight and Sun-Thu 10am-10pm, Amex, BC, DC, MC, V.
Phillip's Foote, 101 George Street, The Rocks, ©9241 1485. Licensed (it is actually a pub), cook-your-own steaks, good salad bar, outdoor tables, **budget**, open daily for lunch and dinner, Amex, BC, DC, MC, V.
Restaurant CBD, CBD Hotel, 75 York Street (cnr King Street), ©9299 8911. Licensed, British/Modern Australian, **moderate**, open for lunch and dinner Mon-Fri, Amex, BC, DC, MC, V.
EJ's, 143 Macquarie Street, City (lower ground floor), ©9247 8588. Licensed, cuisine includes a bit of everything from everywhere, **moderate**, open for lunch only Mon-Fri noon-2.30pm, Amex, BC, DC, MC, V.
Capitan Torres, 73 Liverpool Street, City, ©9264 5574. Licensed, Spanish fare, **moderate**, open daily noon-3pm and 6pm-11pm, Amex, BC, DC, MC, V.
Botanic Gardens Restaurant, follow the signs once you are in the Gardens, ©9241 2419. Licensed, good views, casual dining, outdoor tables, **moderate**, open daily noon-2.15pm, Amex, BC, MC, V.
Dendy Bar & Bistro, 19 Martin Place, ©9221 1243. Licensed, extensive menu, **budget**, open 11am-midnight, Amex, BC, MC, V.

Eating Out

Sydney

Zolie's Restaurant, 5 York Street, City, ©9299 3276. European cuisine, **moderate**, open Mon-Fri noon-3pm and nightly 6pm-10pm, Amex, BC, DC, MC, V.

Restaurant Suntory, 529 Kent Street, City, ©9267 2900. Licensed, traditional Japanese cuisine, **expensive**, open Mon-Fri noon-2pm, Mon-Sat 6.30pm-10pm and Sun 6pm-9pm, Amex, BC, DC, MC, V.

Papillon, 71 York Street, City, ©9262 2624. Licensed, French cuisine, **expensive**, open Mon-Fri noon-3pm and Tues-Fri 6pm-9pm, Amex, BC, DC, MC, V.

Don Quixote, 1 Albion Place, City, ©9264 5903. Licensed, Spanish cuisine, **expensive**, open Mon-Fri noon-3pm and Mon-Sat 6pm-11pm, Amex, BC, DC, MC, V.

Kamogawa, Corn Exchange Building, cnr Sussex & Market Streets, City, ©9299 5533. Licensed, Japanese with teppan bar, traditional rooms and conventional dining area, **moderate to expensive** depending on locale, open daily 6.30pm-10am, 6pm-10pm and Mon-Sat noon-3pm, karaoke bar Mon-Fri 8.30pm-1am, Amex, BC, DC, MC, V.

Amar's, 44 Bridge Street, City, ©9247 9930. Licensed, Indian cuisine, **moderate**, open Mon-Fri noon- 2.30pm and 5.30-10.30pm, Amex, BC, DC, MC, V.

Chinatown (Haymarket)

Golden Harbour, 31 Dixon Street, ©9212 5987. Licensed & BYO (corkage fee per bottle), Cantonese, **budget**, open Mon-Fri 10am-4.30pm, 5.30pm-11pm and Sat-Sun 9am-4.30pm, 5.30pm-1am, Amex, BC, DC, MC, V.

House of Guang Zhou, 76 Ultimo Road, ©9281 2205. Licensed, Chinese, **budget**, open Mon-Fri 11.30am-3pm, Sat-Sun noon-3pm and daily 5.30pm-2am, Amex, BC, DC, MC, V.

Golden Century Seafood Restaurant, 393-399 Sussex Street, Haymarket, ©9212 3901. Licensed, popular venue, fresh seafood with Asian influence, **expensive**, open daily noon-4am, Amex, BC, DC, MC, V.

Marigold, Levels 4 & 5, 683-689 George Street, ©9281 3388. Licensed & BYO (corkage fee per person), Cantonese, **moderate**, open daily 10am-3pm and 5.30pm-midnight, Amex, BC, DC, MC, V.

Malaya, 761 George Street, ©9211 0946. Licensed, Malaysian cuisine, **budget**, open daily noon-3pm, Mon-Sat 5-10pm and Sun 5-9pm, Amex, BC, DC, MC, V.

East Sydney

Beppi's, cnr Yurong & Stanley Streets, ©9360 4558. Licensed, Italian cuisine, **expensive**, open Mon-Fri noon-3pm and Mon-Sat 6pm-11.30pm, Amex, BC, DC, MC, V.

Yutaka, 234 Crown Street, ©9361 4804. Licensed & BYO (corkage fee per person), Japanese cuisine, **moderate**, open Mon-Fri noon-2.15pm, Mon-Sat 6-10.45pm and Sun 6-10pm, Amex, BC. MC, V.

Tre Scalini, 174 Liverpool Street, ©9331 4358. Licensed, Italian cuisine, **expensive**, open Mon-Fri noon-2.30pm and Mon-Sat 6-10.30pm, Amex, BC, MC, V.

Ristorante Mario, 38 Yurong Street, ©9331 4945. Licensed, Italian cuisine, **expensive**, open Mon-Fri noon-3pm and Mon-Sat 6.30-11pm, BC, MC, V.

No Name, 2 Chapel Street, Darlinghurst, ©9130 4898. BYO, Italian pasta and minestrone, **budget**, open for lunch and dinner, no credit cards accepted. There are a few No Name restaurants around Sydney, but this is the original and most people think it is still the best.

Cruising Restaurants

Captain Cook Cruises, ©9206 1111, have lunch and dinner options.

The *Luncheon Cruise* departs Circular Quay at 12.30pm, lasts one and a half hours and in-

Eating Out

cludes a Buffet Luncheon featuring Sydney rock oysters, Tasmanian trout, rare roast beef, ham, chicken, fresh salads, fruit platters and Australian cheeses - $49 adult, $29 child.

The *Sunset Dinner Cruise* leaves from Wharf 6 Circular Quay at 5.15pm daily. The cruise offers a 2 course a la carte menu & wine or local beer. The cost is $69 adult, $55 children. Reservations essential.

The John Cadman Dinner cruises every night of the year and departs Wharf 6 Circular Quay at 7.30pm. The a la carte menu is prepared by international chefs, and there is a selection of Australian and imported wines. Cost of the dinner cruise is $97 adults, $55 children, and reservations are essential, ✆9206 6666.

Captain Cook Cruises also offer *Coffee* and *Explorer Cruises*.

Sail Venture Cruises have luncheon and dinner cruises on their Big Cats, with changing menus. The luncheon cruise departs Darling Harbour Aquarium Wharf at 12.15pm (returning at 2.25pm) and Campbells Cove, Circular Quay, at 12.35pm (returning at 2.05pm) - $55 adult, $28 child.

The dinner cruise departs Darling Harbour at 7pm (returning at 10.10pm) and Campbells Cove at 7.30pm (returning at 9.45pm) - $105 adult, $55 children.

For reservations and enquiries, ✆9262 3595.

Matilda Cruises serve lunch on their two-hour harbour cruises, which leave Darling Harbour Aquarium Wharf at 11.30am and 1.30pm, Campbells Cove Circular Quay at 11.45am and 1.45pm, and Taronga Zoo at 12.45pm and 2.45pm. The cruises cost $56 adult, $28 children, and an Aussie BBQ lunch cooked on board. Reservations are necessary, ✆9264 7377.

Bounty Cruises have lunch and dinner cruises aboard the tall ship *Bounty*, and they always guarantee that part of the cruise will be under sail. The cruises leave from Campbells Cove

The Bounty

Wharf, where you can also inspect the *Bounty*, which is a replica of the one that Captain Bligh sailed on and was built for the movie *Mutiny on The Bounty*. The lunch cruise departs every day at 12.30pm, and costs $65 on weekdays and $95 on weekends. The dinner cruise begins at 7pm and costs $99 for adults. Both cruises offer buffet-style meals. For reservations, ✆9247 1789.

Don't think for one moment that the above lists all the restaurants in Sydney. It is little more than the tip of the iceberg. Often you will find restaurants that we have not listed in the same street as the ones included above. Our list gives you somewhere to start and an idea of what is on offer.

On weekends, it is a wise idea to phone ahead and book a table.

In case you are wondering about the availability of a Big Mac, be reassured that there are 14 *McDonald's* in the city. *Pizza Hut* has two city branches; and *KFC* has one in the city and one at Darling Harbour.

Sydney

Entertainment

As mentioned in the Introduction chapter, the Friday edition of *The Sydney Morning Herald* has 'Metro', and the Thursday edition of the *Daily Telegraph* has '7 Days' which list what's on at all of Sydney's night spots.

It would be lengthy and boring to list all the venues in the city and suburbs, so we took a survey amongst a group of Sydney ragers and the following are their favourites.

Night Clubs

City

Harbourside Brasserie, Pier One, Millers Point, ✆9252 3000. It has two cocktail bars and commands sweeping views of Sydney Harbour.

Paragon Hotel, 1 Macquarie Place, ✆9241 3522. Open ⏲Mon-Thu 9.30am-1am, Fri-Sat, 9.30-5am, Sun 12pm-10pm.

Orient Hotel, cnr Argyle & George Streets, ✆9251 1255. Open ⏲7 days 10am-3am (live bands every night of the week). Nightclub and live bands set out over three floors. Plenty of space. Tourist spot, very popular.

Retro Bar, 20 Sussex Street, City, ✆9212 4868. Open ⏲Thursday to Saturday 6pm-5am. Popular for those who wish to re-live the eighties, or are still there.

Riche, Hilton International Hotel, 259 Pitt Street, ✆9266 0610. Open ⏲Wed 9pm-2am, Fri-Sat 9pm-2am.

Bar Luna, Jackson's on George, 176 George Street, ✆9247 9334. Open ⏲Tues-Sun, afternoon or evening until early the following morning (restaurant service ceases 9.30pm). Very popular. The beer flows freely here.

Riva, Sheraton On The Park, 130 Castlereagh Street, City, ✆9286 6666. Open ⏲10pm to late Wednesday to Saturday. Excellent atmosphere for middle-aged crowds.

Darling Harbour/Pyrmont

The Cave, Star City, Pirrama Road, Pyrmont, ✆9566 4755. Open ⏲9.00pm to late (24 hour licence) 7 days a week. If you're tired of losing money in the Casino nearby, this is a good place to go to forget about it - provided you can still afford the cover charge.

Kings Cross

Round Midnight, 2 Roslyn Street, ✆9356 4045. Open ⏲Tue-Thu and Sun 8am-3pm, Fri-Sat 8am-5pm. Popular venue.

Sugareef, 20 Bayswater Road, Kings Cross, ✆9368 0763. Open ⏲9pm to 6am every day. Popular and often crowded.

Darlinghurst

Kinselas, 383 Bourke Street, Darlinghurst, ✆9331 3100. Open ⏲24 hours, 7 days. This building was once Kinsela's Funeral Parlour. You can find better.

The Cauldron, 207 Darlinghurst Road, ✆9331 1523. Open ⏲Tues-Sat 10am-3am. Very popular venue with the smart, well-dressed crowd, bookings advised.

North Shore

Greenwood Hotel, 36 Blue Street, North Sydney, ✆9964 9477. Open ⏲Monday to Saturday 11am to late. A very good club/bar with a nice atmosphere.

Metropole Hotel, 287-305 Military Road, Cremorne, ✆9909 8888. Open ⏲10pm until 5am(ish) Friday/Saturday only. Very upmarket and popular.

Paddington

Fringe Bar, 106 Oxford Street, Paddington, ✆9360 3554. Open ⏲11.30am to midnight Monday to Thursday, 11.30am to 3am Friday to Saturday.

Bars & Bistros

City

Bridie O'Reilly's, corner Kent and Erskine Streets, ✆9279 3133. Open ⏲11am-midnight (Mon-Thurs), 11am-2am (Fri-Sat), 11am-10pm (Sun). Bistro. Light entertainment includes Irish bands.

Bridie O'Reilly's, cnr George and Hay Streets, ✆9212 2111. Open ⏲11am-midnight (Mon-Thurs), 11am-2am (Fri-Sat), 11am-10pm (Sun). Bistro. Light entertainment includes Irish bands.

Horizons Bar, ANA Hotel, 176 Cumberland Street, The Rocks, ✆9250 6000. Open ⏲Mon-Thu noon-1am, Sat noon-2am, Sun noon-midnight. Light lunch noon-2pm.

Customs House, Sydney Renaissance Hotel, 31 Alfred Street, ✆9247 2285. Open ⏲Mon-Fri 11am-10pm (closed weekends). Lunch is served from noon-2pm, there is no dinner service. The bar is at the rear of the hotel and opens onto Macquarie Place Park where, in summer, a crowd of business movers and shakers spend their evenings. In operation since 1846, it has been said that should a bomb explode in this bar on any Friday evening, the Australian Stock Exchange would not open come Monday morning, not to mention the banking, legal and accounting professions.

Woolloomooloo Bay Hotel, 2 Bourke Street, ✆9357 1177. Open ⏲Mon-Sat 10am-11pm, Sun 11pm-9pm, bistro lunch and dinner 12pm-9pm. The Woolloo-mooloo is a great place to spend a Sunday afternoon in summer. The patrons spill onto the pavement outside whilst the band is playing.

Darling Harbour

Craig Brewery Bar & Grill, Festival Market Place, Darling Harbour, ✆9281 3926. Open ⏲Mon-Wed 10am-noon, Thurs-Sat 10am-3am. Dinner - cook your own steaks on the barbecue.

Pumphouse Restaurant & Bar, 17 Little Pier Street, Darling Harbour, ✆8217 4100. Open ⏲Mon-Fri 11am-late, dinner till 9pm, nightclub and live bands. The pumphouse is known for the fabulous boutique beers available on tap.

East of the city

Kings Cross

Bourbon & Beefsteak, 24 Darlinghurst Road, Kings Cross, ✆9358 1144. Open ⏲24 hours, 7 days a week, dinner 7.30-10.30pm The Bourbon and Beefsteak is an institution. Nearly every Sydneysider has visited the Bourbon at least once.

Kings Cross Main Drag

Sydney

Darlinghurst

Burdekin Hotel, 2 Oxford Street, ✆9331 3066. Open ⏲11am-2pm, and 7.30-10.30pm.

Paddington

London Tavern & Restaurant, 85 Underwood Street, ✆9331 6192 (restaurant), 9331 3200. Open ⏲Mon-Thurs 11am-11pm, Fri-Sat 10am-11:15pm. Pool Tables and card machines.

Pubs

City

Lord Nelson Brewery Hotel, 19 Kent Street, ✆9251 4044. Open ⏲7 days 11am-11pm. The Lord Nelson claims to be the oldest continually licensed hotel, and the only pub brewery in Sydney brewing natural ales.

Mercantile Hotel, 25 George Street, The Rocks, ✆9247 3570. Open ⏲Mon-Thurs 10am-midnight, Fri-Sat 10am-1am. The Mercantile is frequented by Irish travellers and is known as the Irish Pub. It has an Irish flavour and St Patrick's Day, March 17 is a big day for the Mercantile. They even serve green beer!

The Hero of Waterloo Hotel, 81 Lower Fort Street, ✆9252 4553. Open ⏲Mon-Sat 10am-11pm, Sun 10am-10pm. Bistro lunches and dinners available seven days. A museum downstairs shows a tunnel which runs down to the harbour. This pub is the oldest continuously trading pub in Sydney. Built in 1843.

Jazz Venues

The Basement, 29 Reiby Place, City, ✆9251 2797. Open ⏲open nightly for dinner, Mon-Fri for lunch. Features modern local and international artists and serves contemporary Australian food. Excellent music and food. Guaranteed to have a good time. For jazz lovers.

Soup Plus, 383 George Street, City, ✆9299 7728. Open ⏲Mon-Thu noon-midnight, Jazz 7:30-midnight; Fri-Sat noon-1am; Jazz 8pm-12.30am.

Strawberry Hills Hotel, 453 Elizabeth Street, Surry Hills, ✆9698 2997. Open ⏲Mon-Thurs 11am-midnight. Fri-Sat 11am-12.30am. Sun noon-10.30pm.

Cinemas

The main cinema area in the city is in George Street, between Park and Liverpool Streets. Here you will find:

Village Cinema City, 545 George Street, ✆9264 6701; ***Hoyts Centre***, 505 George Street, ✆9273 7431; and ***Greater Union***, 525 George Street, ✆9267 8666.

There are also many cinemas in the large suburban shopping areas.

An independent cinema in the city is ***Dendy***, 19 Martin Place, ✆9233 8558 and 261 King Street Newtown, ✆9550 5699.

As a general rule, Tuesday is half-price night at all cinemas, although some offer discounts on other nights.

The Classics

The Sydney Opera House is *the* venue in Sydney for opera, ballet, and performances by the Sydney Symphony Orchestra.

The newly refurbished Sydney Town Hall is also the scene of musical evenings. The 'Metro' has the information on programs, locations and times.

Theatres

Sydney has a vibrant theatre scene, and the local talent compares favourably with the rest of the world.

Then there are the small theatre groups, and local dramatic and musical societies, whose performances are quite professional and you may see a star in the making. For example, **NIDA**, the National Institute of Dramatic Art (where Mel Gibson learnt his craft) presents plays at ***The Parade Theatre*** at 215 Anzac Parade, Kensington, ✆9697 7613, opposite the main entrance to the University of New South Wales. Prices vary according to the production but range from ✪$17 to $20, not much more than you pay to see Mel in a movie.

Half-tix

Speaking of prices, Sydney has a ***Half-tix booth*** in Darling Park, 201 Sussex Street, at the base of the IBM building, and it sells tickets to major venues at half price on the day of the performance.

It is open between 9am and 5pm Monday to Friday, and 10am-3pm Saturday. The phone number for selections and reservations is 9286 3310 and for the head office, 9966 1723. All major credit cards are accepted. They have a website at www.halftix.com.au

Major Theatres

The Sydney Opera House has two theatres - the *Drama Theatre*, which seats 544, and the *Playhouse*, which seats 398. The Box Office is open Mon-Sat 9am-8.30pm, and charge telephone bookings may be made, 9250 7777. There are several eateries at the Opera House itself, or you can choose from those in the area of Circular Quay.

Her Majesty's Theatre, 107 Quay Street, 9212 3411, is close to Central Railway Station and within walking distance of the restaurants of Chinatown.

Capitol Theatre, 13 Campbell Street, Haymarket, 9320 5000 for recorded show information, or 9266 4800 for bookings. The theatre is in Haymarket, near Chinatown.

The Theatre Royal, MLC Centre, King Street, 9231 6111, is in the heart of the city.

The Ensemble Theatre, 78 McDougall Street, Milsons Point, 9224 8444, is situated in the Lower North Shore and has its own restaurant.

The Wharf Theatre, Pier 4, Hickson Road, Millers Point (The Rocks), 9250 1700, also has a restaurant, 9250 1761.

Belvoir Street Theatre, 25 Belvoir Street, Surry Hills, 9699 3444, doesn't have a restaurant, but does have a licensed bar offering light snacks before and after the show.

Seymour Theatre Centre, cnr Cleveland Street & City Road, Chippendale, 9531 7940, has three theatres - the *York*, *Everest* and *Downstairs*, and a very good restaurant, 9692 4138. There is also a coffee and snack bar in the foyer.

The Footbridge Theatre, Sydney University, Parramatta Road, Glebe, 9692 9955 or 9266 4800 (bookings), is actually in the grounds of Sydney University.

Opera Theatre, Sydney Opera House

Small Theatres

Stables Theatre, 10 Nimrod Street, Kings Cross, 9361 3817.

Bay Street Theatre, 75 Bay Street, Glebe, 9692 0977.

New Theatre, 542 King Street, Newtown, 9519 3403.

Pilgrim Theatre, 262 Pitt Street, City, 9261 8981.

Enmore Theatre, 116 Enmore Road, Enmore, 9550 3666.

These small theatres may not have a current presentation when you are in town, and others not mentioned here may have something that you would be interested in seeing. Check 'Metro' for details. More live cinemas are found in the suburbs.

Rock Concerts

The main venue for these is the ***Sydney Entertainment Centre***, near Chinatown, ✆1900 957 333 for recorded information or ✆9320 4200 for enquiries.

The Sydney Entertainment Centre is also used for ice shows, tennis tournaments, boxing matches, etc.

An increasingly popular venue for concerts and other large entertainment events is Olympic park in Homebush. These venues are now used for a variety of events, from big sporting matches, to the annual Royal Easter Show.

Gambling Venues

Star City Casino, 80 Pyrmont Street, Ultimo, ✆9777 9000, is close to Darling Harbour, and can be reached by ferry and bus. There are the usual assortment of blackjack tables, roulette tables, and so on, and hundreds of poker machines where people queue up to lose their money 24 hours a day.

There are plenty of other places to go if you feel like a flutter. Firstly there are the **Clubs** - Leagues Clubs, RSL (Returned Servicemen's League) Clubs, Bowling Clubs, Worker's Clubs, Golf Clubs - which all have poker machines (that seem to offer better odds than those at the Casino), and most have keno.

A lot of people go to the club to get a reasonably priced meal, and enjoy whatever entertainment is on offer.

Every suburb has one or more clubs, but if you are a first-time visitor to Sydney, I suggest that you stick to the suburban League Clubs. They are bigger, brighter, busier, and you can experience a good cross-section of Sydney life. Clubs are listed in the Yellow Pages Telephone Directory under *Clubs - Social and General*.

Although the clubs are there primarily for the use of members, visitors are always made welcome, as long as they are suitably dressed - no thongs, a collar with a shirt, and in the evening, long pants are preferred. Those dress rules are of course for men. Women must be 'decently' attired. Remember to sign the visitor's book in the foyer.

The clubs also have TAB facilities and SKY Channel television. This means that you can study the form guide in the comfort of a well-appointed club with a cold glass of whatever you fancy, place bets on your favourite horses, watch the race live, then collect your winnings (or tear up your ticket). Perhaps it should be mentioned that SKY Channel is only available to TAB agencies and licensed premises.

The Horse-racing venues are:

Randwick Racecourse, Alison Road, Randwick, ✆9663 8400.

Canterbury Racecourse, King Street, Canterbury, ✆9930 4000.

Rosehill Gardens Racecourse, Grand Avenue (off James Ruse Drive), Rosehill, ✆9930 4070.

Warwick Farm Racecourse, Hume Highway, Warwick Farm, ✆9602 6199.

Races are held every Saturday and Wednesday at one of the above courses.

The first race is usually around 12.30, but during January and February the first race starts around 2.30pm. These are called *Twilight Meetings*, as the last race is around 6.30pm. The daily newspapers have details of race times, starters and jockeys, comprehensive form guides, TAB numbers and post positions.

Harness-racing venues are:

Harold Park Paceway, Ross Street, Glebe, ✆9660 3688. Meetings are held on Tuesday and Friday nights, and first race is 7pm.

Bankstown City Paceway, 178 Eldridge Road, Bankstown, ✆9708 4111. Meetings are held on Monday nights, and first race is 7pm.

Fairfield Paceway, Fairfield Showground, ✆9604 4559.

Meetings are not held on a regular basis, so either phone the club or look in the newspapers for forthcoming races.

Greyhound racing is held at ***Wentworth Park***, Wentworth Park Road, Glebe, ✆9660 6232. Meetings are held every Monday and Saturday nights and the first race is 7.30pm.

Shopping

The City

Sydney has a large shopping area in the city, stretching from Park Street in the south to Hunter Street, with shops along George, Pitt, Castlereagh and Elizabeth Streets, which run south-north, and Market, King and Hunter Streets, which run roughly east-west. The section of Pitt Street between Market and King Streets is a pedestrian mall, with many arcades connecting it to both Castlereagh and George Streets. The closest railway stations to the shopping areas are Town Hall, Wynyard, St James and Martin Place.

Shops are normally open Mon-Wed 9am-5.30pm, Thurs 9am-9pm, Fri 9am-6pm, Sat 9am-5pm, Sun 11am-4pm, but this is not a hard and fast rule. Some open earlier and close later, particularly on Sunday, and many suburban supermarkets are open until late at night six days a week, and until around 6pm on Sunday. The shops in the tourist areas are open every day, usually with extended hours.

Souvenirs

If you are only interested in buying souvenirs, such as cuddly koalas and kangaroos, T-shirts, etc, it is probably best to head for the tourist areas, such as The Rocks, Darling Harbour or Circular Quay.

Other 'typically Sydney' souvenirs are found in the range of goods at the Done Art & Design Shops at The Rocks, Darling Harbour, Queen Victoria Building and the departure level of the International Airport.

Buying Opals

If you have your heart set on some opal jewellery, you should grab your passport and airline ticket and head for a duty free store, or a jewellery shop that has a 'Tax Free for Overseas Visitors' sign in the window. In the case of opals, which are mined in Australia and set in jewellery locally, there is no duty, therefore in both establishments you would avoid the 10% GST.

Australia produces more than 90% of the world's opals, and the three main areas where they are found are Lightning Ridge in NSW which produces the Black Opal; Quilpie, where the Queensland Boulder Opal originates; and Coober Pedy in South Australia, which has the White or Milk Opal.

Opals

When buying opals there are a few important terms you should know:

Solid Opal - this is the most valuable, and is good for investment purposes. The more colourful and complete, the greater its value.

Doublet - this is comprised of slices of opal glued together, and is of medium value. It has no investment value.

Triplet - slices of opal covered with quartz, perspex or glass. This is the least expensive with no investment value.

If your pocket can't stretch as far as a solid opal, but you still would like a piece of opal jewellery, remember that anything that is glued can come unstuck, and that condensation can form under perspex or glass. The less expensive types of opal are not suitable for rings, unless you are going to remember to take them off every time you wash your hands.

Department Stores

David Jones

David Jones has two stores in the city - one bounded by Elizabeth, Market and Castlereagh Streets, the other diagonally opposite on the corner of Market and Castlereagh Streets. The Elizabeth Street store is devoted mainly to ladies' wear.

Queen Victoria Building

The Market Street store is known as the men's store, but it also has the Food Hall on the lower ground floor, and both stores have the same phone number: ✆9266 5544.

David Jones stores are ⏲open Mon-Fri 9am-5.30pm (Thurs to 9pm), Sat 9am-4pm, Sun 11am-5pm, and all major credit cards are accepted.

Grace Bros

Situated on the corner of George and Market Streets, Grace Bros is more of a family store and sells literally everything under one roof. It has seven floors of shopping and is ⏲open Mon-Wed 9.30am-6pm, Thurs 9am-9pm, Fri 9.30am-6.00pm, Sat 9am-6pm, Sun 11am-5pm, ✆9238 9111.

Argyle Stores

Sydney's newest department store is situated in The Rocks. For more information see The Rocks section in the *City Sights* chapter.

City Shopping Centres

Town Hall Arcade

Situated underground in the Town Hall Station, there are two arcades of specialty shops. The shorter of the two from the station leads to Bathurst Street, near Kent Street, and the other continues under the Queen Victoria Building to Grace Bros.

The Queen Victoria Building

The QVB was built in 1898 in the Byzantine style, and originally housed the city markets. Bounded by George, Market, York and Druitt Streets, its prosperity was short-lived, and it fell into disrepair. At one stage it was used as part offices and part Municipal Library, and the partitions that succeeded in making the building into a rabbit warren were actually nailed onto the beautiful tiled floors. Both the inside and outside of the building were decidedly tacky, and in 1959 there was much debate about demolishing the entire structure and building another shrine to modern architecture. Fortunately, common sense prevailed and the wreckers were not allowed to move in, but it was not until 1982 that a 99-year lease was granted and over $75 million invested to restore the building to its original state. It even has replicas of the Crown Jewels on the top level.

The Royal Automata Clock 'performs' on the hour between 9am and 9pm daily, and you need to get there early to see the moving Royal Pageant. (It is a good idea to keep a firm grip on your handbag and wallet while waiting in this crowd.)

The QVB is open seven days a week. Apart from the range of boutiques and specialty shops, there are several restaurants and cafes, both in the QVB and in the underground walkway to Grace Bros.

Centrepoint

Known as 'the heart of the city', Centrepoint is located on Pitt Street Mall, beneath Sydney Tower, and connects Grace Bros with David Jones. It has over 170 shops on four levels, including hairdressers, beauticians, leather shops, jewellery and accessory outlets, boutiques, and several coffee shops and takeaways. The lifts for Sydney Tower are found on the elegant Gallery Level of Centrepoint.

The lower ground floor is the Centrepoint Tavern, a good spot for a quick lunch, or a happy-hour drink.

Centrepoint is open daily, but not all the shops are open outside normal shopping hours.

Imperial Arcade

The Imperial runs between the Pitt Street Mall and Castlereagh Street, and has 114 specialty shops on 3 levels. It is also connected to Centrepoint.

Glasshouse on The Mall

Located in the middle of the Pitt Street Mall, the Glasshouse has three floors of shopping, with the usual collection of boutiques.

Skygarden

A very up-market shopping experience, Skygarden has three levels of prestigious shops under a huge crystal dome. The mosaic entrance arch is made of thousands of Venetian glass tiles, and depicts the day and night theme of the complex. The top dining level is nothing to write home about.

Strand Arcade

The Strand opened in 1892 and is an *olde worlde* walk-through with mosaic tiled floor and Victorian architecture. It connects Pitt Street Mall with George Street and is open Mon-Wed and Fri 9am-5.30pm, Thu 9am-9pm, Sat 9am-4pm and Sun 11am-4pm.

Mid City Centre

This centre connects Pitt Street Mall and George Street, and is between the Strand Arcade and Grace Bros, with an entrance from Grace Bros. It has four levels of shopping with over 40 fashion boutiques, more than 50 specialty shops, and first class restaurants and coffee shops.

MLC Centre

The MLC Centre has entrances from Martin Place, Castlereagh Street and King Street, and has fashion boutiques, coffee shops and restaurants, and the Theatre Royal. The outdoor cafes overlooking Martin Place are popular lunchtime places.

Royal Arcade

Located under the Sydney Hilton Hotel, the Royal Arcade is between Market and Park Streets, and connects Pitt and George Streets. It has a range of rather expensive shops, typical of those found in hotel arcades.

Piccadilly Arcade

The Piccadilly is near the Pitt Street Cinema Centre, and connects Pitt and Castlereagh Streets. It also has overhead walkway connections to the Sydney Hilton and Sheraton on the Park Hotels. This is another rather upmarket shopping experience.

At the other end of the shopping district, near Wynyard Station, there are a few more places waiting to be discovered.

Wynyard Arcade

Fairly recently renovated, this arcade is situated inside the station and has specialty shops of its own as well as access to Westpac Plaza and the Hunter Connection.

Chifley Plaza

Situated on Hunter, Elizabeth and Phillip Streets, Chifley Square is home to, among other not-so-well-known names, the local branch of *Tiffany's*.

If after visiting all of the above you are still in a shopping mood, return to the city centre and hop on the monorail for Darling Harbour.

Harbourside, Darling Harbour

After undergoing an extensive renovation upgrade, the Harbourside Festival Marketplace has a new look for its 200 shops from boutiques to souvenirs, sportswear to art, and restaurants, cafes and bars. It is a bazaar for overseas visitors rather than for Sydneysiders, and the refit was no doubt pitched at attracting the Olympic crowds.

Markets

The Rocks Market

Every Saturday and Sunday, at the end of George Street in The Rocks, a sail-like canopy transforms the area into a Portobello Road.

Paddy's Markets

There are two locations:

The original Paddy's is in Haymarket, on the corner of Hay & Thomas Streets, near Chinatown. It is open Fri-Sun 9am-4pm.

The other is on Parramatta Road, Flemington, and it is open Fri 10am-4.30pm and Sun 9am-4.30pm.

There are over 1000 stalls in each location selling fashion garments, footwear, jewellery, household and electrical goods, takeaway foods, fresh fruit and vegetables, poultry, seafood, and heaps and heaps of souvenirs. Paddy's is the biggest market in Australia, and for further information, phone the Hotline - ✆1300 361 589.

Paddington Bazaar

Located at the corner of Oxford and Newcombe Streets, Paddington, in the grounds of the Uniting Church, this bazaar is held on Saturdays 10am-4pm, ✆9331 2646. There are over 250 stalls offering all types of clothing, crafts, jewellery and food.

While you are in Paddington you could visit *Coo-ee Aboriginal Art*, 98 Oxford Street, ✆9332 1544. They have a large display of Aboriginal Art, and are agents for Tiwi Design fabrics.

Balmain Saturday Market

Held in the grounds of St Andrew's Congregational Church, corner Darling Street and Curtis Road, Balmain, every Saturday 8.30am-4pm, ✆0418 765 736 (mobile).

Glebe Markets

These are held in Glebe Public School, cnr Glebe Point Road & Derby Place, on Saturday 9.30am-4.30pm. Many people think this Market has a lot of atmosphere.

City Sights

It is not possible to see the sights of the city of Sydney in one day on a walking tour, even if you are super-fit. Apart from the distance, Sydney is not a flat city, and the hills would slow you down. By taking advantage of **The Sydney Explorer** bus (see *Local Transport*) you could catch a glimpse of everything, but you still wouldn't have time to appreciate what you saw. It is best to allot at least a few days for the city itself before you spread your wings to the outer attractions. So this guide is set out in areas, perhaps you should allow one day per area. Note that all museums are closed on Christmas Day and Good Friday.

The grid references shown below refer to the colour map of Sydney on the following pages.

Circular Quay Area

Sydney Harbour Bridge E11

Affectionately known to Sydneysiders as 'The Coathanger' the Sydney Harbour Bridge dominates the city skyline. It is 503m long, and was completed in 1932 after nine years of construction. It was built from either shore, and when the two halves met they were only 7.6cm (3 inches in the old measurements) out of alignment! The Bridge opened with a piece of drama. The dignitaries were lined up, the Premier, Jack Lang, stepped forward to cut the ribbon, and up rode Captain de Groot on a noble steed. He slashed the ribbon with his sword, and all and sundry stood speechless, at least for a few seconds. The miscreant was apprehended, the ribbon was rejoined, and the ceremony continued.

You can walk over the bridge, and you can climb up the south-east pylon for some of the best harbour views. The pylon is ⏲open daily

10am-5pm and admission is around ✪$2 adult.

A recent enterprise which has proved extremely popular is offered by *BridgeClimb*, 5 Cumberland Street, The Rocks. Included in the three hour package is a safety briefing and a magnificent walk up and across the great steel span. From the top of the bridge, spectacular views of Sydney by day or night are the reward for making it to the top, ✆9252 0077 for tickets, ⏲7am-7pm, 7 days a week.

Sydney Opera House G10

This magnificent performing arts complex is situated on Bennelong Point, which was named by Governor Phillip after an Aboriginal he befriended, taught English, and actually took back to England. This spot is apparently where Bennelong resided in his humpy.

Shrouded in controversy during its construction, Sydney Opera House was finally completed in 1973, and has since become almost the symbol of Australia. Instantly recognisable anywhere because of its unique architecture, this extraordinary building can only really be appreciated when acknowledged as part of its surroundings. The design encapsulates the concept of architecture mimicking its environment: the white sails give the vague impression that the building is a cluster of vessels on the waters of Port Jackson.

The Opera House has four theatres, four restaurants and six bars, and is surrounded by wide walkways. Details of current programs are published in the daily newspapers, and the Box Office is ⏲open Mon-Sat 9am-8.30pm and two hours prior to the start of a Sunday performance. Phone bookings may be made up to seven days prior to the performance, and the booking clerk will advise when payment must be made, or you can use your credit card. Front of House tours are held ⏲daily from 9am-4pm, departing every 30 minutes, and cost ✪$15 adults, $10 concession, ✆9250 7111. There are also tours on some Sundays that take visitors backstage and cost ✪$23 per person with no concessions

Sydney Harbour Bridge

(the tour is unsuitable for children under 12). The availability of the backstage tours depends on whether there are rehearsals in the house. It is best to contact *Guided Tours*, on the Saturday before you would like your tour, on the above number.

Bus no 438 travels down George Street to the concourse. Circular Quay Railway Station is the closest stop for train passengers.

Surely one of the world's greatest marine backdrops, the combination of Sydney's premier icons, the Opera House and the Sydney

SYDNEY

KEY
Information centre
Hospital
Pool
Swimming pool
Railway, underground
Central
Railway station
Major road
Other road
Park
Mall or public space
Ferry route
Monorail line
THE ROCKS
DAWES POINT
MILLERS POINT
BALMAIN EAST
McMAHONS POINT
GOAT ISLAND
PORT JACKSON
DARLING
Farm Cove
Sydney Cove
Walsh Bay
Woolloomooloo Bay
Opera House
Government House
Conservatorium of Music
Royal Botanic Gardens
Observatory Park
Observatory
Circular Quay
Ferry Wharves
Sydney Harbour Bridge
Sydney Harbour Tunnel
Bradfield Highway
Cahill Expressway
Milsons Point
Kirribilli
Blues Point Reserve
Blues Point
Dawes Point
Millers Point
Peacock Point
Darling Street Wharf
Illoura Res
Wynyard
NORTH
0
200
400m

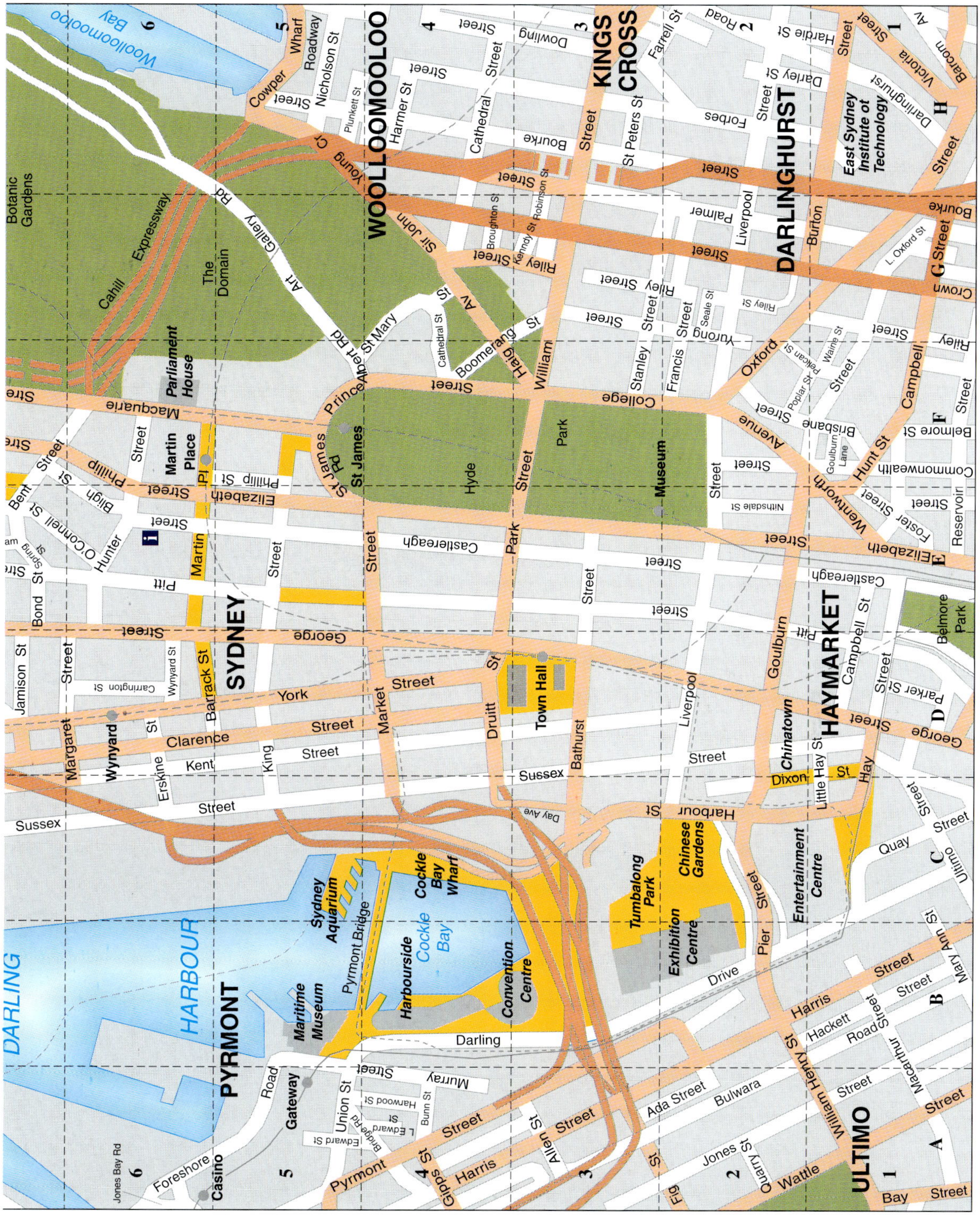
SYDNEY
WOOLLOOMOOLOO
KINGS CROSS
DARLINGHURST
HAYMARKET
ULTIMO
PYRMONT
DARLING HARBOUR
Woolloomooloo Bay
Botanic Gardens
The Domain
Parliament House
Martin Place
St James
Hyde Park
Museum
Town Hall
Chinatown
Chinese Gardens
Tumbalong Park
Exhibition Centre
Entertainment Centre
Convention Centre
Harbourside
Cockle Bay
Cockle Bay Wharf
Sydney Aquarium
Pyrmont Bridge
Maritime Museum
Casino
East Sydney Institute of Technology
Belmore Park
Wynyard
Cahill Expressway
Art Gallery Rd
George Street
Pitt Street
Castlereagh Street
Elizabeth Street
Macquarie Street
Phillip Street
College Street
Oxford Street
William Street
York Street
Clarence Street
Kent Street
Sussex Street
Harris Street
Darling Drive
Bourke Street
Crown Street
Riley Street
Liverpool Street
Park Street
Market Street
Druitt St
Bathurst
Goulburn
Campbell Street
Harbour St
Wentworth Avenue
Foreshore Road
Pyrmont Street
Murray Street
Pier Street
Cowper Wharf Roadway
Victoria Street
Darlinghurst Road
Jones Bay Rd
Wattle Street
Bay Street
Jones St
Fig St
Allen St
Ada Street
Bulwara Road
William Henry St
Macarthur Street
Mary Ann St
Ultimo Road
Quay Street
Hay St
Dixon St
Little Hay St
Day Ave
Gateway
Union St
Harwood St
Bunn St
Edward St
L Edward St
Bridge Rd
Gipps St
Hackett Street
Jamison St
Margaret Street
Carrington St
Wynyard St
Barrack St
Erskine St
King Street
Bond St
Hunter St
Spring St
O'Connell St
Bent St
Bligh St
Phillip St
Prince Albert Rd
St Mary Rd
St James Rd
Boomerang St
Cathedral St
Haig Av
Sir John Young Cr
Harmer St
Plunkett St
Nicholson St
Dowling Street
Cathedral Street
Broughton St
Kennedy St
Robinson St
Stanley Street
Francis Street
Yurong Street
Seale St
Palmer Street
St Peters St
Farrell St
Forbes Street
Burton Street
Hardie St
Barcom Av
Pelican St
Poplar St
Waine St
Brisbane Street
Goulburn Lane
Belmore St
Commonwealth Street
Foster Street
Reservoir Street
Nithsdale St
Hunt St
L. Oxford St
Parker St
Quarry St
A
B
C
D
E
F
G
H
1
2
3
4
5
6

Harbour Bridge, must be appreciated at every angle. The source of Sydney's beauty in a nutshell.

Circular Quay F8

It doesn't seem to matter when you visit the Quay, there are always lots of people around, but it is on weekends and holidays that you have the added colour and noise of all the buskers. From men playing classical pieces on violins, to little kids belting it out on a range of brass instruments, to Aborigines and (non-Aborigines) playing didgeridoos and teaching people to perform kangaroo and emu dances - it's all captivating entertainment.

The Quay is the heart of the Sydney Ferry network. At any given time, at least one of these green-hulled vessels will be visible at the docks, either accepting passengers or waiting for them to disembark. They then make their way slowly to and from the middle harbour on routes that stretch north-east to Manly and west towards Parra-matta River.

It is a real *mezcla* of people milling in anticipation of their ferry; people hurrying to catch their train at the railway station; some buying tickets for harbour cruises; some fishing in the doubtful water near Wharf 5; others, the well-dressed ones, beginning their walk around to the Opera House for a ballet or opera matinee.

A fairly recent and certainly controversial development has been established along the eastern promenade, stretching most of the way to the forefront of the Opera House. It is lined with up-market cafes, restaurants, shops and a movie cinema. The top levels are exclusive apartment residences. This imposing complex has been dubbed 'The Toaster'.

Circular Quay Railway Station, although not underground, is part of the City Circle, and the Cahill Expressway on top of the railway takes traffic from the Bridge to the Eastern Suburbs and Macquarie Street.

Justice & Police Museum F8

This museum, at 9 Phillip Street, ✆9252 1144, is almost directly opposite Wharf 5, and if you look across you will see figures of 'burglars' apparently trying to break into the building on the corner. It is only ⏲open Sunday 10am-5pm, but is worth a visit if you are in the area, and interested in phrenology or medieval-style weaponry. It is now housed in a former police station and court house, and has displays of relics from police investigations and trials, as well as record sheets of some of Sydney's most notorious felons. Admission is ✪$7 adults, $4 children.

Museum of Sydney F7

Situated on the corner of Phillip and Bridge Streets, on the site of First Government House, this modern museum is ⏲open daily 10am-5pm and admission is ✪$7 adults, $4 children, $17 family, ✆9251 5988. It has an excellent cafe and a good bookshop, both of which can be visited without entering the museum. The bookshop specialises in architecture and design titles. There are also exhibits in the forecourt, and in the entrance foyer the foundations of Australia's first Government House are visible. Over the years there has been some controversy about the exhibits on show, and about the quotations of famous people that are on display throughout the galleries.

Museum of Contemporary Art (MCA) E8

The MCA is the Art Deco building on the waterfront around from Wharf 5. It formerly housed the Maritime Services Board. The museum is run as a non-profit company by a joint venture between Sydney University and the NSW Government. The museum's brochure proclaimed:

> *"This is a museum about the beautiful under our noses, the unusual, the weird and wacky in the visual, electronic, sound and tactile world we all live in."*

And that just about sums it up! The museum is ⏲open daily 10am-5pm every day except Christmas. Admission is free. Entrance is from the Quay or from George Street. Volunteer-led guided tours are available for free, and curator-led tours cost $25 a head ad must be

Museum of Contemporary Art (left)

booked two weeks in advance. For details of current exhibitons phone ✆9252 4033 or the Infoline on ✆9241 5892.

Cadman's Cottage E9

Continuing along the waterfront, the cottage is situated in a reserve on the corner of Argyle Street. It is the oldest remaining house in Sydney, and was home to John Cadman, the last Government Coxswain.

The two-storey sandstone cottage was finished in early 1816, and its building was possibly supervised by Francis Greenway, the convict architect, who lived nearby. At that time the house stood two metres from the water, on a small sandy beach, and had a wharf on its northern side. Its present position resulted in the late 1840s when ten acres of land were reclaimed to form Circular Quay.

It is presently an information centre for Sydney Harbour National Park, ✆9247 5033, and has plenty of brochures on walks and trips in Sydney parks and those further afield. It is open seven days a week.

The waterside walk continues around the back of the Overseas Terminal. There is a new upmarket bar and restaurant here over two levels, with great views. Continue on to Campbell's Cove, which has many restaurants in converted storehouses, and the wharf from which the *Bounty* and other cruise ships depart. Nearby is the Park Hyatt Sydney Hotel.

The Rocks E9-E10

The Rocks nestles on the western edge of Circular Quay, the initial point of colonial settlement. Preservation of the area's heritage was the subject of conflict during the 1970s, but eventually common sense prevailed and the region has undergone restoration and improvement to become popular with both locals and tourists. The architecture transports the visitor to a previous era, and even products of modern consumerism attempt to blend in with the nostalgic theme.

The Sydney Visitor Centre E9

Steps beside Cadman's Cottage lead up to George Street, and if you turn right at the top of the steps you will come to the old Sailors' Home which now houses The Rocks Visitor Centre, ✆9255 1788. The Centre is ⏱open daily 9am-5pm, and has a very good video presentation on the first floor, of the growth of Sydney from a small penal colony to a thriving modern city. They carry brochures and maps for tourist attractions all over Sydney.

George Street E9-E10

Continuing along George Street, there are many old historic buildings and pubs, and on the weekends the Bridge end of the street is closed off and The Rocks Markets are held (see *Shopping* section).

In the building on the right hand side of the markets there are some interesting craft displays and shops.

Westpac Museum E9

Retrace your steps along George Street, walk past the Old Sydney Parkroyal Hotel, then turn up Playfair Street. Here at no 6-8 is the Westpac Museum, ✆9763 5670, which traces the history of the bank from its beginnings in 1817 as the Bank of NSW, to the present day of technological banking. There are also temporary exhibitions featuring subjects as diverse as the Royal Flying Doctor Service and Antarctica. The museum is ⏱open Tues-Fri 10.30am-4pm, Sat-Mon 1-4pm and admission is free.

By the way, Playfair Street bends to the left, and straight ahead from the museum is Atherden Place, with four terrace houses. It is the shortest street in Sydney.

The Rocks Square E9

The square is in the middle of Playfair Street (which is closed to traffic) and this area has many outdoor eateries, little shops, jazz or rock bands, and several lanes sprouting in all directions. Following Playfair Street to its end brings you to Argyle Street.

The Rocks Puppet Cottage E8

The cottage is situated in Kendall Lane, and can be reached from George Street through a lane at no 77. It is ⏱open 10am-5pm Wed-Sun, ✆9241 2902. There are hundreds of puppets on display, and shows are held at 11am, 12.30pm, 2pm and 3.30pm on weekends, and other days during school holidays. Admission is free, and the cottage is sponsored by the Sydney Cove Authority.

Susannah Place D8

Situated at 58-64 Gloucester Street, Susannah Place, ✆ 9241 1893, is a terrace of four brick houses that was built in 1844. It is now a museum of the lifestyle in the area from the 1840s until the turn of the century. Included is a shop that stocks the type of goods that would have been available then.

The Rocks Centre E9

The centre is on the corner of Playfair & Argyle Streets and offers two floors of boutiques and eateries.

Argyle Stores E9

The Rocks' newest addition is Argyle Stores, 18-24 Argyle Street, ✆9251 4800, which has around 5000 square metres of upmarket shopping. Modelled along the lines of France's Galleries Lafeyette, the different departments are managed by individual operators, but blend to give the appearance of one entity.

The building was initially completed in 1828 using convict labour, and was the first Customs House in Australia. Over the years it has had several uses, and names, until in 1993 it was completely restored by the Sydney Cove Authority at a cost of around $9 million. In 1994 it was offered for lease as a department store, and back in October 1996 the Argyle opened its doors to customers.

A few doors up Argyle Street is *The Argyle Restaurant*, which is ⏱open daily 11.30am-3pm, 7.30-10.30pm, ✆9247 7782. This is a real Aussie theatre-restaurant, that serves good old fashioned tucker (food) with large helpings of fun and laughter.

Clocktower Square E9

The square is the building on the corner of Argyle and Harrington Streets with the clocktower, and it contains several souvenir shops, a Japanese restaurant, and **The Rocks Opal Mine**, ✆9247 4974.

Millers Point E11

Millers Point is the suburb on the opposite side of the Harbour Bridge (and the Bradfield Highway which crosses it) to The Rocks. It can be reached by following Hickson Road from the Park Hyatt Sydney Hotel around the base of the south-east pylon of the Bridge to Dawes Point; by following George Street to its end, then walking down steps to Hickson Road; or by continuing along Argyle Street and passing under the Bradfield Highway.

Holy Trinity (Garrison) Church D9

The Church is in Argyle Street. It was built in 1848 and is called the Garrison Church because it was compulsory for the soldiers of the 50th Regiment stationed at Dawes Point Battery to attend the morning service. There is a leaflet available for a small purchase fee at the rear of the church which details its complete history.

Argyle Place D9

The little park just up the street, is Sydney's oldest village green.

Sydney Observatory D8

The Observatory is on Watson Road, Observatory Hill, and can be reached by following Argyle Street, then walking up some steep steps. The Observatory, ✆9217 0485, has a regular program of exhibitions, films, talks and night viewings, and a hands-on exhibition. During the day it is open Mon-Fri 2-5pm, Sat-Sun 10am-5pm and admission is free. It is also open nightly, except Wednesday, and has two programs in winter (6.15 and 8.15pm) and one in summer (8.15pm). Bookings are necessary for the night sessions, and charges are $10 adults, $5 children, $25 family.

S.H. Ervin Gallery D8

The Gallery is in the National Trust Centre, almost next door to the Observatory. The building was erected in 1815 as a military hospital, then for many years was home to one of Sydney's leading girls' high schools.

The Gallery has changing exhibitions, and for current programs and entry charges, ✆9258 0173.

The Royal Botanical Gardens & Macquarie Street

The Gardens are a popular lunchtime spot for city workers, and weekends see many family picnics. They are situated on the edge of Farm Cove, where the early colonists first tried to grow vegetables.

As you enter through the gate near the Opera House and climb the slight slope, the astonishing building to your right is **Government House**. It is the state's finest example of sophisticated Gothic Revival and took eight years to build, finally completed in 1845. Although the battlements, turrets and arches present it for all intents and purposes as a castle, defence was not one of the building's intended functions, and it was instead

Sydney Observatory

given over to the administration of colonial affairs. Surrounded by scenic gardens in one of the city's finest corners, it now acts as a pleasant welcoming venue for the Governor's official receptions. It is open to the public Fri-Sun 10am-3pm, 9931 5222. The garden belonging to the House is open every day 10am-4pm.

The building at the end of the driveway leading from Government House is the **Conservatorium of Music**, which was originally the Governor's stables.

Signposts point the way to **Mrs Macquarie's Chair**, a rock outcrop where the Governor's wife apparently sat to watch for ships arriving from England.

The small remote island you can see in the centre of the harbour is **Fort Denison**. For a short time it was regarded notoriously among early convicts as the most inescapable gaol of the colony and the destination of wayward miscreants. The nickname 'Pinchgut' evolved from the starvation men unlucky enough to spend time on the island experienced.

Tours of Fort Denison leave from Wharf 6, Circular Quay, but must be booked in advance, 9247 5033 (NPWS at *Cadman's Cottage*). The tour costs $16 for adults, $10 for children and concession and $40 for families. Back on land, the footpath by the sea wall leads to the Visitors Centre and shop, a kiosk, and a restaurant; and signposts show the way to the herbarium, the pyramid glasshouse and other exhibits. There are two exits near the pyramid, one on to Macquarie Street, the other leads to the Art Gallery. The Royal Botanical Gardens are open daily 8am to sunset, 9231 8125.

Art Gallery of New South Wales G5

The Art Gallery is in Art Gallery Road, in the Botanical Gardens, and faces The Domain. It is a spectacular building, housing a vast contemporary collection of Australian, European and Asian Art, and a fine collection of Aboriginal paintings and artefacts. The names of famous artists are set in stone on the front of the building, upon the tier just below the roof level. Two statues of mounted horseman grace the patches of lawn on either side of the entrance.

Many special exhibitions are held at the Gallery, and for recorded information on current exhibits, 9225 1744 or 9225 1790. Free guided tours of the Gallery are available - check at the information desk on your left as you walk into the gallery through the vestibule. There is no charge for admission to the Gallery and its permanent collection, but a fee is levied for special exhibitions.

There is a restaurant and a coffee shop, and the Gallery is open daily, 10am-5pm.

In this enriching environment, you can immerse yourself in culture and history before relaxing and reflecting among the flora of the Domain across the road or in the Botanical Gardens nearby.

The Domain G5

The Domain is the large grassed area between the Art Gallery and the Public Library. It is a peaceful park setting for soap box orators on Sundays, and the venue for a number of Sydney's free summertime open-air concerts, such as *Opera In The Park* and *Symphony in the Park*.

State Library of New South Wales F6

The original, imposing building of the Library faces Shakespeare Place, on the corner of Macquarie Street. The new section has been built behind, but can also be accessed from Macquarie Street. The hushed ambience of the library envelops you upon entering.

The Library, commonly referred to as the Mitchell Library, contains the nation's finest collection of Australiana and an amazing wealth of historical records. The accumulation of this stored knowledge continues to grow with the obligation under law placed on all publishing houses to supply the library with a copy of each of their publications.

There is a magnificent reading room with wood panneling and tiered shelving, complete with matching stairs and narrow walkways. There is also an excellent Reference Library. The new wing contains the latest technology for reading and learning. The information desk has a self-guided tour sheet with information on every part of the library, and it is worth obtaining.

There is a restaurant and a bookshop, and the Library is open Mon-Fri 9am-9pm, Sat 9am-5pm, Sun 11am-5pm, and admission is of course free, 9230 1414. The Library has changing exhibitions, usually of an historic nature, and information on current programs can be obtained by calling the above number.

Parliament House F6

Situated in Macquarie Street, Parliament House has experienced several additions, removals, renovations and upgrades since its initial construction in 1816. It is a combination of styles - from Georgian to Victorian to contemporary - which have been carefully designed over the years to blend the variety and preserve the pleasant small scale of the building despite necessary expansions.

The House is open to visitors, and they can even attend a session. Parliament generally sits from mid-February to early May, and from mid-September to early December, on Tues, Wed and Thurs. For information on hours, 9230 2111.

The Mint F5

The Mint is further south of Parliament House and next to Sydney Hospital (which was once a wing of Governor Macquarie's Rum Hospital). Built in 1816, it was the 1850s that earned the building its name for it was here that gold sovereigns were coined. Visitors can visit the Mint's former vaults, strike their own souvenir coin, and learn how raw gold was turned into bullion and currency. The Mint is open daily 9am-5pm and admission is free, 9217 0311.

Hyde Park Barracks F5

The Barracks is a Georgian building designed by convict architect Francis Greenway, and was intended for convict accommodation when it was built in 1819. It now houses an impressive collection which shows how the convicts spent their daily lives; where and how they slept, ate and worked. The Barracks also has the Greenway Gallery, which has changing exhibitions of historical and cultural interest. The Barracks Cafe is in the original confinement cell area and has an imaginative menu, but it's a bit on the expensive side.

Art Gallery of NSW

The Historic Houses Trust of New South Wales has control of the Barracks which is in Queens Square, adjacent to The Mint and north-east of Hyde Park itself. The museum opens daily (except Christmas Day and Good Friday) 10am-5pm, ✆9223 8922. Admission is $7 adults, $3 children, $17 family.

Francis Greenway also designed St James' Anglican Church on the other side of the street from the Barracks.

St Mary's Cathedral F4

The Cathedral, on the corner of College Street and St Mary's Road, ✆9220 0400, is a magnificent example of revival Gothic architecture in Hawkesbury sandstone, out-matched in its style only by Government House.

Begun in 1866, after a fire destroyed the previous church, the workmen laid down their tools in 1928, standing back to admire the legacy of a 62-year project. The twin spires over the southern nave were added in early 2000, rectifying the unfinished look the exterior bore for seventy years.

Vaulted ceilings, intricate statues, period-piece gargoyles and crafted side altars make the church interior both beautiful and fascinating.

Perhaps the pinnacle of the labour is the outstanding stained-glass window features, depicting scenes from the life of the Blessed Virgin Mary, and the early days of the Catholic Church in Australia. Under the Cathedral is a crypt where the Catholic Archbishops of Sydney are interred, and there is also an exhibition on the background of the Cathedral and the plans for its future.

The Chapter Hall, commissioned by John Bede Polding, Sydney's first Bishop, is the earliest building on the site. Built in Gothic Revival style between 1843 and 1845, it was to form part of a Benedictine Monastery planned to include the original cathedral. The monastery was never completed.

Another attraction of the Cathedral is its world-famous choir which sings every Sunday at the 10.30am Mass.

Hyde Park F5-F2

Opposite Hyde Park Barracks is Queen's Square with an imposing statue of Queen Victoria, and adjoining that is Hyde Park. Further south into the park is the impressive **Archibald Fountain.** Its fanning peacock-spray captures the attention of people strolling through the northern section of Hyde Park.

Hyde Park is bounded by Queen's Square, College Street, Liverpool Street and Elizabeth Street, with Park Street running through the centre, and changing its name to William Street as it crosses College Street. The western boundary of the park adjoins the hectic commerce-and-trade climate of Market and Elizabeth Streets while St Mary's Cathedral to the east encourages quiet contemplation and prayer.

At the Queen's Square end of the park there are entrances to the underground **St James Station** from Macquarie Street, Elizabeth Street (at the end of Market Street) and Queen's Square. At the Liverpool Street end of the park there are entrances to the underground **Museum Station** from Elizabeth Street (at the end of Bathurst Street) and near the corner of Elizabeth and Liverpool Streets.

The **Anzac War Memorial**, with the tomb of the Unknown Soldier and the Pool of Reflection, is in the southern section. Protruding from its lush surrounds, this enormous monument commemorates those Australians who gave their lives in wars - a significant proportion of the population each time. The poignant carvings on the Memorial pitch solemm order against the rage of battle, evoking a sense of reflection and an awareness of great loss. It is a remarkable feature with outstanding architecture that should be viewed.

The Australian Museum F3

The Museum is at 6 College Street, and is open daily, except Christmas Day, 9.30am-5pm, ✆9230 6000. General admission to the museum is $8 adult, $3 child (5-15), $19 family, but for special temporary exhibitions there may be an extra fee. There is no charge

Archibald Fountain, Hyde Park

after 4pm each day. Phone the above number for all details of current attractions, special programs for children, information on guided tours and any other query you could possibly have.

The Australian Museum is recognised as one of the foremost museums of its type in the world. There is a bookshop and restaurant in the complex.

Parking

It is not really recommended that you take your car to the city if you intend to visit several places. Wherever you find a place to park, you will be walking quite a distance away from it, then have to retrace your steps to retrieve it. There is very limited long term street parking, and although there are parking stations in The Rocks area (behind the Regent Hotel), it could end up costing you more for the car than for your day out.

Another alternative is the council-run **Domain Parking Station**, which is entered from Sir John Young Crescent, east of St Mary's Cathedral. If a car is a necessity, ✆9232 6165 for current opening times and daily charges and flat rates. Take note of the closing time because a fee exceeding $50 will be levied against you if you are forced to call the emergency number on the ticket and to open the station for you to retreive the car.

There is a moving underground footway from the parking station to the intersection of St Mary's Road, Prince Albert Road and College Street, in the front of the Cathedral. Privately-owned parking stations in other parts of the city are more expensive than the Domain.

Sydney

City Centre

Pedestrians flock through city centre thoroughfares for many reasons. Most shop at the many lavish malls, plazas, arcades and complexes. Others hunt for a snack in an elegant food court, a fresh seafood meal by the waterside, or dinner with a view at one of the upper-floor restaurants in the middle of the CBD. Still more stroll on their way to relax with friends over coffee at a promenade cafe. And all enjoy the sights and sunshine of a remarkable city, drawn like moths to a flame.

Though this is principally a shopping area, here are a few sites worth visiting.

Martin Place E6-F6

A traffic thoroughfare until 1973, Martin Place, or Martin Plaza as it is sometimes called, is a wide pedestrian mall that stretches for five blocks from George Street to Macquarie Street. At the George Street end near the GPO is the **Cenotaph**, where a Military Memorial Ceremony takes place on the last Thursday of the month at 12.30pm. On other Thursdays the Army Band plays near the monument. It is near the Cenotaph that Sydney's official Christmas Tree is erected (very tall and impressively decorated, it is disappointingly artificial nevertheless).

Between Pitt and Castlereagh Streets, near the *MLC Centre*, there is a sunken amphitheatre where free lunchtime entertainment is sometimes staged.

The entrance to Martin Place Railway Station is between Phillip and Macquarie Streets.

Sydney Tower E5

Sydney Tower soars over 300m above the city. It is located above the Centrepoint Shopping Complex, bounded by Pitt, Market and Castlereagh Streets. From the Market Street foyer take the lift to the Podium Level, then board one of three double-decker lifts that will take you to the Observation Level (Level 4). Here there are high-powered binoculars, an illuminated display of Sydney Harbour's water traffic, a tourist booking and information service, audio and guided tours.

Level 3 has the highest coffee lounge in Australia; Level 2 has a self-service revolving restaurant; and Level 1 has an a-la-carte up-market restaurant.

The Observation Level is ⏱open daily 9am-10.30pm Sun-Fri and 9.30am-11pm on Saturday. A general tour is available, lasting between 30 and 45 minutes. The 76-floor ascension costs adults ✪$20, children $14, and $55 for a family, ✆9223 0933.

The Queen Victoria Building D4

From the outside it gives a visually comparative insight into Sydney's architecture, which is an eclectic mix of old and new. The ostentatious towers, arches, angelic figureheads and pale green domes of the restored QVB contrast with the streamlined walls and dominant glass of the typical modern skyscrapers occupying the background. Yet somehow the clash pleasantly co-exists.

The QVB is located at 455 George Street, ✆9264 9209. See the Shopping Section.

Sydney Town Hall D3

Situated on the corner of George and Druitt Streets, the Town Hall was built between 1868 and 1889 in French Renaissance style. Its concert hall houses a pipe organ which ranks with the biggest and best in the world.

The steps of Town Hall are often crammed with people catching their breath, snacking on food, making a protest, selling something suspect or busking with limited talent. At night, the building's spires and recesses are aesthetically floodlit.

Centrepoint Touring Company conduct tours of the building when there are no functions taking place, ✆8223 3815 for further information.

Town Hall Railway Station has entrances to the underground on both sides of George Street.

St Andrew's Cathedral D3

The Cathedral has twin towers reminiscent of York Minster, and is the oldest cathedral in Australia. The foundation stone was laid on May 17, 1837 by Governor Bourke. Work

Sydney Town Hall

stopped in 1842 due to lack of funds; a three year drought had caused the colony financial problems. The Cathedral was finally completed in 1868.

Cinema District D3

The next block on George Street, between Bathurst and Liverpool Streets, a large cinema complex jointly run by three different chains, a couple of McDonald's, a Pizza Hut, and other varieties of fast food outlet-. There are also arcade parlours, restaurants and coffee shops. In short, this is a very busy part of the city.

Chinatown D2

Continue down George Street, turn right at Goulburn Street, and the first turn on the left will bring you to Chinatown, which has the usual amount of restaurants, delicatessens and herbalists.

From here it is a short walk to **Paddy's Markets**, the **Entertainment Centre** and the restored **Capitol Theatre**.

Darling Harbour

Darling Harbour is Sydney's newest area, and is nearly half the size of the Sydney Business District at 54ha (133 acres). It was originally a shipping and storage area for the Port of Sydney. Now, Darling Harbour is rapidly becoming the entertainment hub of Sydney. The Conference Centre, Exhibition Centre, Maritime Museum, Aquarium, IMAX Theatre, Chinese Gardens and Sega World can all be found here. A short distance away is the Entertainment Centre, the penultimate venue for concerts. In recent years, the Harbourside Festival Marketplace upgrade and construction of Cockle Bay Wharf has raised the profile of the location further.

On weekends families can be seen strolling along the walkways, picnicing on the grass and having a pleasant time.

There is always something on at Darling Harbour. Every weekend there is a program of entertainment, and almost every yearly festival or show has changed its venue to this central area - the Home Show, the Boat Show, Navy Week, Music Festivals, Book Fairs, Antique Fairs, and the list goes on.

For information on special events when you are in town, phone the Darling Harbour Infoline on, ✆1902 260 568. Alternatively, you can visit the Darling Harbour Information Centre, situated right near the IMAX Theatre, or phone them directly on, ✆9286 0111. Their web site is at www.darlingharbour.com.au

How to Get There

By Monorail, the closest station to the Pitt Street Mall is near the corner of Pitt and Market Streets. There is a stop on both sides of Darling Harbour: Darling Park Station on the city side and Harbourside Station on the other.

The monorail operates 7am-10pm Mon-Thu, Fri-Sat 7am-midnight and 8am-10pm on Sundays (see also under *Local Transport*).

By Light Rail, which runs from Central Station to Darling Harbour, in the middle of the circuit.

By Bus no 456 from Circular Quay via Town Hall to Darling Harbour, Mon-Fri 10am-2.30pm, Sat-Sun 11.30am-5pm, every 30 minutes.

By Sydney Ferries from Wharf 5 at Circular Quay to the Aquarium via Pyrmont Bay (Casino and Maritime Museum).

By Sydney Explorer Bus, which stops at Harbourside and the Chinese Gardens.

By Train, the nearest stations are Town Hall, from where you can walk down Market or Bathurst Streets then across Pyrmont Bridge; and Central Station, from where you can catch Bus 469, or take any bus travelling north along George Street and alight at Chinatown.

Parking

Although several thousand car parking spaces are available on the western side of Darling Harbour - off Quay Street, adjacent to the Sydney Entertainment Centre; off Murray Street behind Harbourside; off Darling Drive under the Sydney Exhibition Centre; and off Sussex Street underneath Darling Park through to Cockle Bay Wharf - it is an expensive operation to park your car for a whole day, so the best advice is to leave the car at home, or at a railway station on the outskirts of the city.

Darling Harbour Super Ticket

Several of the attractions at Darling Harbour have banded together to offer reductions in the form of the Darling Harbour Super Ticket, which can be purchased at any of the information booths at Darling Harbour, the Sydney Aquarium, the Monorail, the Chinese Garden, or at Matilda Cruises. The cost is ✪$45 adults, $30 children under 12, which

Darling Harbour

may sound a bit expensive, but this is what you receive:

A two hour Matilda Harbour Cruise.
Entry to Sydney Aquarium.
Discount entry to IMAX theatre.
Discount entry to the Powerhouse Museum.
A ride on the Monorail.
A visit to the Chinese Gardens.
Lunch at the Shark Bite Restaurant at the Aquarium.

When you add all that, the ticket is definitely worth considering.

Cockle Bay Wharf C4

Located on the city side of Darling Harbour, this is the area's latest development. Modern, innovative and precise architecture is a feature of the construction, complemented by the space-age IMAX Theatre hovering at its southern end. Cockle Bay, behind the wharf, has many cafes, bars and restaurants along its trendy strip. Both a nightclub and a pub can also be found along the promenade, and the restaurants are outstanding. It is definitely a recommended place to dine, and two excellent choices are *Coast*, ✆9267 6700, and *Nick's*, ✆9264 1212.

Sydney Aquarium C5

The Aquarium is located near the city end of Pyrmont Bridge, and is one of the largest and most spectacular in the world. The numerous tanks and tunnels allow the visitor to experience life on the ocean floor, surrounded by hundreds of different species of marine life. There are also displays of river systems, crocodiles, rocky shores, and the Great Barrier Reef. A touch pool allows you to get your hands onto some rough and spiky creatures.

The Aquarium is ⏲open daily 9.30am-9pm, and admission is ✪$22 adult, $10 child, $48 family (2 adults and up to 3 chil-dren), ✆9262 2300. The *Shark Bite Restaurant* has plenty to tempt your taste buds while you are here.

Australian National Maritime Museum B5

The museum, at the western end of Pyrmont Bridge, is dedicated to helping people understand and enjoy Australia's ongoing involvement with the sea. Among the craft moored at the museum are yachts, warships, tugboats, and a refugee boat.

Free guided tours of the Museum building are available at regular intervals throughout the day, and a booking must be made at the Information Counter on arrival. Audio tours are also available from the Information Counter - $3 adults, $5 for 2 adults sharing, $2 children.

The museum has a program of changing exhibitions, and information can be obtained by phoning the recorded information line on, 1900 962 002, or for general information, 9298 3777. There is also a library, a kiosk on the waterfront, and a shop with a wide range of nautical gifts. The museum is open daily 9am-5pm (closes at 6pm in January), and minimum general admission is $10 adult, $6 child, $25 family. There are extra charges for special exhibitions.

Harbourside B4

Harbourside Darling Harbour is a shopping centre with 200 shops that include 54 waterfront restaurants and food places. There are no department stores, and many of the shops sell for the tourist trade although there are branches of fashion outlets that seem to find their way into every shopping centre in Sydney.

Harbourside shops have longer trading hours than in any other complex in the city - Mon-Sat 10am-9pm, Sun 10am-6pm - the restaurants, of course, stay open even longer.

Harris Street Motor Museum A3

The building next to Harbourside is the **Convention Centre**, and for people that are interested in cars, motoring and associated memorabilia, their next stop should be the **Motor World Museum Gallery**, Level 1, 320 Harris Street, a short walk from the Convention Centre Monorail Station, 9552 3375. Here you will find a spectacular array of classic machines from the earliest to the latest, with lots of hands-on exhibits, in an historic old Woolstore building. The museum and carpark cover almost 4ha on two levels. It even has a place where you can 'park' the kids for a while under supervision. *The Cadillac Cafe* is available for roadside snacks, and the bookshop stocks everything ever written about cars, and some out-of-the-ordinary souvenirs. The museum is open Wed-Sun 10am-5pm, and admission is $11 adults, $6 children, family $22, 9552 3375.

The Powerhouse Museum B2

While you are in Harris Street, you continue in the direction away from the water until you arrive at Australia's largest museum, The Powerhouse Museum, on your left. Created from the shell of an old Sydney power station, the museum is alive with dynamic exhibitions, hands-on fun and special performances. There is so much to see that some people spend the whole day wandering through this incredible exhibition. Tours, talks, films, performances, demonstrations and workshops are continually in progress, and there is the *Ken Done Restaurant* (painted by, guess who?) and a kiosk when you need sustenance. As always, there is a souvenir/book shop, but this one offers some unusual merchandise. The Powerhouse Museum is open daily 10am-5pm. Admission is $8 adults, $2 children, under 5 free, $18 family, and the first Saturday of every month is free, 9217 0100.

Back at Darling Harbour proper, the **Exhibition Centre** is the next group of buildings, and information on current shows is available from the Infoline.

In front of the centre is **Tumbalong Park**, and then it is a short walk to the next attraction.

The Chinese Garden C2

The Garden was specially designed by landscape architects from Guangdong Province, and is the largest and most elaborate outside China. It covers a full hectare, and has a two-storey pavilion above a system of lakes and waterfalls. It is a serene retreat from the mayhem of the waterfront.

The Garden is open daily 9.30am-5pm and admission is $4.50 adults, $2 children.

Across Pier Street from the Chinese Garden is the **Sydney Entertainment Centre**. Chinatown is opposite the main entrance to the Centre, in Harbour Street.

From the Chinese Garden walk back towards the waterfront, and you will come to **Darling Walk**, opened in 1997. It covers 20,000 square metres of mainly restaurants, bars, clubs and shops.

Panasonic IMAX Theatre C3

There is no way you could miss this building - it is the strangely-shaped monolith painted with yellow and black squares. The theatre has a 900m^2 movie screen, the largest size in the world, and seating for over 500 people. For programs contact IMAX on 9281 3300. Admission is $17.50 adults, $12.50 children, and $50 for a family pass.

The complex also contains the *Wockpool Noodle Bar*, 9211 9888.

Star City Casino A5

An $867 million testament to the Aussie love affair with luck and misfortune and a mecca for the nocturnal, this enormous complex sprawls over almost three-and-a-half hectares and consists of a five star hotel, an apartment complex, a huge gaming room, the Lyric Theatre, the Showroom, 20 bars and restaurants, shops and a nightclub.

The casino is at 80 Pyrmont Street, Pyrmont, a short stroll from Darling Harbour, and its doors are open 24 hours, 9777 9000.

Sydney Jewish Museum

Over in Darlinghurst to the east, the Sydney Jewish Museum is worth the trip across town. It is the corner of Darlinghurst Road and Burton Street, south of Kings Cross Station, and is open Mon-Thurs 10am-4pm, Fri 10am-2pm, Sun 11am-5pm (closed Saturday and Jewish Holidays). Admission is $7 adult, $5 child, $16 family, 9360 7999.

The Chinese Garden

The exhibits are spread over three floors with six mezzanine levels. The mezzanines contain the permanent exhibition of The Holocaust, and survivor volunteers are present on each level to offer a rare insight into the displays. However, Catholics argue that the role of the Vatican during World War II is inaccurately recounted by the Museum, and that the aid which Pius XII gave to thousands of Jews at the time unfortunately goes unacknowledged.

The museum has a shop with a wide range of souvenirs, and on the lower ground floor the excellent *Cafe Macc* offers traditional European and Israeli cuisine at reasonable prices.

Sydney

Sydney Beaches

Sydney's coastline stretches for approximately 65km, from Palm Beach in the north, to Cronulla in the south.

Most of the ocean beaches are patrolled during the summer months on the weekends and during school holidays. The lifesavers, who know what they are doing, erect flags in the safest part of the beaches, and people are requested to make sure they swim between these flags. If they don't, and get into difficulties, the lifesavers are not going to let them drown, but under reasonable circumstances it should not come to this point.

If the beach is considered unsafe, perhaps because of a strong undertow or a very high tide, the lifesavers will close it and erect a sign warning people not to enter the water. Take notice of such signs and decide to spend the day somewhere else.

Board riders are given their own stretch of beach, so that they don't interfere with swimmers, and swimmers should keep out of designated board areas.

On weekends, Lifesavers in this country are not paid for the hours they spend on duty. They are willing volunteers who give freely of their time to keep our beaches safe.

Harbour beaches are not patrolled. It must not be assumed that the harbour is one giant swimming pool. There are several places where shark-nets have been strung across inlets, and these are the only places where you should venture into the water. You won't see one, but there are sharks in Sydney Harbour. It is generally believed that old sharks, unable to fend for themselves in the open sea, come into the harbour for easy feeding.

There has not been a shark attack in Sydney since 1963, when two children were taken whilst swimming in Middle Harbour.

Ocean Beaches

Listed below are the beaches stretching from Palm Beach in the north to Bundeena in the south, with the closest main road, and the public transport that gives access.

Also included is the following information for each venue:

Dressing Shed - usually will include showers and toilets.

Patrolled - in summer on weekends and during school holidays, ie from the first weekend in October to Easter the following year.

Pool - rock pool suitable for children.

Board - surf is suitable for board riders.

Surfers - surf is suitable for body surfers.

Usually beaches back onto a park or a reserve, and there are clear directions on the major roads indicating the way to the beach. Most beaches tend to have some topless sunbathers during the hottest parts of the day.

North of the Harbour

Palm Beach, off Barrenjoey Road, was once mainly frequented by the wealthy and yuppy set. It has now become very popular with British tourists because it is the setting for the TV series *Home and Away*. Dressing shed, patrolled, surfers and board, pool south end. About one-and-a-half hours drive from the city centre.

Bus no 190 from Wynyard.

Whale Beach, off Barrenjoey Road. Dressing shed, patrolled, surfers, board, pool south end. Bus 190 from Wynyard, Bus 193 from Avalon (infrequent service).

Avalon Beach, off Barrenjoey Road. Dressing shed, patrolled, surfers, board, pool south end. Bus 190 from Wynyard.

Bilgola Beach, off Barrenjoey Road. Dressing shed, patrolled, surfers and board.

Bus 190 from Wynyard.

Newport Beach, off Barrenjoey Road. Dressing shed, patrolled, surfers and board.

Bus 190 from Wynyard.

Bungan Beach, off Barrenjoey Road. Patrolled, board.

Bus 190 from Wynyard.

Manly Beach

Mona Vale Beach, off Barrenjoey Road. Top end not patrolled (Bongin Bongin). Dressing shed, patrolled south end, surfers south end, board north end.
Bus 157 from Manly, Bus 184 from Wynyard (peak hour).

Warriewood Beach, off Pittwater Road. Dressing shed, patrolled surfers and board.
Bus 157 from Manly.

Turimetta Beach, off Pittwater Road. Not patrolled, board.
Buses 155 and 157 from Manly.

Narrabeen Beach, off Pittwater Road. Dressing shed, patrolled, surfers and board.
Buses 182 and 190 from Wynyard, Buses 155 and 157 from Manly.

Collaroy Beach, off Pittwater Road adjoining Narrabeen Beach. Dressing shed, patrolled, surfers and board, pool at southern end.
Buses 182 and 190 from Wynyard. Buses 155 and 157 from Manly.

Collaroy Basin, off Pittwater Road. Surfers, little swell.
Via Collaroy Beach.

Long Reef Beach, off Pittwater Road. Dressing shed, patrolled, surfers and board.
Bus 182 and 190 from Wynyard, Bus 155 and 157 from Manly.

Dee Why Beach, Howard Street, off Pittwater Road, adjoins Long Reef Beach. Dressing shed, patrolled, surfers and board, pool south end.
Bus 178 and 180 from Queen Victoria Building, Bus 190, 182, 184 from Wynyard.

Curl Curl Beach, Oliver Road, off Pittwater Road. Dressing shed, patrolled, surfers and board, pool south end.
Bus 136 from Manly.

Freshwater (Harbord) Beach, Oliver Road, via Pittwater Road. Dressing shed, patrolled, surfers and board, pool north end.
Bus 139 from Manly.

Queenscliff Beach, off Pittwater Road. Dressing shed, patrolled, surfers and board, pool north end.
Bus 136 and 139 from Manly.

North Steyne Beach, off Pittwater Road, adjoins Queenscliff Beach. Dressing shed, patrolled, surfers and board.
See *Manly Beach* for travel information.

Manly Beach, off Pittwater Road, adjoins North Steyne Beach. Dressing shed, patrolled, surfers and board.
Bus 169 from Wynyard or Buses 143 and 144 from Chatswood, ferry from Circular Quay, JetCat from Circular Quay. Peak hour bus services available from Wynyard.

Sydney

Shelly Beach, off Darley Road. Sheltered area with little swell, suitable for swimmers. Between Shelly Beach and Manly Beach there is a pool at Fairy Bower.
Via Manly Beach.

South of the Harbour

Bondi Beach, via Bondi Road off Old South Head Road. Dressing shed, patrolled, surfers and board, sanctioned topless area south end, pool at south end.
Bus 380 and 389 from Circular Quay, 365 from Edgecliff.

An internationally famous beach, **Bondi** can attract more than 40,000 people on a sunny Sunday afternoon.

The 1km strip of beach has a long history of development, since the local government authority gained control of it in 1881. By 1907 it was very popular with the neck-to-knee fraternity, although bathing time was limited to half an hour to avoid loitering. In 1928, the Bondi Beach Pavilion was built and then contained changing rooms for 1200 people, turkish baths, shops, a gymnasium and a ballroom. Today it is a community centre.

Surf life saving had its origins here and at nearby Bronte, with these clubs claiming to be the world's oldest. Surf Carnivals are often held at the beach, but the standard of the surf depends on the wind, and can range from enormous waves one day to a mill-pond the next. In the event that the swell is disappointing, there are plenty of cafes and restaurants to attend, or some casual street shopping to enjoy. Bondi has its own distinct lifestyle, and the pace slows as soon as you cross into its suburban boundary.

Tamarama Beach. Off Bronte Road. Dressing shed, surfers and board.
Bus 360 and 361 from Bondi Junction.

Bronte Beach, off Bronte Road. Squeezed between Tamarama and Clovelly it can experience some rough surf at times. Dressing shed, patrolled, surfers and board, pool south end.
Bus 378 from Railway Square.

Clovelly Beach, off Clovelly Road. Dressing shed, patrolled.
Bus 339 and 340 from Millers Point. Although Clovelly has a sandy foreshore, it is more like a pool than a beach. Good for children.

Coogee Beach, off Coogee Bay Road. Dressing shed, patrolled, surfers and board, pool south end.
Bus 372 from Railway Square, Bus 373 from Circular Quay (Pitt Street).

Maroubra Beach, Fitzgerald Avenue, off Anzac Parade. Dressing shed, patrolled, surfers and board.
Bus 395 from Railway Square, Bus 396 from Circular Quay.

Wanda Beach, off The Kingsway. Dressing shed, patrolled, surfers and board.
Catch a train to Cronulla and then make the short walk to beach.

Elouera Beach, adjoins Wanda Beach. Dressing shed, patrolled, surfers and board, pool south end.
Train to Cronulla, walk to beach.

North Cronulla Beach, adjoins Wanda and Elouera Beaches, off The Kingsway. Dressing shed, patrolled, surfers, board, pool south end.
Train to Cronulla, walk to beach.

South Cronulla Beach, off The Kingsway. Dressing shed, patrolled, surfers and board, pool north end.
Train to Cronulla, walk to beach.

Shelly Beach, off Cronulla Street. Dressing shed, patrolled, surfers, board, pool south end.
Train to Cronulla, walk to beach.

Harbour Beaches

There are hundreds of coves and bays around the harbour, but we are only including those that have shark-proof nets, changing facilities, takeaway food outlets, and picnic areas. Obviously the beaches on the harbour do not have waves.

Clifton Gardens, Chowder Bay. The bay is two bays north-east of Taronga Park Zoo, and not easy to get to by public transport.
Take Bus 228 from Milsons Point (Mon-Fri), Bus 247 from Wynyard/QVB to Taronga Zoo,

alight at Thompson Street and follow the signs.

Balmoral, Hunter's Bay. This is quite a pretty beach and is divided into two by Rocky Point, a tree-covered outcrop. Balmoral is very popular and has takeaway food bars as well as coffee shops and an up-market restaurant. The rotunda on the beach is used for many shows on summer evenings, the 'Shakespeare on the Beach' programs in particular have a large following.

Bus 238 from Taronga Zoo, Bus 257 from Chatswood, or Bus 233 from Mosman Wharf.

Manly Cove, Manly. The swimming enclosure is adjacent to Manly Wharf, where the ferry from Circular Quay docks.

Travel by Ferry, or Bus 144 from Chatswood.

Nielsen Park, between Vaucluse Road and Greycliffe Avenue, Vaucluse, in the eastern suburbs. During the swimming season (October to April) a shark-proof net is erected at Shark Beach. Experience has shown that this net must be taken down during the colder months because it cannot withstand the winter storms and heavy seas. There are dressing sheds and showers for swimmers, and a kiosk is situated opposite the beach.

Ferry from Circular Quay, Bus 325 from Circular Quay.

Botany Bay Beaches

Botany Bay was where Captain James Cook landed, and where Captain Phillip was sent to begin the new colony. Phillip, unable to find a fresh water supply, sailed further north to Sydney Harbour. Nowadays Botany Bay is a densely populated area, and if you arrived in Sydney by air, you have already spotted it; Kingsford Smith Airport is situated on its shores.

The Bay also has its share of sharks, so if you feel like a swim, stick to:

Brighton-le-Sands Baths, off Grand Parade. It has wire netting for protection, although the rest of the Lady Robinson Beach is not protected and is frequented by swimmers.

Ocean baths, Coogee Beach

There are dressing sheds. Bus 302-303 from Circular Quay, Bus 478 from Rockdale.

Bundeena

South of Botany Bay is Port Hacking. Cronulla is on its northern side, and Bundeena on the southern side borders the Royal National Park. Access is by ferry from Cronulla.

Surrounding Bundeena are Hordens, Gunyah and Jobbons, pleasant but small beaches which have little swell and are suitable only for swimming. They have no safety nets and are not patrolled.

Inner-City Suburbs

As an introductory note, it is recommended that if you wish to explore the inner suburbs and outlying regions of Sydney by car, you should use a detailed Street Directory to find you way around. The directions listed in the *How To Get There* sections below are based on that premise; they are street-specific and really require the aid of a comprehensive map. Several Street Directories are available from book stores, newsagencies and information centres.

Terrace housing is a quaint and common feature of inner-suburban dwelling. Density of living in popular regions with close proximity to the CBD means that town houses, duplexes and apartments are basically the only form of accommodation on offer. Sometimes these linked buildings stretch the distance of a whole street, separated in appearance only by exterior colours and the barest architectural trimmings. Although the frontal facade of these places is standard and often unimpressive, the interior is typically where owner's exert their effort, and they are often breathtaking. A pleasant stroll through these quiet, leafy back-streets can be worth the trip.

The inner-suburban people will most likely draw your interest. The clash of fashion, status and ideology within a small geographical radius is fascinating. Paddington east of Sydney is known for its concentrated gay community while Newtown to the city's south is the cultural centre of liberal alternative youths epitomising New Age living. A half-hour walk can take you between worlds.

NORTH

Although the Lower North Shore harbour front now contains some of the most valuable and exclusive real estate in Australia, it was originally the burial ground of the infant colony because it was considered to be far enough away to prevent the spread of disease.

How To Get There

Whatever form of transport is used, visitors must first cross the Sydney Harbour Bridge.

By Train

Trains from Central Station pass through Town Hall, Wynyard and Milsons Point to North Sydney. If you are on a train that is going to travel the City Circle, you must change trains at Town Hall or Wynyard for one on the Northern Line.

After North Sydney, the service continues through many suburban stations to Hornsby, where it may terminate, or link up with the main northern line to Newcastle, Dungog and Scone.

There is no rail service to the Lower North Shore suburbs, but buses from the city stop at North Sydney Station.

By Bus

Buses to the Lower North Shore begin in Carrington Street, at Wynyard Station. There are several to choose from, but there is a route map there, and a ticket machine. Some buses travel via North Sydney Station, while others take the Freeway and exit the Bridge on Military Road.

By Car

There are signs on all roads leading to the city that direct you to the Bridge or the Cahill Expressway. Once on the Bridge, Lane 1 has an exit for Lavender Bay, Milsons Point, and access under the Bridge to Kirribilli; Lanes 1 and 2 allow cars to exit to North Sydney, and Lane 2 also allows travel to the next exit for Crows Nest and Manly. To reach Military Road, and the suburb of Neutral Bay, follow the signs leading to Manly. Lane 4 also has an exit for Neutral Bay and Kirribilli, but this is not as easy to follow.

By Ferry

Ferries leave from Circular Quay Wharf 4 for the Lower North Shore suburbs. Buses meet the ferries to take passengers to the main street, Military Road.

Attractions

On the eastern side of the Bridge lies **Kirribilli** and the stately mansions, *Admiralty House*, Sydney residence of the Governor-General, and *Kirribilli House*, Sydney residence of the Prime Minister. These two imposing buildings can be seen from the Harbour, and about twice a year they are opened for public inspection.

Neutral Bay is the first suburb over the Bridge if you have used the Expressway, and the main street is lined with designer shops and restaurants. The side streets on the right hand side lead to the Harbour.

Military Road, still with door-to-door shops and restaurants, continues through the **Cremorne Junction** to **Spit Junction**, where Spit Road branches off towards **Manly**, and Military Road continues on its way to **Mosman**, where the biggest attraction has to be Taronga Zoo. There is a lovely walk along the foreshores of the Harbour between Cremorne Point Wharf and Mosman Bay Wharf.

Taronga Park Zoo

The Zoo, ✆9969 2777, has Australia's best collection of native and exotic animals. Its main entrance (for car and bus access) is on Bradley's Head Road, but it is only a pleasant 12 minute ferry ride from Wharf 4 Circular Quay (leaving every half hour). Admission prices are ✪$21 adults, $15 children and $55 for families.

Taronga has Australia's best collection of native and exotic animals, and also offers some of the finest views of the city, particularly from near the giraffe enclosure. There are seal shows, a rainforest aviary, a nocturnal house, all the usual animals, and Friendship Farm, where children can pat baby animals. Throughout the park there are plenty of food outlets, and there is also a licensed restaurant.

Probably the best way to explore the exhibits is to take the air cable from the lower wharf to the main entrance at the top of the hill and work your way down to catch the ferry back at the end of your journey. Of course, if you use the main entrance to begin with, walk at your leisure to the bottom of the zoo and remember to catch the air cable back in order to save your legs.

A *ZooPass* ticket is available from the ticket office at Circular Quay, and it costs ✪$28 adult, $14 child, with no combination ticket for a family. The pass includes the ferry to the Zoo, a bus up to the main entrance, and the admission fee.

Taronga is ⏲open every day, including Christmas Day, 9am-5pm, ✆9969 2777.

Manly

The *Manly Visitor Information Centre*, ✆9977 1088, is at North Steyne, on the beach opposite the Steyne Hotel. There are two websites to visit for this locality: www.pcn.com.au and the official website of Manly Council, which is www.manly.nsw.gov.au with an email address at vic@manly.nsw. gov.au

Probably the most popular attraction at Manly is **Oceanworld**, West Esplanade, ✆9949 2644. You have three options for getting close to the sea creatures: viewing them through the safety of glass, handling them in touch pools or - for the fearless - rubbing skin against scale with the sharks in the diving tank. Seals perform at 11.45am and 2pm. Oceanworld is open ⏲10am-5.30pm and entry fees are ✪$16 adults, $8 children.

EAST

Travelling to the inner eastern suburbs may seem that you have never left the city. The reason for this is that you really haven't. It is just that most of the streets have changed their names.

How To Get There

By Train

The Eastern Suburbs line runs to Kings Cross, Edgecliff and Bondi Junction.

By Bus

Buses to the eastern suburbs leave from Circular Quay and Railway Square.

By Car

Drive up William Street from the Australian Museum. At the top of the street, turn left into Darlinghurst Road to tour Kings Cross, or continue straight ahead for New South Head Road.

To get to Paddington, follow Oxford Street from Hyde Park.

By Ferry

Ferries travel from Circular Quay Wharf 4 to Double Bay, Rose Bay and Watsons Bay.

Attractions

The first suburb on this trip is **Kings Cross**, probably one of the best-known Sydney areas. The Cross is sleazy, of that there is no doubt, with its strip joints, sex shops and ladies of the night. But, if you drive through during the day mid-week, it may seem like any other suburb. It is when the sun drops that it comes into its own. There are some excellent restaurants and night spots, and there are some places where you have to be brave to enter. It is not the type of place where you talk to strangers, and believe me, there are some strange people walking the streets. Nevertheless, there are people who would think they had not seen Sydney if they hadn't been to the Cross. It is a haven for backpackers because of the number of cheap hostels, and it is certainly a central area, but it is probably not a good idea to stay there if you are travelling with children.

Having said that, there are a couple of landmarks. The **El Alamein Fountain**, on the corner of Darling-hurst Road and Macleay Street, was built to commemorate the men of the Australian 9th Division who fought in North Africa during World War II. It is an unusually shaped ball of a fountain, and there are always hundreds of people in the park surrounding it.

A short walk away, although in a different suburb, is **Elizabeth Bay House**, at 7 Onslow Avenue, Elizabeth Bay, ✆9356 3022. It was built for the Colonial Secretary, Alexander Macleay and his wife Eliza, and is presently furnished to the period, 1839-1845. In its day it was considered to be the finest house in the colony, and its views over the harbour would have been even more impressive then than they are now. It is a two-storey house with a grand winding staircase, and is maintained by the Historic Houses Trust. It is ⏲open Tues-Sun (Monday when a public holiday) 10am-4.30pm (except Christmas Day and Good Friday) and admission is ✪$7 adult, $4 child, $17 family.

Paddington is another suburb that seems to be part of the city, but it is a charming part. It has many crooked streets lined with pretty terrace houses that are decorated with Paddington Lace, a distinctive wrought-iron trimming. The original village was established in the 1840s and housed the workers building the Victoria Barracks. Parts of the original little town can be seen in the area bounded by Shadforth, Prospect and Spring Streets.

Terrace Housing in Paddington

Darlinghurst Road links Kings Cross with Paddington, or you can follow Oxford Street from the city.

Attractions in the area include numerous antique shops along Queen Street, and art galleries sprinkled along Oxford Street and the side streets. The Paddington Village Bazaar is held in the Uniting Church grounds every Saturday (see *Shopping*).

Victoria Barracks in Oxford Street, next to the Town Hall, ✆9339 3170, is a Georgian-style building (1841-1848) and a living history of Australia's military. The Army Museum is ⏲open on Sunday 10am-3pm.

The **Sydney Cricket Ground** is a little further south, in Driver Avenue, Moore Park, ✆9360 6601. This famous and historic site continues to play host to many notable sporting events. A *Sportspace Tour* is available, guiding visitors through the complex and its memorabilia for ✪$20 adults, $13 children and $52 for families, ✆9380 0383 (bookings essential).

Centennial Park in Oxford Street, was founded in 1888 to celebrate the centenary of the colony. The park is open daily sunrise-sunset, and there are facilities for hiring horses and bikes (see *Sport*).

Double Bay, one of the most up-market suburbs in Sydney, is reached in a car by following New South Head Road from Kings Cross; or by bus from Elizabeth Street; or by train to Edgecliff and walking down New South Head Road.

Known by Sydneysiders who can't afford to shop here as 'Double Pay', it is the most exclusive shopping area in Sydney, and all the well-known, top-class designers have outlets. The surrounding areas of Darling Point, Point Piper, Vaucluse, etc, are populated by people who *can* afford to shop here, and it is worth a visit.

New South Head Road continues through **Rose Bay** and on to **Vaucluse** where it is worth visiting **Vaucluse House**, which dates from 1803. It was the home of William Charles Wentworth, one of the intrepid trio who first crossed the Blue Mountains, and the father of the Australian Constitution. He, and his wife Sarah and their children, lived here from 1829 to 1853, and it's furnishings still recall that period. The house is set in 11ha with gardens, bushland and a harbour beach frontage, and has out-buildings and stables. The house is ⏲open Tues-Sun 10am- 4.30pm and Monday if it is a public holiday. Admission is ✪$6.50 adults, $2.50 children, $15.50 family. There are tearooms in the grounds, and they serve a-la-carte lunches, and Devonshire teas that you would die for. If you are not driving, Bus 325 from Circular Quay stops at the front gate.

The end of New South Head road is **Watsons Bay**, which is on the Harbour, near South Head and the Harbour entrance. The area's most famous landmark is not, as some would say, the pub, nor is it Doyle's restaurant - it is **The Gap**, a cliff from which there are great views, and from where people have committed suicide by jumping into the ocean below.

Nearby is the anchor from the ill-fated *Dunbar*, a barque which was wrecked on the rocks of The Gap on its second voyage in August 1857. It was Sydney's worst shipping disaster, with 121 lives lost and only one survivor.

From Watsons Bay you can follow Old South Head Road to **Bondi Junction**, or turn off Old South Head Road left onto Military Road and head for **Bondi Beach** and the other beaches to the south. Bondi Junction is about 2km from the beach, and is the main bus/train link for public transport throughout this area. It is also quite a good shopping centre. Bus no 280 runs between Bondi Beach and Bondi Junction.

SOUTH

The southern suburbs are for the most part either industrial or residential, and if you arrived by air, you have already travelled through parts of them. However, there are a few places that are historically interesting on the shores of Botany Bay. The two main areas are **La Perouse**, on the north head of Botany Head, and **Kurnell** on the south head.

How To Get There

By Train

There is no direct train route to *La Perouse*.

To get to *Kurnell*, take the train to Cronulla, then local Bus 67 from the depot opposite the station, near Munroe Park.

By Bus

Bus no 398 runs from Circular Quay to *La Perouse*.

The best transportation route to *Kurnell* is detailed above.

By Car

To get to *La Perouse*, follow Anzac Parade all the way from Taylor Square in Oxford Street. To get *Kurnell* from there, drive around the foreshores of the bay, crossing Endeavour Bridge and Captain Cook Bridge.

It is difficult to get to both places in one trip without a car.

Bare Island Fort, Botany Bay

Attractions

La Perouse

La Perouse is named after Jean-Francois de Galaup, Comte de Laperouse, who was commissioned by Louis XVI in 1785, to set out on a voyage of discovery. The expedition consisted of two ships, *L'Astrolabe* and *La Boussole*. Two and a half years later, the two ships arrived in Botany Bay, a week after the arrival of the First Fleet. La Perouse and Captain Phillip apparently became good friends, and the Frenchman gave Phillip reports and letters to be sent back to his king. The French ships stayed in Botany Bay for a period of six weeks, then La Perouse set sail, never to be heard from again.

The whereabouts of the ships remained a mystery until the two wrecks were discovered on the reefs of Vanikoro, off the Solomon Islands, by Peter Dillon, an Irish trader and adventurer.

The **La Perouse Museum**, ✆9311 3379, is housed in the Cable Station, inside a circle formed by the end of Anzac Parade. It contains many artefacts from the wrecks, as well as relics from their time in the Bay.

The **Cable Station** was designed and built between 1880 and 1881 to provide accommodation, offices and telegraph facilities for the officers of the Eastern Extension Australasia and China Telegraph Company. The company's submarine cable between La Perouse and Wakapuaka in New Zealand terminated here.

On the bay foreshore, where La Perouse landed, there is an obelisk to commemorate his visit, and close by is the grave of Pere L.C. Receveur, a chaplain and naturalist with the expedition who has the honour of being the first Frenchman to be buried on the Australian continent.

A causeway from the tip of the point leads to **Bare Island**, on which the fort was built in 1881, following Britain's decision to give self governing colonies the responsibility for their own defence. It only operated as a means of defence for 27 years, then it became a war veterans' home, then a museum with exhibits associated with its early history.

The **Macquarie Watchtower**, also in the circle formed by the road, was built between 1820 and 1822, to prevent smugglers entering Botany Bay.

Kurnell

Kurnell has **Captain Cook's Landing Place**, an historic site of over 400ha. Cook landed at 3.00pm on April 28, 1770, and tradition maintains that the first person to step ashore was his wife's young cousin, Isaac Smith. The spot where he scrambled onto dry land is marked with a small obelisk, and there is a larger one dedicated to the discovery nearby.

The site is also a monument to the Gwiyagal People, the Aboriginal tribe who inhabited the area at the time of European discovery.

The **Discovery Centre**, in Captain Cook Drive, is ⏲open Mon-Fri 11am-3pm and 10am-4pm on weekends and public holidays, ✆9668 9111. It is one of the major features of the site, with exhibits detailing Cook's life, exploits and achievements, including his notes and opinions on the country he had discovered.

There are also scenic walks, picnic and barbecue areas, and an historic walk, and the visitor centre has maps and leaflets on everything you can see and do.

WEST

The inner western suburbs were settled in the early days of the colony and therefore have many buildings and homes from a bygone era.

How To Get There

By Bus

Buses 438, 440, 470 travel south along George Street and pass the beginning of Glebe Point Road, Glebe, but the buses that actually drive down Glebe Point Road are 431, 433, and 434. Bus no 433 continues on to Balmain.

Bus 440 connects the city with Rozelle, passing through the suburbs of Camperdown, Annandale and Leichhardt.

By Road

To get to Glebe, drive south along George Street, which becomes Broadway, then turn right at the traffic lights on the corner of Glebe Point Road. Incidentally, at that point Broadway becomes Par-ramatta Road and the Great Western Highway.

Or, if you are crossing the Harbour Bridge, take the Western Distributor, stay in the left lane, follow the sign to the Western Suburbs, then take the first exit onto Bridge Road. The Fish Markets are off to the right and if you continue on you will find yourself in the heart of Glebe.

The best way to get to Balmain from the city is to drive south along George Street to Leichhardt, turn right at Norton Street, follow that street to its end, turn left, then right at the first traffic lights, and follow this street, which undergoes a few name changes before it becomes Darling Street and travels through the heart of Balmain.

If you are coming over the Harbour Bridge, take the Western Distributor, continue over the new Glebe Island Bridge, go with the major flow of traffic turning right into Victoria Road, then right into Darling Street, Balmain. This way by-passes Leichhardt.

By Ferry

Sydney Ferries travel between Circular Quay and three wharves in Balmain - Darling Street, Thames Street and Elliott Street.

Attractions

The word 'glebe' means 'a gift to the church', and the suburb of **Glebe** was first settled in the late 1700s as a church-owned estate. The church in question was St John's Church, and it still stands on the corner of Glebe Point Road and St John's Road. Apparently by the 1820s the church had fallen on hard times, and the land was sold and subdivided. The high portions of Glebe, away from the insect-ridden Blackwattle Swamp (now known as Blackwattle Bay) were purchased by wealthy families. Grand houses with names such as Hereford House, Forest Lodge, Toxteth House and Lyndhurst were built. The land that was not so valuable became as area for worker's cottages, many of which have recently been restored.

Glebe has become a trendy place to live again, and it has a small shopping centre with lots of art galleries and heritage shops.

The University of Sydney, on Parramatta Road, adjoins Victoria Park, and is a sandstone blend of Tudor and Gothic architecture, with acres of green lawns. The Great Hall has a Royal Window which illustrates the monarchy from the Normans to Queen Victoria. The University's Fisher Library, ✆9351 2993, contains more than 400,000 volumes, and the Nicholson Museum has a quality collection of Egyptian, Etruscan, Greek and Roman art.

Leichhardt has a large Italian population, and consequently a large number of Italian restaurants are found in the main streets of Parramatta Road and Norton Street. Leichhardt Park, at the end of Mary Street, has several football ovals, acres of parkland, and an attractively sited public swimming complex, ✆9555 8344, with views over Iron Cove.

Trendy Norton Street's newest addition is the **Italian Forum**.

The suburb of **Balmain** gets its name from Dr Balmain, who received the whole of the peninsula as a land grant. Balmain is a trendy area now, rivalling Paddington with its quaint terraces, art galleries and alternative lifestyle shops, but it wins hands down in the restaurant department. There are also many pubs that have outdoor beer gardens and live entertainment.

Balmain Saturday Market is held in the grounds of St Andrew's Congregational Church, on the corner of Darling Street and Curtis Road, ⌚every Saturday 9am-4.30pm, ✆0418 765 736.

Outlying Attractions

Parramatta

Parramatta Road terminates at Parramatta, the second oldest settlement in the country. The area was first visited by Governor Phillip and

Cafe in Glebe

a party of explorers on April 24, 1788. It had become obvious that the soil in the area of Sydney Cove would not produce sufficient crops to feed the infant settlement, and in September 1788, Governor Phillip announced his intention to found another settlement. On November 2, 1788, he chose this area, and named the settlement Rose Hill, but on June 4, 1791, he renamed it Parramatta.

Parramatta became the site of Australia's first orchard, vineyard, tannery, legal brewery, woollen mills, observatory, steam mill, market place and fair. It also was the terminating point of the first road, ferry and rail links out of Sydney. And, most importantly, it saw the beginning of Australia's wool industry.

Although, strictly speaking, Parramatta is a suburb of Sydney, it is a city in its own right with a population of about 130,000. The *Parramatta Visitors Centre* has been incorporated into the Parramatta Heritage Centre, 346 Church Street, ✆9630 3703, and is ⌚open Mon-Fri 10am-5pm, Sat-Sun 10am-4pm. The Centre has a wealth of information on the important historic houses of *Experiment Farm Cottage*, *Elizabeth Farm* and *Hambledon Cottage*. To take both tours requires a full day, and a certain amount of fitness, as there are many points of interest.

Parramatta Park is within easy walking distance of the central business area, and comprises about 85ha. In the Park are found Old Government House, the Governor's Bathhouse, The Tudor Gate House, Australia's first Observatory, and a kiosk with boat and cycle hire. Nearby are *Parramatta Stadium* and the *Swimming Centre*.

The city's main festival is the Wistaria Garden Festival, held in September each year. North of Parramatta, in the suburb of **West Pennant Hills**, is *Koala Park Sanctuary*, 9484 3141. Set in 4ha, the Park not only has plenty of koalas, there are also kangaroos, wallabies, wallaroos, wombats, dingoes, echidnas and emus. The Park is open daily 9am-5pm, and photo sessions with koalas are available at intervals throughout the day. Admission is $14 adults, $8 children and $32 for families. The Sanctuary is on Castle Hill Road, and to get there from Parramatta follow Pennant Hills Road to the Castle Hill Road turn-off. To get there from Sydney by road, travel along Epping Road which becomes Beecroft Road (or along the M2 to the Beecroft Road exit), to its end, then turn left onto Pennant Hills Road and a short distance along on the right is the Castle Hill Road turn-off. From Sydney by train, travel to the Pennant Hills Station, then take Bus 655 to the Park.

Ku-ring-gai Chase National Park

Located 24km (15 miles) north of the city, the Park has numerous bushwalks and some magnificent Aboriginal rock carvings in accessible spots. The higher parts of the park afford magnificent views across Pittwater.

On the edge of the park is *Waratah Park*, 13 Namba Road, Duffys Forest, home of 'Skippy the Bush Kangaroo' and many of her friends, including Tasmanian Devils, dingoes, wombats, wallabies, emus and koalas. Feeding times are on the hour between 11am and 4pm. There is a restaurant, a snack bar, and a souvenir shop, and the Park is open every day 10am-5pm, 9450 2377. Admission is $12.90 adults, $6.50 children and $34.90 for families. To get there by car, proceed north on the Pacific Highway to the suburb of Pymble, then turn right onto Mona Vale Road. Take the left turn to Duffy's Forest off Mona Vale Road at Terrey Hills, and follow the signs.

Wonderland Australia

Located near the M4, in outer western Sydney, Wonderland is 219ha (540 acres) of landscaped grounds in Wallgrove Road, Eastern Creek, and has Australia's longest wooden roller coaster, the Bush Beast. Other rides include The Demon, Space Probe and Snowy River Rampage. There are also many different kinds of theme shops, live shows and picnic spots. It is open 10am-5pm every day, 9830 9100 or 9830 9106 (recorded information). Admission is adults $39 and children $27.

The *Australian Wildlife Park*, 9830 9187, also at Wonderland, is open daily 9am-5pm. Entry fees are $18 adults, $12 children and $46 for families.

Shuttle buses run to the fun park from Mt Druitt, Fairfield, Blacktown and Rooty Hill train stations.

Also in Eastern Creek is the **Eastern Creek Raceway**, Brabham Drive, 9672 1000. This venue has accommodated the 500cc Motorbike Grand Prix, and hosts other races around the year.

Hawkesbury River

The River is 45km (28 miles) north of Sydney, and is dotted with historic towns such as Windsor, Richmond, Wilberforce, Pitt Town and Wisemans Ferry. It winds around Sydney's western outskirts through a natural forest area until finally meeting the sea at Brooklyn. One of the best ways to see it is to join the *Riverboat Postman* near the Hawkesbury River

Hawkesbury River

Railway Station in Brooklyn. This four hour cruise includes commentary and snacks. The cost is ✪$35 adults, $18 children and $72 for families, ✆9985 7566.

An alternative is to hire a house boat from the many on offer at Brooklyn, at the southern end of the Hawkesbury Bridge. Two such companies are Holidays Afloat Houseboats, ✆9985 7368, and House Boats Prestige, ✆9985 7744.

Royal National Park

The Park is situated south of Port Hacking, about 29km from the centre of Sydney, and covers 16,000ha of vegetation and landscape typical of the Sydney Basin sandstone.

Tourist Information

A Visitor Centre and Wildlife Shop is on Farnell Avenue, Audley. Call into the centre for advice on all aspects of your park visit. Permits for camping are obtained here. It is ⏲open daily 8.30am-4pm, ✆9542 0648. The shop sells books, film, maps, posters, gifts and souvenirs.

Park Entrance Fee

There is no charge for traffic travelling through and not stopping in the Park from Sutherland to places south of the Park.

For those that intend to stop within the park the following charges apply:

Bus - ✪$3.00 per adult, $1.00 for each school age child, under the age of 5 free, pensioners free. Must display pensioner card.

Cars - ✪$9.00 per vehicle.
Motor Bikes - ✪$3.00 per bike.
There is no charge for people who hike into the park for the day.

Sydney Tramway Museum

If you are visiting the Royal National Park on a Sunday or Wednesday, you might like to check out the Sydney Tramway Museum in Pitt Street, Loftus, ✆9542 3646. It is ⏲open Sunday and Public Holidays 10am-5pm, Wednesday 9.30am-3.30pm, but no one is admitted in the hour prior to closing.

Admission is ✪$12 adult, $6 child, and includes unlimited tram rides and use of facilities.

Festivals

The **Festival of Sydney** is held during the entire month of January each year, and features include twilight and open-air concerts in the Domain, contemporary music at Hyde Park and Darling Harbour, outdoor movies at the Opera House, bike rallies, street theatre, and classical theatre performances at the Opera House, the Belvoir Theatre and the Seymour Centre.

Australia Day, January 26, sees the city come alive, especially around the harbour, with all kinds of displays, and a Ferrython in which all the Sydney ferries compete.

The Mardi Gras is organised by representatives of the gay and lesbian community, and is held on the first Friday in February each year. For visitors who are new to this scene, be aware that nudity and sexual insinuation are always prevalent here.

The Royal Easter Show is now held at Homebush Bay, the venue of the 2000 Olympics. The Show begins on the Friday before Good Friday and finishes on Easter Tuesday.

Anzac Day commemorates the actions of Australian and New Zealand troops involved in the conflict of the First World War, and the lives they sacrificed. The day falls on the 25 April, the same date that the soldiers landed on the shores of Gallipoli in 1914 and were overwhelmed by the Turkish resistance.

The **National Folkloric Festival** is held in June.

On the 17 March, thousands don a green item of clothing for **St Patrick's Day**.

The Sydney to Hobart Yacht Race generates a lot of excitement every Boxing Day.

In addition to the above, each municipal area of Sydney has its own festival, and there are other special annual events, such as the blessing of the fishing fleet.

Public Holidays

Christmas, Boxing Day, New Year and Easter are obviously celebrated at the same time as everywhere else in the world.

Other holidays that are enjoyed in Australia are:

Australia Day - January 26.
Anzac Day - April 25.
Queen's Birthday - the second Monday in June.
Labour Day - the first Monday in October.

Another day is *Bank Holiday*, which is held on the first Monday in August, but only banks, government offices, insurance companies and the like are closed.

Sport and Recreation

Boating

It should be noted that a licence is required to drive any mechanically driven vessel capable of 10 knots or more. There are several places around the harbour foreshores where bare boats can be hired. Here are a few names and addresses:

Abbotsford Point Boat Hire, 617 Great North Road, Abbotsford, ✆9713 8621.

Australian Sailing School & Club, Parrawi Road, Mosman, ✆9960 3077.

Balmoral Sailing and Kayaking School and Hire, 2 The Esplanade, Balmoral, ✆9969 5344.

Sailing on Rushcutters Bay

Eastsail, d'Albora Marinas, New Beach Road, Rushcutters Bay, ✆9327 1166.

Rose Bay Marina, 594 New South Head Road, Rose Bay, ✆9363 5930.

If you are a marine enthusiast and wish to admire the yachts in the harbour, there are several wharfs along the shoreline. The ***Cruising Yacht Club*** at Rushcutters Bay is close to the city.

Cycling

Australian Cycle Co., 28 Clovelly Road, Randwick, ✆9399 3475, are ⏱open seven days and are close to Centennial Park. They hire out bikes at reasonable prices.

Golf

Although Sydney has about 40 public golf courses, few are located close to the city centre. Here is a selection:

Moore Park Golf Club, is on the corner of Cleveland Street and Anzac Parade, ✆9663 1064. This is the closest course to the city. It comprises 18-holes and is par 71 for 5790m. Eighteen holes will cost you ✪$24 on a weekday and $27 on weekends.

Cammeray Golf Course is located in Park Avenue, Cremorne, ✆9953 2089. Another 9-hole course, at 2417m, par 33, Cammeray is built on quality terrain that is always well-kept. A nine-hole round is ✪$11 and can be played between designated hours daily.

Bondi Golf Course, 5 Military Road, North Bondi, ✆9130 7170. This course is only a 2500m nine-hole course, but its hills and freak peninsula winds provide some challenges. Famous Bondi Beach sprawls below - a soothing sight after a terrible shot. It costs adults ✪$9 to play, and a further $9 to hire clubs. Children play for $5.

Balgowlah Golf Course, 506 Sydney Road, Balgowlah, ✆9949 2057, is another terrific nine-holer. This popular spot is not far from Manly Beach and is difficult enough to test good golfers whilst not crushing the dreams of intermediates. It is green and lush and can make for a pleasant couple of hours. The course is par 34, 2321m long, and costs ✪$12 for nine holes. Non-members have access to the course daily at designated hours.

Wakehurst Golf Club is on Upper Clontarf Street, Seaforth, ✆9949 3188. This is a full 18 hole, par 72 course built in the middle of cleared scrubland and dotted with water hazards. Its length is just over 6100m and its terrain can be tricky for any golfer to negotiate. A round on this scenic course will set you back ✪$22 on weekdays and $25 on weekends. Club hire is an additional ✪$15 and you can pick up a golf cart for $25.

The Australian in Rosebery and ***Royal Sydney*** in Rose Bay are nearby, while the ***New South Wales Golf Club*** is in La Perouse further south. However, the only way to make a divot on these exclusive fairways is to quickly make friends with a member, if you can find one.

For further information on Sydney's courses, find the listing in the Yellow Pages Telephone Directory or use the golf guide at sydney.sidewalk.com.au

Horse Riding

Superior Horse, Pavillion A, Driver Avenue, Moore Park, ✆9360 5650, has horses for hire daily 9am-5pm. Centennial Park and adjoining Queens Park have a combined area 220ha (543 acres) - more than enough room to have a decent ride.

Lawn Bowls

There are bowling clubs in almost every suburb of Sydney, and one in the city. If you are not sure which club is the closest to where you are staying, you could contact the Royal NSW Bowling Association, ✆9283 4555.

Scuba Diving

Gear can be hired and dives arranged from the following places:

Dive 2000, 2 Military Road, Neutral Bay, ✆9953 7783.

Deep 6 Diving, 1057 Victoria Road, West Ryde, ✆9858 4299.

Pro Dive, Head Office, 34/330 Wattle Street, Ultimo, ✆9281 6166.

Swimming

The closest public swimming pools to the city centre are:

North Sydney Olympic Pool, Alfred South Street, Milsons Point, ✆9955 2309;

Andrew (Boy) Charlton Pool, The Domain, Woolloomooloo, ✆9358 6686;

Prince Alfred Park Swimming Pool, Chalmers Street, Surry Hills (near Central Railway Station), ✆9319 7045.

The new ***Cook and Phillip Park Recreation Centre***, is on the corner of Haig & Boomerang Streets, near St Marys, ✆9326 0444. It has a 50m underground pool among its facilities.

The larger hotels have swimming pools, usually heated all year round.

Tennis

Tennis courts abound in Sydney's suburbs and most have lights for night play. Pages of available courts can be found in the L-Z Yellow Pages Telephone Directory, appropriately enough under *Tennis Courts For Hire*.

For spectators, the NSW Tennis Open is played at ***White City*** in Rushcutters Bay, ✆9360 4113.

Ten Pin Bowling

The bowling centres close to the city are: ***Balgowlah Bowling Centre***, Condamine Street, Balgowlah, ✆9948 7656. Other centres can be found in the A-K Yellow Pages Telephone Directory under *Ten Pin Bowling*.

Sydney Olympic Park

Situated roughly in the geographic heart of metropolitan Sydney, the Olympic Park is 14km from the CBD, in the suburb of Homebush.

Facilities include Stadium Australia, Bicentennial Park, the Sydney International Aquatic Centre, the State Sports Centre, as well as Tennis, Hockey and Archery facilities. Other features include a major metropolitan park, called Millennium Park, a golf driving range and an Olympic Village which accommodated 15,000 athletes.

A concentration on modern architecture is the definitive element of the Olympic site. From a distance the domes, arcs and cylindrical shapes of the venue seem to make it spring like a spaceport from science fiction out of its green surrounds.

Stadium Australia

This enormous stadium was the venue for the Opening and Closing Ceremonies, and will host many other notable competition events into the future. It has a seating capacity of 100,000 people.

State Sports Centre

The Centre is a multi-purpose venue designed to present a full spectrum of events. For information about current programs at the Centre, phone the information line on, ✆9763 0111.

Transport to Homebush

Transport to the Olympic Site is by car, bus, river cat or rail (Olympic Park station).

Guided tours of the Olympic Site are available, and perhaps the best way to explore this venue and all of the others in close proximity, is on the Olympic Explorer Bus (see under *Local Transport*).

Stadium Australia

Lostock
Bandon Grove
Wootton
151
Bluey's Bea
Liddell
Allynbrook
Stroud Road
avensworth
Dungog
Bulahdelah
Gresford
Myall Lake
Booral
Wallarobba
Hwy
MYALL LAKES NATIONAL PARK
Singleton
Hunter R
43
Paterson
Karuah
Greta
Grahamstown Res
Port Stephens
MAITLAND
Nelson Bay
20
Raymond Terrace
28
Cessnock
Kurri Kurri
Bellbird
Paxton
NEWCASTLE
NORTH
Pacific
Rathmines
0
25
Wangi
85
Swansea
Lake Macquarie
Mannering Park
Gwandalan
Budgewoi
Toukley
Wyong
Noraville
The Entrance
Tuggerah Lake
Bateau Bay
Long Jetty
Gosford
Terrigal
Avoca Beach
Woy Woy
Broken Bay
Kuring-Gai Chase NP
Berowra
Terrey Hills
SYDNEY
Colo Heights
Wisemans Ferry
Hawkesbury R
Bilpin
North Richmond
Wilberforce
Mount Victoria
Nepean
Richmond
Windsor
Blackheath
Katoomba
Springwood
Riverstone
Leura
Glenbrook
Emu Plains
78
Western
Hwy
Parra
BLUE MOUNTAINS NATIONAL PARK
Mulgoa
Prospect Reservoir
Warragamba
Bringelly
Narellan
Liverpool

Central Coast

The Central Coast is located north of Sydney. It begins at the Hawkes-bury River and stretches northwards to the southern shores of Lake Macquarie, and westwards to historic St Albans.

The area is roughly divided into two - the City of Gosford with Brisbane Waters, and the Shire of Wyong with Tuggerah Lakes. Within these two districts there are many seaside and holiday centres.

Gosford City

Population 129,000
The City of Gosford is 88km (55 miles) north of Sydney. The natural beauty of the district and its close proximity to the major cities of Sydney and Newcastle has made it an attractive living and recreation area on the east coast of Australia. There are many popular surfing beaches and the Brisbane Waters are legendary for fishing, sailing and other recreational pursuits. Although for many years, it has been a popular holiday and retirement area, many young families are now settling in the district as an alternative to living in the outer suburbs of Sydney and Newcastle.

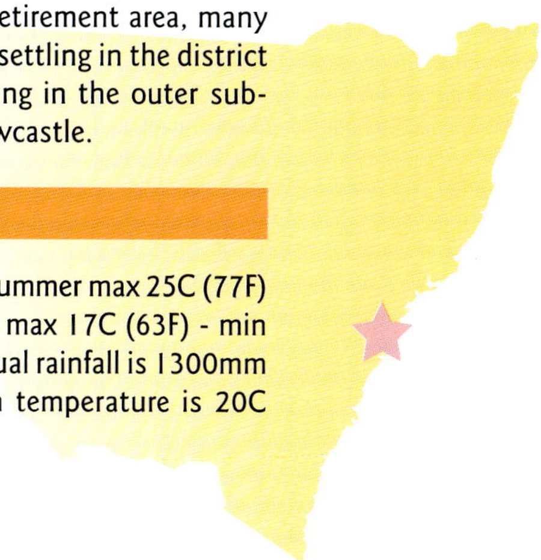

Climate

Average temperatures: summer max 25C (77F) - min 18C (64F); winter max 17C (63F) - min 10C (50F). Average annual rainfall is 1300mm (51 ins), average ocean temperature is 20C (68F).

Central Coast

How to Get There

By Bus

Interstate coachlines call at Gosford.

By Rail

There is a good electric train service from/to Sydney, and the State Rail Authority has mini-fares, family fares and combined rail/coach fares, ✆131 500.

By Road

From Sydney via the Pacific Highway all the way to Gosford, or the F3 expressway from Hornsby to the Gosford turn-off, then the Pacific Highway.

Visitor Information

The Gosford Visitor Information Centre is in 200 Mann Street, Gosford, ✆(02) 4385 4430 or ✆1800 806 258, open Mon-Fri 9am-5pm, Sat-Sun 9am-2pm. Their email address is thecoast@c ctourism.com.au and the web page is at www.cctourism.com.au

If you are in Terrigal, the Visitor Information Centre is in Rotary Park, Terrigal Drive. It is open 9am-5pm Mon-Sat and 9am-3pm on Sunday during summer. They share contact details with the Gosford Centre.

The Centre has compiled some very good self-drive tours of the area, which encompass all the attractions. Visitors are well-advised to pick up these brochures.

Accommodation

Accommodation is not a problem in the area, although it is wise to book in advance during the summer holiday period. Here is a selection with prices for a double room per night, which should be used as a guide only. The telephone area code is 02.

Gosford

Metro Motor Inn Gosford, 512 Pacific Highway, ✆4328 4666. 50 units, licensed restaurant, swimming pool, spa, barbecue - $105.

Bermuda Motor Inn, cnr Henry Parry Drive & Pacific Highway, North Gosford, ✆4324 4366. 17 units, swimming pool, barbecue - $65-95.

Gosford Motor Inn, 23 Pacific Highway, ✆4323 1333. 36 units, heated swimming pool, barbecue - $70-100.

Rambler Motor Inn, 73 Pacific Highway, West Gosford, ✆4324 6577. 55 units, playground, swimming pool, spa, barbecue - $75-100.

Wyoming Caravan Park, 520 Pacific Highway, Wyoming, ✆4328 4358. (No pets allowed) - powered sites $19 for two, cabins $55 for two.

Woy Woy

Glades Country Club Motor Inn, 15 Dunban Road, ✆4341 7374. 23 units, swimming pool, barbecue - $80-120.

Ettalong

Motel Paradiso, cnr Schnapper & Ocean View Roads, ✆4341 1999. 1 room, licensed restaurant - $75-140.

Ettalong Beach Village, Fassifern Street, ✆4344 2211. (No pets) - powered sites $20-32 for two, cabins $60-110 for two.

Avoca

Bellbird Resort, 360 Avoca Drive, ✆4382 2322. 36 units, licensed restaurant, swimming pool, tennis court - $80-100.

Avoca Beach

The Palms at Avoca, Carolina Park Road off the Round Drive, ✆4382 1227. (No pets allowed), barbecue, sauna, pool - cabins ✪$80-145 for two, villas $75-125 for two.

Terrigal

Country Comfort Terrigal, 154 Terrigal Drive, ✆4384 1166. 40 units, 7 suites, licensed restaurant, swimming pool, spa, sauna, tennis, barbecue - ✪$175-220.

Clan Lakeside Lodge, 1 Ocean View Drive, ✆4384 1566. 26 units, licensed restaurant (closed Sunday & Monday), barbecue - ✪$100-220.

Terrigal Beach House, 1 Painter Lane, ✆4384 1423. 9 units - ✪$45-90.

Bellbird Caravan Park, 61-69 Terrigal Drive, ✆4384 1883. (No dogs allowed) - unpowered sites ✪$20-25 for two, on-site vans $50-60for two, cabins $80-95.

Wamberal

Apollo Country Resort, 871 The Entrance Road, ✆4385 2099. 42 units (private facilities), licensed restaurant, swimming pool, spa, barbecue, tennis, gym - ✪$95-160.

Kincumber

Figtree Cottages, 247 Avoca Drive, ✆4368 3056. 2 rooms, unlicensed restaurant, solar heated saltwater pool, fireplace, spa - ✪$120-130.

Eating Out

Central Coast

No matter which locality of the Central Coast you choose to stay in, you will find excellent restaurants. Here is a brief list, and the Information Centre can advise you further if you desire.

Gosford

Gosford Shoreline, Masons Parade, ✆4325 0644. Fully licensed seafood restaurant with an a-la-carte selection. Open midday-2pm and 6pm-8.30pm Mon-Sat, and until 9.30pm Friday and Saturday nights, lunch only on Sundays, closed Public Holidays.

Gee Kwong Chinese Restaurant, 197 Mann Street, ✆4325 2489. Open 11.30am-3pm and 4.30pm-9pm Mon-Sat, and until 10pm on Friday and Saturday nights, closed Sunday and Public Holidays.

Tohn Oor Sian Classic Thai, 26 Adelaide Street, Gosford East, ✆4324 2887. Take-away available, dine-in BYO wine only. Open midday-2.30pm and 5.30pm-10.30pm 7 days.

Jaceys, 45 Imperial Centre, ✆4324 2558.

Da Vincis, 1-2 Brisbane Waters Drive, Gosford West, ✆4322 8000.

Saltwater, Shop 6 Brisbane Waters Drive, West Gosford, ✆4323 7744.

Curry House, 104 Mann Street, ✆4322 0223.

Peking Garden, in the Central Coast Leagues Club, Dane Drive, ✆4324 3788.

Surrounding Areas

Paceys, 172 Avoca Drive, Avoca Beach, ✆4382 3588. Seafood, a-la-carte. Open 6pm-9pm 7 days and midday-3pm weekends and Public Holidays.

Sirens, 1 Kurrawyba Avenue, Terrigal, ✆4385 2602. Open 5pm-midnight every day.

Pizza One, 80 Ocean View Drive, Wamberal, ✆4385 3311.

Ghandi Indian Restaurant, 189 Ocean View Road, Ettalong, ✆4341 1994.

The Don's Italian Restaurant, 28 Kincumber Village, Avoca Drive, Kincumber, ✆4363 1900.

Fishermans Wharf, The Boulevarde, Woy Woy, ✆4341 1171.

For Pizza Hut deliveries, ✆13 1166. Branches of McDonalds and KFC are found in all the major towns.

Points of Interest

The town site of Gosford was first referred to as the Township at Point Frederick, then in February 1839, when the plan was sent to Governor Gipps for approval, as the Township of Brisbane Water. The Governor returned the plan in April marked as the Plan of Gosford, with no explanation for its name. It was later discovered that the Governor had served with the Earl of Gosford in Canada, and had taken the opportunity to honour his friend.

Originally, timber cutting was the main economic product of the district, then from the 1880s, citrus orchards began to dominate the local farms in the Narara, Lisarow, Wyoming, Holgate and Ourimbah areas. These farms were close to the railway, but later as roads developed, farming spread on to Somersby plateau. By 1928-29, the district supplied 34% of the state's citrus crop.

The 1880s also saw the Gosford area become a tourist venue, with the completion of the railway in 1887, and visitors coming for the

fishing, and for hunting trips.

In recent times Gosford's development has been influenced by other factors, such as the metropolitan expansion of Sydney, improvements to the roads, and changes in lifestyles.

The majority of people visit the area now for the surf, sun and sand, but there are quite a few attractions worth visiting.

Above: *Woy Woy.*
Left: *A Fisherman on the Brisbane Waters*

Henry Kendall Cottage & Historical Museum, 218 Gertrude Street, Gosford, ✆4325 2270, was built for the famous poet in 1836 by Peter Fagan. It is now an historical museum with displays of various items from the past. ⏲Open Wed, Sat & Sun, and public and school holidays, 10am-4pm.

The Australian Reptile Park was the first major tourist attraction on the Central Coast, and is a popular science exhibit. Crocodile feeding in the impressive crocodile enclosure is by far the highlight of the day. Watch as the trainer holds a long pole over the water's edge while a croc emerges, leaps into the air, takes the dangling chicken from the end of the pole into its jaws, and thrashes back into the water again. The park supplies venoms to countries all over the world for antivenenes and other research. There are picnic and barbecue facilities, but note that the place is overrun by kangaroos, and the joy of their company can quickly turn into despair if one bounds up and pinches your lunch while you pat her! The park is hopen daily 9am-5pm, ✆4340 1146, and is on the Pacific Highway, Somersby. Admission prices are ✪$16 adults, $8 children, $40 families.

The Starship Cruise & Ferry Service, 100 John Whiteway Drive, ✆4340 1146, has two venues for cruises. The *Lady Kendall* departs from Gosford Wharf, Wed, Sat & Sun to cruise on the Brisbane Waters, and the *Trinity Queen* leaves from The Entrance Wharf for cruising Tuggerah Lakes and Wyong River, Wed-Sat 10.15am and 1pm. Both vessels operate daily during school holidays.

The Fragrant Garden, 25 Portsmouth Road, Erina, ✆4367 7322, has a very large collection of fragrant plants, crafts, pot-pourri in an olde-worlde garden. There is a mud-brick gallery, waterfall and a herb roof, and souvenirs are for sale.

Central Park Family Fun Centre, The Entrance Road, Forresters Beach, ✆4386 2466, has something for everyone - ten-pin bowling, five giant waterslides, a mini golf centre, senior and junior Grand Prix cars, BMX track, maze, mini bikes, Sunday markets. ⏲Open daily 9am-5pm, Sat and holidays 9am-10pm.

Festivals

Gosford's Australian Springtime Flora Festival is held in September.

Facilities

Fishing, swimming, boating, diving, wind-surfing, water skiing, horse riding, ten-pin bowling, squash, lawn bowls, golf and tennis. The Tourist Information Centre will give you all the information for directions and bookings.

Outlying Attractions

Beaches

The coastal beaches in the Gosford area are Killcare, McMasters, Copacabana, Avoca, Terrigal, Wamberal and Forresters. They each have their own attractions, and all are patrolled on weekends from October to April, with daily patrols during the school holiday periods. Apart from McMasters and Forresters, they have a choice of takeaway food outlets close to the beachfront.

The crystal clear waters right along the Central Coast offer some of the best diving in Australia, and there are fascinating wrecks off Terrigal in reasonably shallow water. If you are interested in learning how to dive, the ***Terrigal Diving Centre***, The Haven Terrigal, ✆4384 1219, or ***Pro Dive***, 96 The Entrance Road, The Entrance, ✆4334 1559, are the places to visit. They teach diving, and after 5 days tuition, which costs around $450, you are awarded a C card. If you are already a qualified diver and have your certificate with you, a diving charter can be arranged instead. Fishing tours are also available for those who prefer to catch fish rather than rub noses with

The Entrance

them (unless you are one of those fanatics who performs this ritual *after* catching a fish); one option is ***Haven Fishing Charters***, 12 Lexington Parade, Green Point, ✆4369 5673. The **Blue Bead Arabian Stud**, ✆4382 2346, is located at Razina Park in Picketts Valley Road, 5 minutes from Terrigal and Avoca Beaches. They have mountain trails for the experienced, and instruct beginners and improvers. Bookings are essential, and the stud is open 7 days.

Tuggerah Lakes

The administrative centre of the Tuggerah Lakes district is Wyong, 22km (24 miles) north of Gosford on the banks of the Wyong River. The Lake system extends from Killarney Vale in the south to the township of Lake Munmorah in the north, and consists of three lakes - Tuggerah, Budgewoi and Munmorah. Tuggerah Lake is the biggest and has the only opening from the ocean, appropriately at The Entrance. There are no sharks in the lakes.

Characteristics

One of the most popular holiday places in New South Wales, Tuggerah Lakes has grown like Topsy. Once it was strictly a fisherman's paradise with basic fishing shacks. Now there are first class motels, hotels, restaurants and sporting facilities.

How to Get There

By Rail

There is a regular electric rail service from Sydney to Wyong, and local buses from the station to the other areas.

By Road

From Sydney, via the Pacific Highway, or the F3 from Hornsby following the turnoffs.

Visitor Information

The Entrance Visitor Information Centre has its office in Marine Parade, and is open daily 9am-5pm. It shares its contact details with the Gosford Visitor Information Centre.

Central Coast

Accommodation

As with any holiday centre, there is a great deal of accommodation to choose from in the Tuggerah Lakes district. Here is a selection with prices for a double room per night, not including GST, which should be used as a guide only. The telephone area code is 02.

Wyong

Central Coast Motel, cnr Pacific Highway & Cutler Drive, ✆4353 2911. 17 units, swimming pool - ✪$60-80.

The Entrance

El Lago Waters Resort, 41 The Entrance Road, ✆4332 3955. 40 units, licensed restaurant, swimming pool, spa, sauna, tennis - ✪$70-120.

Ocean Front Motel, 102 Ocean Parade, ✆4332 5911. 31 units, barbecue, undercover parking - ✪$80-150.

Sapphire Palms Motel, 180 The Entrance Road, ✆4332 5799. 20 units, swimming pool, spa, barbecue - ✪$55-95.

Tienda Motel, 309A The Entrance Road, ✆4332 3933. 30 units, swimming pool, spa - ✪$55-110.

Lake Front Motel, 16 Coogee Avenue, ✆4332 4518. 14 units, swimming pool, barbecue - ✪$55-110.

Blue Bay Camping and Caravanning Park, cnr Bay Road & Narrawa Avenue, ✆4332 1991. (No dogs allowed), 48 sites - powered sites ✪$23-30 for two, on-site vans $50-80 for two, cabins $60-100.

Dunleith Caravan Park, Hutton Road, North Entrance, ✆4332 2172. 180 sites - powered sites ✪$18-35 for two, cabins $65-180 for two.

Long Jetty

The Coachman Motor Inn, 33 Gordon Road, ✆4332 3692. 7 units, swimming pool, barbecue - ✪$50-110.

Palm Gardens Resort, 44 Kitchener Road, ✆4333 1000. 23 suites, swimming pool, spa, sauna, barbecue - ✪$70-170.

Buccaneer Motel, 398 The Entrance Road, ✆4334 3100. 14 units, swimming pool, barbecue - ✪$68-120.

Jetty Motel, 353 The Entrance Road, ✆4332 1022. 22 units, swimming pool, spa, barbecue ✪$60-110.

Bateau Bay

Palm Court Motel, 61 Bateau Bay Road, ✆4332 3755. 10 units, unlicensed restaurant, swimming pool - ✪$60-110.

Bateau Bay Hotel/Motel, The Entrance Road, ✆4332 8022. 6 units, licensed restaurant - ✪$60-70.

Sun Valley Caravan Park, Bateau Bay Road, ✆4332 1107. (No pets allowed), 342 sites - powered sites ✪$21-30 for two, holiday flat $65-110 for two.

Budgewoi

Hibiscus Lakeside Motel, 2 Diamond Head Drive, ✆4390 9100. 13 units, barbecue - ✪$65-110.

Sunnylake Caravan Park, 2 Macleay Drive, ✆4390 9471. 130 sites - powered sites ✪$15-30 for two, cabins $90-170 for two.

Budgewoi Tourist Park, Weemala Street, ✆4390 9019. (Pets allowed on leash), 380 sites, barbecue - powered sites ✪$12-18.

Noraville

Sea'n'Sun Motel, 115 Budgewoi Road, ✆4396 4474. 12 units, mini golf, barbecue - ✪$55-100.

Toukley

Toukley Motor Inn, 236 Main Road, ✆4396 5666. 13 units, swimming pool - ✪$56-80.

Twin Lakes Motor Inn, 57 Main Road, ✆4396 4622. 11 units, swimming pool - ✪$50-85.

Eating Out

The district has several licensed RSL and bowling clubs, and these usually offer reasonably priced meals. There are also many takeaway and fast food outlets, both in the towns and on the beachfronts.

Rus Chinese Rendevous, 120 Railway Street, Wyong, ✆4353 2494.

Wyong Golf Club Restaurant, Pacific Highway, Wyong, ✆4352 1999.

Sounan Thai, 27 The Entrance Road, The Entrance, ✆4332 8806. Fully licensed restaurant with waterside views. Open 6pm-11pm 7 days and midday-3pm Wed-Sun, closed Public Holidays.

Jetty Indian Tandoori, 509 The Entrance Road, Long Jetty, ✆4334 2477.

Jans Chinese Malaysian Restaurant, Shops 5-6, 227-229 The En-trance Road, The Entrance, ✆4334 1333.

Mantas Seafood Restaurant, 347 The Entrance Road, Long Jetty, ✆4332 2548.

Beach Point, 19 Point Street, Bateau Bay, ✆4334 5070.

Carmelos Italian Restaurant, 61 Bateau Bay Road, Bateau Bay, ✆4334 5155.

Pizza Pit, 65 Scenic Drive Budgewoi, ✆4399 1035.

Silver Moon Chinese Restaurant, 105 Scenic Drive, Budgewoi, ✆4390 0489. Licensed, open 5pm-9pm 7 days and for lunch midday-2pm every day except Monday.

Cactus Blues Mexican Restaurant, 245 Main Road, Toukley, ✆4397 1557.

Starfish Seafood Restaurant, 200 Main Road, Toukley, ✆4397 1300.

Points of Interest

The Forest of Tranquility, Ourimbah Creek Road, Ourimbah, is the home of Willy Wombat's rainforest walk, the best walk in a rainforest in the Sydney environs. There are gas barbecues, a children's playground, and picnic area, and rainforest plants are for sale. ⏲Open Wed-Sun 10am-5pm and all public holidays, ✆4362 1855.

Crackneck Lookout, in Hilltop Avenue, Bateau Bay, offers sweeping views of the coastline to Norah Head and Bungary Point, over the three lakes and the three power stations.

Bateau Bay Golf Practice Range, 468 The Entrance Road, ✆4332 3277, is the largest golf range on the Central Coast, and venue of Australian Golf Schools. Practice facilities include grass tees, target greens, bunker and distance markers. ⏲Open 7 days.

Long Jetty Catamaran Hire, cnr Tuggerah Parade and Pacific Street, Long Jetty, ✆4332 9362, hires out catamarans, sailboards, canoes and pedal boats. They also have lessons in water skiing, and sell fishing tackle and bait.

The Entrance Aquaslide, ✆4334 3151, adjacent to the Lakeside Plaza carpark, 19 Taylor Street, The Entrance, has The Space Spiral, Outer Orbit and Cosmic Crusher rides, and the good news is, the pool is heated.

Each afternoon at 3.30pm, near the children's playground in the **Memorial Park**, The Entrance, everybody gathers to feed the pelicans.

The pelican has been adopted as the symbol of the tourist industry on the Central Coast, and the daily feeding ensures that this symbol doesn't disappear. There is no doubt that they are fascinating creatures, with wing spans up to 2m, and those incredible beaks, but there are many locals who are not exactly enamoured of them. To start with, they eat fish and are not well mannered enough to limit themselves to the afternoon meals supplied

Central Coast

by humans, but tend to fish for themselves in the lakes. And, they are much better at it than those people sitting in boats and on the shore with hooks and lines. Then they have lice, which they shed in the water to bite anyone who dares to swim in the area. It is not that the pelicans do this on purpose, but try selling that to a kiddy who is suffering from itchy bites. Of course, the pelicans came before people starting feeding them, but not in such large numbers.

At **Dunleith Caravan Park**, Hut-ton Road, North Entrance, ✆4332 2172, there is a Shell Museum, with an extensive display of shells and early photographs of the area, along with models of aquatic animals.

Norah Head Lighthouse, circa 1903, is open for visitors only by arrangement with the Visitor Centre. At Cabbage Tree Bay, the tiny settlement where the road to the light house commences, there are steps leading down to a lovely little rock pool, which is very popular with children. You can also drive down the steep road before the steps, but parking is usually a problem. There is a surfing beach alongside, but it is not patrolled, and there is a dangerous riptide.

Edward Hargraves Homestead, in Elizabeth Drive, Noraville, is not open for inspection, but can be viewed from the road. Edward Hargraves discovered gold near Bathurst in 1851, causing the first gold rush in Australia.

Toukley has a good-sized shopping centre, and the Toukley & District Senior Citizens Club in Hargraves Street, has loads of entertainment and things to do. Toukley RSL is also a very busy club, and visitors are always welcome, as they are at Toukley Bowling Club.

Warnervale Airfield, near the expressway (follow the road through Toukley, crossing the Pacific Highway) offers joy-flights every Sunday, and other days by appointment. Contact ***Central Coast Helicopters***, Lot 1, Sparks Road, Warnervale, ✆4352 2222, or ***Warnervale Air***, Jack Grant Avenue, ✆4392 5174.

Smokey Mountain Steam Railroad, in Mountain Road, Warner-vale, offers a different day out for all the family with steam train rides through the surrounding picturesque valleys 🕒between 11am and 4pm. It operates on Sundays and public holidays from Boxing Day until the last Sunday in October, except Good Friday and days of total fire ban. For further information, contact them on, ✆4392 7644.

Beaches

The coastal beaches in the Tuggerah Lakes area are: Bateau Bay; Shelly Beach; Toowoon Bay; The Entrance; North Entrance; Soldiers Point; Cabbage Tree Bay; Jenny Dixon; The Lakes Beach.

Jenny Dixon Beach and Cabbage Tree bay are not patrolled, and Jenny Dixon has some nude bathers, but the other beaches are patrolled every weekend, and all through the school holidays, and have handy food outlets. From the Lakes Beach, miles of sand and surf stretch northwards, but it should be remembered that the site of the beach club was chosen because it is the safest part of that stretch.

Newcastle

Population 138,200
Newcastle is situated on the Hunter River, 171km (106 miles) north of Sydney, and 827km (514 miles) south of Brisbane.

Climate

Average temperatures: January max 27C (81F) - min 18C (64F); July max 17C (63F) - min 6C (43F). Average annual rainfall: 1134mm (45 ins), and the rain falls quite evenly throughout the year.

Characteristics

Newcastle is the second largest city in New South Wales, and the sixth largest in Australia. The site was discovered when Lt Shortland was searching for convict escapees in the late 18th century, and discovered coal, which together with steel dominated Newcastle to the mid-1960s.

Newcastle is a city with international-style hotels, motels and shopping centres. It is an ideal base for visiting the holiday areas of Lake Macquarie, Port Stephens and the Hunter Valley.

The city was hit by a shocking earthquake on December 28, 1989, with the loss of lives and many buildings. A swift Novocastrian recovery has meant that few signs of the disaster remain.

Newcastle

How to Get There

By Air

The Newcastle Airport is at Williamtown, 23km from the city, and there are plenty of taxis available for transport to and from the city centre.

Qantas, ✆13 1313 have regular flights to Newcastle.

By Bus

Greyhound Pioneer, ✆13 2030, and McCaffertys, ✆13 1499, are among the coach companies that stop at Newcastle.

By Rail

Newcastle is on the Sydney/Murwillumbah line with regular services, and connections from Murwillumbah to Brisbane and the Gold Coast, ✆13 2232.

By Road

From Sydney, via the Pacific Highway and the F3 Expressway.

From Brisbane via the Pacific Highway through Tweed Heads and along the coast, or via the New England Highway through Glen Innes and Armidale.

Visitor Information

The Tourist Information Centre is located at 363 Hunter Street, ✆(02) 4974 2999 or ✆1800 654 558. Opening hours are 9am-5pm Mon-Fri and 10am-3.30pm on weekends. The internet references for Newcastle are newtour@hunterlink.net.au or you can try: mail@ncc.nsw.gov.au for email, and also www.ncc.nsw.gov.au for the website.

Accommodation

As with any large city, moderately-priced accommodation places are in the suburbs, and the Tourist Office has a complete list of what is available. Here is a selection with prices for a double room per night, which should be used as a guide only. The telephone area code is 02.

City

Holiday Inn Esplanade Newcastle, Shortland Esplanade, ✆4929 5576. 72 rooms, licensed restaurant - $170-260.

Junction Motel, 121 Union Street, ✆4929 6677. 30 units, licensed restaurant, pool - $130.

Ridges City Central Hotel, cnr King & Steel Streets, ✆4926 3777. 122 units, 6 suites, licensed restaurant, swimming pool, gym, spa - $120-160.

Noah's On The Beach, cnr Shortland Esplanade & Zaara Street, ✆4929 5181. 90 units, 1 suite, licensed restaurant - $140.

Novocastrian Motor Inn, 21 Parnell Place, ✆4926 3688. 47 units, licensed restaurant - 140-200.

Newcomen Lodge, 70 Newcomen Street, ✆4929 7313. 1 room, unlicensed restaurant, pool - $115.

Suburbs

Apollo International Hotel, 290 Pacific Highway, Charlestown, ✆4943 6733. 42 units, 8 suites, tennis, swimming pool, barbecue - $140-240.

Hospitality Motor Inn, 418 Maitland Road, Mayfield, ✆4967 1977. 28 units, licensed restaurant - $120-130.

Sovereign Motor Inn, 309 Maitland Road, Mayfield, ✆4968 4405. 34 units, licensed restaurant, swimming pool - $90-100.

Aloha Motor Inn, 231 Glebe Road, Merewether, ✆4963 1283. 29 units, barbecue - ✪$95-105.

Tudor Inn, cnr Tudor & Steel Streets, Hamilton, ✆4969 2533. 31 units, unlicensed restaurant - ✪$90-100.

Panorama Motor Inn, 256 Pacific Highway, Charlestown, ✆4943 3144. 33 units, licensed restaurant, barbecue, pool - ✪$65-80.

There is a **Youth Hostel** in 30 Pacific Street (cnr King Street), ✆4925 3544. They have 22 rooms at ✪$24 per person twin share.

Caravan Parks

Tomago Village Van Park, Pacific Highway & Tomago Road, Tomago, ✆4964 8066. (No pets allowed) - powered sites ✪$19 for two, cabins $45-70 for two.

Redhead Beach Holiday Park, 1A Kalaroo Road, ✆4944 8306. (No pets allowed) - powered sites ✪$19-25 for two, cabins $45-95 for two, on-site vans $45-55 for two.

Stockton Beach Tourist Park, Pitt Street, Stockton, ✆4928 1393. (No dogs allowed) - powered sites ✪$16-20 for two, cabins $35-60 for two.

Newcastle

Eating Out

Finding somewhere to eat in Newcastle is not a problem. There are the licensed clubs (Newcastle Workers, Western Suburbs Leagues Club, Tubemakers Recreation Club, etc) which all offer restaurants, bistros and snack bars. There are also the hotels and motels, most of which have licensed or BYO restaurants, and coffee shops and takeaway food outlets. The Tourist Information Office has a complete list of restaurants, but here are some you might wish to try.

Hawaiian Sunsets, 171 Darby Street, ©4926 1264. International menu, licensed. Open 6pm-midnight 7 days, closed Public Holidays.

Lans, 146 Darby Street, ©4929 1565. Open 5pm-10pm every day except Mondays and Public Holidays (closed).

Delaney Hotel, 134 Darby Street, ©4929 1627. Open 10am-midnight Mon-Sat and Sunday midday-10pm.

San Marco on the Park, 10 Pacific Street, ©4926 3865. Fully licensed, open 12pm-3pm and 6pm-9pm Mon-Sat, closed Sunday.

Harry's on Hunter, 672 Hunter Street, ©4926 2165.

Mercury Cafe, Mercury Hotel, 23 Watt Street, ©4929 2025.

Queens Wharf Brewery Restaurant, 150 Wharf Road, ©4929 6333.

Signatures, Radisson Hotel, cnr King & Steel Streets, ©4926 3777.

Thara Tong Thai, 541 Hunter Street, ©4929 6722.

Taco Bills Mexican Restaurant, 80 Darby Street, ©4929 2971.

Maharaja Indian Restaurant, 653 Hunter Street, ©4926 1665.

Elizas, Shortland Esplanade, ©4929 5576.

Newcastle Happy Gardens Chinese Restaurant, 133 Scott Street, ©4926 2707.

McDonalds are on the corner of King & Steel Streets. KFC is at 227 Hunter Street and Pizza Hut is located at 500 Hunter Street, ©13 1166 for delivery.

Queen's Wharf

Points of Interest

City Hall, in King Street, is the office of Newcastle's Lord Mayor, and is an impressive sandstone building with a tall clock tower. Opened in 1929, it was completely refurbished in 1970-80, and is now a Convention Centre.

Civic Park, opposite the City Hall, is a large park that is a favourite place for Newcastle's business people to relax during the lunchbreak. The special trees planted at the eastern and western ends are gifts from Newcastle's Sister City, Ube in Japan.

The Captain Cook Memorial Fountain forms a backdrop to Civic Park. It was built in 1966, and is illuminated at night.

The multi-million dollar **Queen's Wharf and Harbour** is a pleasant attraction. You can walk along the promenade, metres away from ships from all over the world, or hire a Daisy Trike or bike and pedal your way around. The complex is only 50m from the Hunter Mall, and includes a marina, a seafood restaurant, a boutique brewery, the Tourist Information Centre and variety shops. From the top of the tower in the complex one has a view of the city, harbour and beaches north up to Port Stephens, and west to the Watagan Mountains. On weekends there are horse-drawn carriage rides available, bands playing, and a complete holiday atmosphere. Unique little 'shop barrows' are located along its foreshores.

At **Harbourside Markets**, cnr Wharf Road & Merewether Street, there's everything to buy, in the classic market style.

William the Fourth was the first Australian-built coastal steamship, and is now anchored at Queen's Wharf. It is available for historical cruises around Newcastle Harbour. See the Tourist Information Centre for all the details.

The Newcastle Regional Art Gallery, in Laman Street, ✆4974 5100, was opened in 1977 by Her Majesty, Queen Elizabeth II. It houses the city's Art Collection and features visiting exhibitions regularly. In front of the building is another gift from Ube, a stainless steel sculpture, 'Space Two'. The gallery is open Tues-Sun 10am-5pm and entry is free.

Christ Church Anglican Cathedral overlooks the city from the top of **the hill**, and can be seen from harbour, sea and suburbs. The foundation for the first cathedral was laid in 1817 and was in use until 1884 when another (now the Cathedral Hall opposite) was erected. The present cathedral was dedicated in 1902, and was eventually completed, tower and all, in 1979. It is open from early morning until 6pm. Guides are available on Sat and Sun afternoons.

Hunter Mall became a pedestrian arcade in 1980, and is framed by fine Victorian and Edwardian buildings. As well as David Jones department store, it has many specialty stores.

Fort Scratchley, on Nobbys Road, is Australia's only fort that went to war. An historical fort, it was built in the mid-1880s near the site where Lt Shortland first landed on September 9, 1879. It is one of two remaining 19th century closed fort complexes in NSW. Believing that Newcastle was a place likely to be attacked from sea, the Government decided a major fort should be built on Signal Hill. It was largely completed in 1882. In June 1942, it was involved in an attack by a Japanese Submarine. The guns, now on display in the fort, returned the fire, causing the submarine to break off. This was the only time in Australian history that heavy guns were fired in hostility from coastal defences. The fort houses the **Newcastle Region Maritime Museum**, which has many interesting exhibits, and is open week-ends and Public Holidays from midday-4pm.

The Ocean Baths, located at Newcastle Beach and at Mere-wether Beach, are the two largest saltwater baths in the Southern Hemisphere.

The Obelisk, up the hill just to the south of the city, is in the park bounded by Bindle Reserve Road, Ordnance Street & Wolfe Street. It marks the site of Newcastle's first windmill. The mill was erected in 1820 and became a navigational mark for ships approaching Newcastle. It was demolished in 1847, and the obelisk erected in 1850. In early 1987 it was struck by lightning, but has since been repaired.

Newcastle Regional Museum, 787 Hunter Street, ✆4962 2001, is the leading Regional Museum in the country. It features exhibits about the industrial and technological heritage of the surrounding region, its social history, lifestyle and environment. The redevelopment of the former Castlemain & Wood Bros Brewery into the museum was a major Bicentennial project. The museum is open Tues-Sun and public holidays 10am-5pm.

Supernova, Newcastle's Science and Technology Fun Centre is housed within the Regional Museum. It is hands-on science, a museum where kids are encouraged to touch the displays. Supernova is open the same hours as the Museum, and there is a moderate admission fee.

Nobbys Head was first described by Captain Cook as a "small clump of an island". It was reduced in 1826 by half its size to im-

Nobbys Beach

prove access by ships to the harbour. In 1846, it was connected to the mainland by the breakwater. On top of Nobbys is a lighthouse signal station, and Nobbys Beach is a popular surfing beach with the Novocastrians.

The Heritage Centre, ✆4925 2265, next door to the Post Office in Hunter Street, is Newcastle's former Police Station (1859), and is operated by the Hunter Region National Trust. The centre features an environmental Gift Shop, ⏲open Mon-Fri 9am-5pm.

Beaches

Newcastle Beach offers safe swimming from the rocks at the northern end to the front of the club pavilion, and surfboard riding to the southern end. *Surfest*, one of the world's leading surfing events takes place here every November. The floodlit and patrolled Ocean Baths are here also.

Nobbys Beach is an excellent family beach. There is good surfing on the reef, at the northern end and at Cowrie hole to the south (patrolled).

Horseshoe Beach is Newcastle's only harbour beach, and is popular with trainers and their racehorses. It is also a good fishing spot.

Stockton Beach, is opposite the city, and offers safe swimming from the breakwater to Hereford Street, and good surfing from there to the north. The main beach is patrolled. Here you can check out the wreck of the *Sygna* (1974).

Bar Beach to the south of Newcastle Beach and the Bogey Hole, is also a good family beach with safe swimming from the northern end (Bar area) to the front of the pavilion, and surfboard riding from there to the southern end. There is plenty of parking. The beach is patrolled and floodlit.

Susan Gilmore Beach, is accessed from the extreme northern end of Bar Beach, via a path down the cliff face, or over the rocks at low tide. The beach was named after an American ship that was wrecked here. It is a nudist beach, and is not patrolled.

Merewether Beach is an excellent swimming beach with good beachbreak surfboard riding south of the club house. The beach is patrolled and floodlit. There are Ocean Baths here too.

Dixon Park Beach offers safe swimming in front of the clubhouse, and is good for surfing, board and ski, in front of the cliff. The beach is patrolled.

Burwood and **Dudley Beaches** are excellent for swimming and board riding, but these nudists beaches are not patrolled.

Out-of-City Attractions

Shortland Wetlands Centre. The Centre is situated on 65ha (160 acres) of wetland along Sandgate Road, Shortland on the edge of Hexham Swamp. More than 170 species of birds have been recorded here. Canoes can be hired for exploring the 7km of waterways around Hexham Swamp.The Visitors centre is open daily 9am-5pm, with extended hours during holiday seasons. An small admission price applies. Phone 4951 6466 for more information. The Information Centre in Newcastle can arrange half day tours and twilight walks to Shortland Wetlands.

Blackbutt Reserve. A reserve of approximately 180ha, Blackbutt is situated in the middle of Newcastle's suburbia. It consists of open forest land intersected by four valleys running from west to east. One of the area's greatest attractions, apart from vegetation, animals and uncommon birds, is its seclusion from the City around it. The Reserve is a popular spot with the locals and a source of interest for overseas tourists keen to observe the exhibition of Australian indigenous wildlife, including wombats, koalas, kangaroos, emus, wallabies and native birds. It is open all year, 10am-5pm for the wildlife exhibits, and there is no admission fee. The Maritime Model Club launch their ships on the biggest pond every Saturday. The Tourist Office has a leaflet setting out the various bushwalks and all the attractions, or you can call direct on 4952 1449.

Tours

The Tourist Office has details of tours in and around Newcastle, and of Hunter River and harbour cruises that are available. Here are two worth enquiring about:

Australian Scenic Tours, 50 Hunter Street, 4929 4333.

Free Spirit Charters, Level 4, 175 Scott Street, 4929 1908.

Scenic Helicopter Flights, cnr Hannel and Cowper Streets, Wickham, 4962 2240, is one company operating in the area.

Hunter Vineyard Tours, 4991 1659, and ***The Wine and Cheese Tasting Tour***, 4938 5031.

Festivals

The Matarra Festival is held each September.

Facilities

Newcastle has all the facilities you would expect of a city its size. Theatre and cinema programmes are in the daily newspapers, and the Yellow Pages Telephone Book has details of all sporting facilities. The Tourist Information Centre has all the details.

Outlying Attractions

Forster - Tuncurry

North of Newcastle, about 161km (100 miles), are the twin towns of Forster and Tuncurry, which are the major tourist areas of the Great Lakes, and are renowned for their beaches, fishing, seafoods and temperate climate all year around.

On land there is the **Booti Booti National Park** to explore, and the **Cape Hawke Bicentennial Walk** with its panoramic viewing platform. The popular beaches and lakes provide ample opportunites for swimming, fishing and sailing.

Black Head Beach, north of Forster

Forster has the Great Lakes Visitor Centre located in Little Street, ✆(02) 6554 8799 or &1800 802 692. It is hopen Mon-Fri 9am-5pm. They have a web page located at the address: www.greatlakes.org.au and their email address is tourglc@tpgi. com.au

Barrington Tops

The Barrington Tops National Park is about 110km (68 miles) north-west of Newcastle, travelling through Raymond Terrace and Dungog. The area is on the World Heritage List.

A wonderful website covers this area in great depth: www. barringtons.com.au

Dungog Visitors Information Centre is on the corner of Dowling and Brown Streets, Dungog, ✆4992 2212, or you can email: dungogvc@midac.com.au. It is open Mon-Fri 9am-5pm and Sat-Sun 9am-3pm.

The Gloucester Visitor Information Centre is on the corner of Church & Denison Streets, Gloucester, ✆6558 1408, or you can send an email to: glosinfo@tpg.com.au. It is open 7 days 9.30am-4.30pm.

Port Stephens

Port Stephens is a 45 minute coastal drive north of Newcastle, and is regarded as one of the most attractive and unspoilt waterways anywhere in Australia. It proclaims itself as the 'Dolphin Capital of Australia', since more than 140 bottlenose dolphins reside in the port, which is more than twice the size of Sydney Harbour. Further upstream from where the Myall River flows into the Port are the Broadwater and the Myall Lakes systems with lovely waterways, tiny uninhabited islands, abundant bird life, a national park, and unpolluted beaches stretching north to the Smith's and Wallace Lakes systems.

The main centres are Shoal Bay, Nelson Bay, Salamander Bay and Soldiers Point, and the smaller, and somewhat newer areas are Lemon Tree, Mallabula, Tanilba Bay and Oyster Cove.

On the waterway's northern reaches are the holiday centres of Tea Gardens and Hawks Nest, both offering good accommodation, beaches and facilities.

Nelson Bay is the Port Stephens service centre, with a variety of shops, a movie cinema, a supermarket, restaurants, banks, a pub, and plenty more. People flock to the scenic **Marina** for shopping, dining and entertainment.

The area also has theme parks catering for children, including **Toboggan Hill Park** in Salamander Bay, ✆4984 1022; **Tomteland Australia** in Williamtown, ✆4965 1500; and **Oakvale Farm and Fauna World** in Salt Ash, ✆4982 6222.

The Port Stephens Visitor Information Centre is on Victoria Parade, Nelson Bay, ✆(02) 4981 1579 or ✆1800 808 900. It is ⏲open 9am-5pm Mon-Fri and 9am-4pm Sat, Sun and Public Holidays. You will find it at the driveway entrance to the Marina. Email them at tops@hunterlink.net.au or find the website at www.port stephens.org.au

Hunter Valley

The beauty of the Hunter, with its rolling hills covered in rows of grape-vines and surrounded by tall mountains, surprises many visitors. There are over 1500ha (3705 acres) of vineyards under cultivation in the Lower Hunter-Pokolbin district near Cessnock, and more than 1600ha (3952 acres) planted in the Upper Hunter, centred around the towns of Muswellbrook and Denman.

It is renowned for the production of top quality table wines. The main Tourist Information Centre for the area is located on Main Road, Pokolbin (near the AirField), ✆(02) 4990 4477, www.winecountry.com.au. There is another in Maitland, in King Edward Park, Banks Street East, ✆(02) 4933 2611.

The Hunter Regional Tourism Organisation has a web page at www.huntertourism.com/ Online/ home/main.html

Murrurundi

The town of Murrurundi on the Pages River occupies the northernmost point of the Hunter Valley, and has historic old buildings, many classified by the National Trust. Tales of bushrangers are intertwined with the region. Ben Hall was born here, and Thunderbolt roamed in the area in the latter part of the last century.

Sheep, cattle and horse breeding are the major interests, and the mountain scenery of the Liverpool Ranges, at the town's doorstep, gives an unparalleled view of the valley.

Scone

Scone was first settled during the 1830s by Scottish settlers who likened the countryside to their homeland, and named many spots after their birthplaces. The town is now a thriving commercial centre supporting important rural industries, and is well known for its thoroughbred horses, cattle and sheep from stud properties in the area. Scone is also the inland gateway to the Barrington Tops region, via the Scone-Gloucester Road.

Nearby **Glenbawn Dam** is well stocked with freshwater fish, and is ideal for boating, yachting, water skiing and swimming.

The **Burning Mountain**, off the New Eng-

Hot Air Ballooning in the Hunter Valley

land Highway between Scone and Murrurundi, turn-off just north of Wingen, has been burning for thousands of years. Today the mountain is easily reached via a two kilometre walking track.

Travelling south through **Aberdeen**, which once housed a thriving abbatoir, one comes to Muswellbrook.

Scone has a Visitor Information Centre on the corner of Susan & Kelly Streets, open daily 9am-5pm. Email them at stic@scone.nsw.gov.au or phone (02) 6545 1526.

Muswellbrook

The Muswellbrook area has benefitted in recent years with the growth of the mining and power industries, and as well, the wine industry. The major rural activity, though, is dairy farming. Produce is supplied through the Hunter Valley Co-operative Dairy Company's processing plant at Muswellbrook.

The area boasts a number of **Art and Craft Galleries**, and the **Rainbow Zone Fun Centre** in Industrial Close, 6541 4279.

For more information, the Muswellbrook Visitor Information Centre is in 87 Hill Street,

(02) 6541 4050. Open 9am-5pm daily. A web page lets you explore the area at www.muswellbrook. org.au

Denman

Situated in one of the most fertile areas of the Hunter Region, some 15km south-west of Muswellbrook off the New England Highway, Denman has many fine horse and cattle studs, and has become an acknowledged quality wine producing area.

Vineyards in the area are: **Arrowfield**, 6576 4041, one of the largest in Australia; **Rosemount Estate**, 6549 6400; **McGuigan Wines**, 6547 2422; and **Horsehoe Vineyard**, 6547 3528.

The nearby **Widden Valley** is considered to be second only to America's famous Kentucky Blue Grass region for the breeding of racehorses.

Singleton

Back on the New England Highway we come to the geographical heart of the Hunter Valley, Singleton. It has the Hunter River flowing past its doorstep and irrigating the surrounding rich grazing land.

Nearby **Lake St Clair** offers boating and fishing, and maps of the waterways are available from the Information Centre.

The **Singleton Army Camp** includes the Royal Australian Infantry Corps Museum, which is open to visitors 9am-4pm Wed-Sun.

On the New England Highway, between Singleton and Muswellbrook, are the Liddell (6542 1611) and Bayswater (6542 1611) **Power Stations**, which are two of the biggest thermal power stations in the Southern Hemisphere. Visitor tours are available at certain times by arrangement.

The Singleton Information Centre at the southern entrance to the town, in the Shire Council, Civic Centre on Queen Street. They are open Mon-Fri 8.30am-4.30pm, (02) 6578 7267. The website is: www.singleton.nsw.gov.au and the email address is ssc@singletoncouncil.nsw.gov.au

Cessnock

The town of Cessnock is 52km (32 miles) from Newcastle and 185km (115 miles) from Sydney. It is the gateway to the wineries, with approximately 30 in the area. Cessnock is the major town in the area, but the satellite district of Pokolbin provides the real accommodation treats.

The historic village of **Wollombi**, 31km (19 miles) south-west of Cessnock, has a few interesting buildings worth visiting - the Court House, St John's Anglican Church and the two-storey Post Office.

The Visitor Information Centre is in Turner Park, Aberdare Road, and opens 7 days, Mon-Thu 9am-5pm, Fri 9am-6pm, Sat 9.30am-5pm and Sunday and Public Holidays 9.30am-3.30pm. The Information Centre has a list of all the attractions in the town, and of the wineries which are open for tours and cellar door sales. They can be emailed at info@winecountry. com.au or visited at the website www.winecountry.com.au

Kurri Kurri

Kurri Kurri is the closest notable town in the Hunter Valley to Sydney (150km) and it lies fairly close to the end of the northern freeway, but really there are more picturesque places to stay in the region, so an extra drive is worth the time.

Near the town of Kurri Kurri is the **Richmond Vale Railway Museum** and the **Richmond Main Colliery**, but opening days are limited so phone 4937 5344 or 4936 1124 if you are fascinated by mid-nineteenth century mining and engineering accomplishments. The historic Kurri Kurri Hotel on the corner of Lang and Hampden Streets is also worth a visit.

Taree

Population 16,700
Taree is located on the banks of the Manning River, 330km (205 miles) north of Sydney.

Characteristics

Taree is the commercial centre of the Manning Valley, and offers natural attractions such as scenic lookouts, waterfalls, and some of the East Coast's cleanest, whitest beaches.

Climate

Average temperatures: January max 29C (84F) - min 17C (63F); July max 18C (64F) - min 6C (43F). Average annual rainfall: 1171mm (46 ins).

How to Get There

By Air

Qantas ✆131313, has flights from/to Sydney.

By Bus

McCaffertys, ✆13 1499, and Greyhound Pioneer, ✆13 2030, stop at Taree on their Sydney/Brisbane runs.

By Rail

There is an XPT Countrylink service from Sydney to Taree taking 5 hours, ✆13 2232.

By Road

From Sydney (310km) and Brisbane (8 hours), via the Pacific Highway.

Visitor Information

The Manning Valley Visitor Information Centre is on the Old Pacific Highway, Taree North, 3km north of the Taree Shopping Centre, ✆(02) 6552 1900 or ✆1800 801 522. They are open 7 days a week 9am-5pm, and the complex includes a restaurant, public toilets, and a 70-seat theatrette. The email address is manningvic@gtcc.nsw.gov.au and the web site: www.gtcc.nsw.gov.au/tourism

Taree

Accommodation

Taree has many motels, a few caravan parks, and houseboats for hire (available from Manning River Holidays Afloat, 36 Crescent Avenue, Taree, ✆6552 3162).

Here is a selection of accommodation with prices for a double room per night, which should be used as a guide only. The telephone area code is 02.

Riverview Motor Inn, Old Pacific Highway, ✆6552 2122. 21 units, 1 suite, licensed restaurant, swimming pool - ✪$100.

City Centre Motor Inn, 4 Crescent Avenue, ✆6552 5244. 20 units, swimming pool, barbecue - ✪$80-90.

Best Western Caravilla Motor Inn, 33 Victoria Street, ✆6552 1822. 27 units, licensed restaurant (closed Sunday), swimming pool - ✪$75-85.

In-Town Motor Inn, 77 Victoria Street, ✆6552 3996. 20 units, spa bath, barbecue - ✪$70-80.

Marco Polo Motor Inn, Pacific Highway, ✆6552 3866. 20 units, swimming pool, sauna, barbecue - ✪$100-110.

Agincourt Motel, 9 Commerce Street, ✆6552 1614. 21 units - ✪$45-65.

Jolly Swagman Motel, 1 Commerce Street, ✆6552 3511. 21 units, barbecue - ✪$55-90.

Chatham Motel, Pacific Highway, ✆6552 1659. 10 units - ✪$40-45.

Arlite Motor Inn, cnr Bligh Street & Pacific Highway, ✆6552 2433. 20 units, swimming pool - ✪$50.

Caravan Parks

Twilight Caravan Park, Pacific Highway, ✆0500 854 448. (Pets allowed under control), 65 sites - powered sites ✪$17-20 for two, on-site vans $30-40 for two, cabins $35-70.

Riverside Caravan Park, Reid Street, Croki, ✆6556 3274. (No pets), 38 sites, barbecue - powered sites ✪$15-18 for two, on-site vans $35 for two, cabins $35 for two.

Eating Out

The hotels all have restaurants and snack bars, and some of the motels have licensed or unlicensed restaurants. The local licensed clubs also have dining rooms and bistros. Here are some restaurants you might like to try.

Thai Tarni, Albert Street, ✆6552 2366. BYO dine-in or take-away. Open 5.30pm-9.30pm every day except Monday and for lunch 11.30am-2pm Tue-Fri.

Il Colosseo, 32 Oxley Street, ✆6552 6289. BYO, Italian, also offers free pizza delivery within a 10km radius. Open 6pm-10pm every day except Monday, and until midnight Fri-Sun.

Shades, 23-25 Oxley Street, ✆6552 1455. Fully licensed restaurant with an international menu. Open every day except Sunday 6pm-midnight.

Kowin Chinese Restaurant, 22 Chatham Avenue, ✆6552 3482. Licensed, open 7 nights 5pm-9pm.

East Court Chinese Restaurant, 73 Victoria Street, ✆6552 2465. Licensed, salad bar, banquets, open 7 nights 5pm-10pm.

Silhouettes, Shop 5, 103 Victoria Street, ✆6552 1393.

Pelican, Old Pacific Highway, ✆6552 2122.

Laurents, 33 Victoria Street, ✆6552 5022.

Jin Hong Chinese Restaurant, 91 Victoria Street, ✆6552 7199.

Seafood on Victoria, 166 Victoria Street, ✆6557 8111.

McDonalds is on the corner of the Pacific Highway and Manning Street. You will find KFC at 38 Victoria Street. Pizza Hut is in Manning Mall, Manning Street, ✆13 1166.

Points of Interest

Taree is, as we have mentioned, a holiday town, and there is not a great deal of sight-seeing, just plenty of places to relax and take advantage of the river.

The riverside **Fotheringham and Queen Elizabeth Parks** offer the opportunity to feed the pelicans and seagulls, and to observe the river.

Manning River Cruises, ✆6557 4767, have a cruise boat on the Manning, with informative commentary to accompany your charter. There are regular departures during school holidays.

The Big Oyster, Pacific Highway, North Taree, is like the other striking and largely ludicrous 'Bigs' in the country.

Festivals

The Taree Aquatic Festival is held each January, and the Taree City Festival is held every two years in June.

Facilities

An 18-hole golf course, several tennis courts, 4 bowling clubs, BMX track, Olympic swimming pool, basketball stadium, indoor cricket stadium, squash courts, ten pin bowling, greyhound racing and horse racing, and facilities for rugby league, rugby union, soccer, hockey, and netball.

The Manning Entertainment centre, ✆6551 0555, has a 505 seat auditorium, and clubs have top local and interstate bands throughout the year. There is also a twin cinema.

Outlying Attractions

Harrington

The northern arm of the Manning River reaches the ocean at Harrington, and a long breakwall provides excellent fishing. The town is about 5km south of the east-side turn-off on the Pacific Highway.

Safe lagoon swimming is available, and there are barbecue and picnic areas.

From **Pilot Hill Lookout** there is a good view of the coastline. The graves near the lookout are those of pilots whose jobs were to guide the boats over the treacherous bar to enable the timber to be picked up at the ports of Wingham and Taree.

The Harrington Crowdy Tourist Information Centre is at 85 Beach Street, Harrington, ✆6556 1188.

Crowdy Head

4km (2 miles) north-east of Harrington is the quaint village of Crowdy Head, the home of the local fishing fleet.

There's good fishing from the headland, and a co-op if you don't have any luck yourself. The **lighthouse** is easily reached by a sealed road, and gives excellent views of the coastline, both north and south.

Crowdy Beach sweeps in a long arc through to Diamond Head in the National Park, and offers safe swimming.

The Harrington Crowdy Tourist Information Centre is at 85 Beach Street, Harrington, ✆6556 1188.

Manning Point

The township is a little over 35km (22 miles) from Taree, and is located on an island near the mouth of the river. The sea and the north arm of the Manning River meet at Manning Point, with the ocean providing safe white sandy beaches for swimming, and the river providing excellent fishing.

Wingham

Situated 13km (8 miles) west of Taree, Wingham has a feeling of 'olde England', with its town common that is also the local cricket pitch. There are also about 13 buildings which have been classified by the National Trust for their historical significance, and most have been carefully reconstructed. They include the School of Arts, the Police Station and Court House, the Bank Building, Gibson & Skinner Butchery and the Australian Hotel.

Manning Valley Historical Society's Museum, corner Farquhar & Bent Streets, ✆6553 5823, ⏲open 10am-4pm, is also located within the town square area, and displays include Jimmy Governor's cell, together with various items relating to the history of the area.

Wingham Brush, located 500m from the shopping centre on Farquhar Street, is 7ha (17 acres) of coastal rainforest, with birds and native marsupials. The Brush is adjacent to the Manning River and has picnic tables, barbecues and boat launching facilities.

Use the resources of the Taree Information Centre to obtain further details of Wingham, ✆6552 1900.

Forestry Drives

Bulga Forest Drive is a scenic tour through timbered country north west of Wingham, passing the Ellenborough Falls near Elands. The round trip from Wingham takes visitors through three State Forests - The Bulga, Dingo and Knorrit.

Kiwarrak State Forest is 5km (3 miles) south of Taree, adjacent to the Pacific Highway. Highlights of this 16km (10 miles) sign-posted drive include the Pines picnic area and Breakneck Lookout.

Coopernook State Forest Drive includes Vincents Lookout, Newbys Creek Walk, Newbys Lookout, Starrs Creek, Big Nellie Mountain and Wautui Falls.

Paragliding at Diamond Head

Middle Brother Forest surrounds Middle Brother Mountain (556m -1824 ft). Several walking trails have been established within the Forest, and attractions include the largest Blackbutt trees in the State.

Old Bar

The town centre of Old Bar is only 16km (10 miles) from Taree's closest surfing beach. Old Bar's attractions, apart from the beach, are the mouth of the Manning River and the reserve/picnic area known as **Mud Bishops Reserve**, which offers shaded barbecue facilities.

Hallidays Point – Diamond Beach

Midway between Taree and the Great Lakes region is the coastal area of Hallidays Point - Diamond Beach. The Lands Department has established a **rainforest walk** encompassing the coastal landforms as well as rare tracts of coastal rainforest. The walk takes in two headlands, Black Head and Red Head, and is joined by Black Head Beach. The Visitor Information Centre in Taree has brochures on the Walk. **Nine Mile Beach** stretches southwards.

Above: North of Port Macquarie, *Below:* South of Port Macquarie

Port Maquarie

Population 33,700

Port Macquarie is situated at the mouth of the Hastings River on the North Coast of New South Wales, 423km (263 miles) north of Sydney.

Climate

Average temperatures: January max 25C (77F) - min 18C (64F); July max 18C (64F) - min 7C (45F). Average annual rainfall: 1563mm (62 ins). The CSIRO suggests that Port Macquarie has the most ideal climate in Australia. A warm off-shore current combines with the surrounding barrier of hills to form a pocket, and produce this small range of temperature.

Characteristics

A major coastal tourist resort and retirement area, Port Macquarie is the most historically significant town along the coast between Newcastle and the Queensland border.

In October, 1818, John Oxley reached the mouth of the Hastings River and described the area as "... a beautiful point of land, having plenty of good water and grass, and commanding a fine view of the interior of the port and the surrounding country". He named the inlet Port Macquarie in honour of the Governor of the Colony of New South Wales.

In 1821, the settlement of Port Macquarie was established by a pioneer party of soldiers and convicts.

How to Get There

By Air

Qantas, ✆13 1313 provide flights from Sydney, Melbourne, Brisbane, Newcastle, Taree, Coffs Harbour, Lismore, Ballina and Coolangatta.

Port Macquarie

By Bus

Greyhound Pioneer, ✆13 2030, and McCaffertys, ✆13 1499 stop at Port Macquarie.

By Rail

The XPT service from Sydney stops at Wauchope and a coach service connects with Port Macquarie, ✆13 2232.

By Road

From Sydney, via the Pacific Highway on a 400km trip. From Brisbane, either the Pacific Highway along the coast (510 km), or the Cunningham Highway to Warwick, the New England Highway and then the Oxley Highway back to the coast.

Visitor Information

The Port Macquarie Visitor Information Centre is on the corner of Clarence and Hay Streets, ✆(02) 6581 8000 or ✆1800 025 935. Their opening hours are 8.30am-5pm Mon-Fri, 9am-4.30pm weekends. Their web page is at www.portmacquarieinfo.com.au and emails can be sent to the address: vicpm@midcoast.com.au

Eating Out

There are many restaurants in the town, offering local seafood, French, Italian, Thai, Mexican, Chinese, Vegetarian and Aussie fare. Here are a few you might like to try.

Cray's Restaurant and Fish Cafe, 74 Clarence Street, ✆6583 7885. Seafood specialists, licensed, lunch and dinner, quality takeaway available.

Scampi's on the Marina, Park Street, ✆6583 7200. Seafood, dinner 7 days after 6pm, BYO, 'Seafood to Go' quality takeaway available for dinner 7 days.

Filou Restaurant, Mercure Sand-castle Motor Inn, 16-24 William Street, ✆6583 4646. Licensed, French cuisine, breakfast, lunch and dinner daily.

Zephyrs on Clarence, 2 Clarence Street, ✆6583 6822. Authentic Australian foods including crocodile, kangaroo and barramundi, licensed, open from 6pm.

Spinnakers Resort, Sails Resort, Park Street, ✆6583 3999. A la carte dining, licensed, breakfast, lunch and dinner.

Al Dente, 74 Clarence Street, ✆6584 1422. Licensed Italian restaurant on the waterfront, lunch and dinner.

Cafe 66, 66 Clarence Street, ✆6583 2484. BYO, Italian fare, snacks to meals, open late.

Toro's Mexican, 22 Murray Street, ✆6583 4340. BYO, dine in or take away.

Pancake Place, cnr Clarence & Hay Street, ✆6583 4544. BYO, open seven days from 10am, take-away and home delivery.

McDonalds is on the corner of Bay & Park Streets, opposite Settlement City and on the corner of the Pacific Highway and Oxley Street. KFC is on the corner of Horton and Hayward Streets. The phone number for Pizza Hut deliveries in the area is ✆13 1166.

Points of Interest - *continued*

Peppermint Park, cnr Pacific Drive & Ocean Street (near Flynn's Beach), ✆6583 6111, has landscaped parkland with water slides, pools, mini golf, aviaries, monkeys, 'Twista' Dodgems and roller skating. Barbecue facilities, a milk bar, and a fitness trail are other attractions. The Park is open Tue-Sun, and every day during school holidays. Adults $14, children $14, pensioners $9, family $50.

Sea Acres Rainforest Centre, Pacific Drive, ✆6582 3355, has a 1.3km boardwalk within 6.2ha (15 acres) of coastal rainforest. There is also a theatre with continuous shows, a restaurant, gift shop and picnic area. The centre is open daily 9am-4.30pm. Adults $10, children $6, pensioners $8, family $25.

Port Macquarie

Accommodation

There is a lot to choose from in Port Macquarie itself, and also the nearby resorts of Lake Cathie, North Haven and Laurieton. It is still advisable to book well in advance during the Christmas and school holiday periods.

The prices listed here are for a double room per night, which should be used as a guide only. The telephone area code is 02.

Sails Resort, Park Street, ✆6583 3999 or ✆1800 025 271. 83 guest rooms and suites, spa, sauna, mini golf, tennis, waterfront restaurant, cocktail bar - ✪$150-315.

Country Comfort Port Macquarie, cnr Buller & Hollingworth, ✆6583 2955 or 1800 065 064. 61 units, licensed restaurant, swim-ming pool, spa, barbecue - ✪$115-165.

El Paso Motor Inn, 29 Clarence Street, ✆6583 1944 or ✆1800 027 965. 55 units, licensed restaurant, swimming pool, spa, sauna, barbecue - ✪$100-115.

Best Western Macquarie Barracks Motor Inn, 103 Hastings River Drive, ✆6583 5333 or ✆1800 622 511. 14 units, swimming pool, barbecue - ✪$100-170.

Aquatic Motel, 253 Hastings Drive, ✆6583 7388. 21 units, swimming pools, barbe cue - ✪$80-150.

Rocky Beach Motel, 10 Pacific Drive, ✆6583 5881. 10 contained units, bbq - ✪$65-90.

Arrowyn Motel, 170 Gordon Street, ✆6583 1633. 14 units, facilities, pool - ✪$55-95.

Port O'Call Motel, 105 Hastings River Drive, ✆6583 5222. 13 units, swimming pool, barbecue - ✪$70-115.

Narimba Lodge Motel, 4 Narimba Close, ✆6583 3839. 5 units with en suites and a range of facilities - ✪$55-80.

Holiday Units

Airlie Palms, 50 Pacific Drive, ✆1800 242 992. 6 units, air conditioning, facilities, bbq, undercover parking - ✪$55-140.

Golden Sands Apartments, ✆6583 2067. 5 self-contained suites, barbecue, undercover parking, centrally located - ✪$50.

Blue Pacific Holiday Flats, 37 Pacific Drive, ✆6583 1686. Self-contained units, undercover parking - ✪$45-80.

Bed & Breakfast

Lighthouse Beach B&B Homestay, 91 Matthew Flinders Drive, ✆6582 5149. Self-contained, spa, swimming pool, barbecue, garage parking, guest library, adults only - ✪$110-150.

Belrina B&B, 22 Burrawong Drive, ✆6582 2967. Luxury accommodation with ensuite bedroom, barbecue, pool - ✪$95-110.

Dolphin View B&B, 53 Matthew Flinders Drive, ✆6582 3561. Ensuite rooms, swimming pool, parking, adults only - ✪$110-145.

Joy's Doo Drop Inn B&B, 29 Laguna Place, ✆6583 3405. Situated on canal waters with private jetty available, solar heated swimming pool, barbecue - ✪$75-110.

Caravan Parks

Sundowner Breakwall Tourist Park, 1 Munster Street, ✆6583 2755. Swimming pool, games room, guest lounge, no pets allowed - powered sites ✪$19-32 for two, cabins $50-140 for two.

Hastings River Caravan Park, 268-270 Hastings River Drive, ✆6583 3387. En suite cabins, tent area, powered sites, barbecue, swimming pool - powered sites from ✪$18 for two, cabins from $45.

Lighthouse Beach Holiday Village, 50 Hart Street, ✆6582 0581. 24 self-contained cabins, 91 powered sites, no pets allowed - powered sites ✪$16-30 for two.

Melaleuca Caravan Park, 128 Hastings River Drive, ✆6583 4498. Budget to luxury accommodation, swimming pool and slide, barbecue, central location, no pets allowed - 81 powered sites ✪$18 for two, on-site vans $35-60 for two, cabins from $55-115.

There is a **Youth Hostel** at 40 Church Street, ✆6583 5512. It has 9 rooms at ✪$20 per person twin share.

Points of Interest - *continued*

The Church of St Thomas the Apostle, cnr Hay & William Streets, was built by convicts, completed in 1828, and has the original box pews made from local red cedar. In the church grounds is the old hospital dispensary, now a simple chapel. For a donation of a couple of dollars, two-hour tours are available on weekdays. The hospital was across the road, where St Agnes' Catholic Church now stands.

Fantasy Glades, Port Macquarie's Fantasy World, is in Parklands Close, off Pacific Drive, ✆6582 2506. Situated in 2.5ha (6 acres) of rainforest gardens, the Glades have ghosts, castles, dragons, witches, dwarfs, mini-cars and train rides. There are also barbecue and picnic areas and a coffee shop. A wonderful attraction for families. Open daily from 9am-5pm. Adults $9, children $6.

Kingfisher Park, Kingfisher Road, off the Oxley Highway, has a large collection of Australian fauna and farm animals. There is also a coffee lounge and barbecue facilities. Open daily from 9am, ✆6581 0783. Adults $9, children $6, family $25.

Billabong Koala & Aussie Wildlife Park, near the intersection of the Pacific and Oxley Highways, ✆6585 1060, is another place where you can cuddle a koala or pat a kangaroo. There are also indoor and outdoor displays and activities, a souvenir and gift shop, a barbecue courtyard, and Matilda's Restaurant. The Park is open every day 9am-5pm. Adults $9, children $5.

The **Hastings District Historical Museum**, in Clarence Street near the corner of Hay Street, ✆6583 1108, won the Museum of the Year Award way back in 1981 and 1982. Its 14 rooms are open Mon-Sat 9.30am-4.30pm, Sun 1.30-4.30pm.

Port Macquarie Observatory, in Rotary Park, William Street, allows visitors to observe the Solar System with the aid of a Planetarium and telescope. Open Wed and Sun 7.30-9.30pm (8.15-10pm during Daylight Saving).

Both the **Historic Cemetery Gardens** and **Kooloonbung Creek Nature Park** are situated at the southern end of Horton Street. The cemetery has many old graves dating back over 150 years, and the nature reserve has landscaped gardens and walks along the creek.

Tacking Point Lighthouse, at the end of Lighthouse Beach Road, is the third oldest in the country.

Macquarie Nature Reserve, Roto House off Lord Street, has an historic visitors' centre, and in the grounds you can picnic, spy on some healthy koalas, or visit some sick ones in the yard of the Koala Hospital a short distance away (the public is not permitted inside the complex itself). The koalas are fed daily at 8am and 3pm. The Koala Preservation Society of NSW is a voluntary organisation and your support will help save the koalas in Port Macquarie.

Old World Timber Art, 120 Hastings Drive, ✆6583 2502, is where you can watch craftsmen creating hand-crafted woodware and souvenirs from beautiful Hastings timbers. The complex is open Mon-Fri 8.30am-5pm, and the showroom, Sat-Sun 10am-4pm.

Thrumster Village Pottery, is a pottery and craft centre situated 9km (6 miles) west of Port Macquarie on the Oxley Highway. Pottery, leatherwork, copper enamelling, hand made glassware and hand crafted works are on display. Open daily during school holidays, otherwise Thurs-Sun 9-5, ✆6581 0885.

Cassegrain's Hastings Valley Winery, Pacific Highway, is open daily 9am-5pm, ✆6583 7777. They offer winery inspections, wine tasting and cellar door sales. There are also picnic and barbecue facilities, a children's play area, cooperage and souvenirs.

Surfing beaches are part of the city atmosphere. The best known is Lighthouse Beach, which has magnificent surf.

Sports

Fishing

Mid Coast River Fishing Charters, ✆1800 025 935 for details. 2 people full day, ✪$125.

Odyssey Charters, ✆6586 3132. Long Day Reef/Trolling ✪$155 (minimum 10 people), other packages available.

Port Macquarie Estuary Sport-fishing Tours, ✆6582 2545.

SeaQuest Fishing Charters, ✆6583 3463. ✪$100 adult, $70 child.

Airborne

High Adventure Airpark, ✆1800 025 935 for details. Microlite flight (✪$145 for 1hr), tandem hanggliding (✪$160 for 20mins) and tandem paragliding (✪$145 for 30mins) are a few of the activities available.

Skydiving, ✆6584 3655. ✪$290 for a tandem jump.

Horse Riding

Cowarra Homestead Forest Trails, ✆1800 025 935 for details. 1hr ✪$28, 2hrs $45, several routes to choose from.

Watersports

Port Macquarie Kayak Adventures, ✆1800 025 935 for details. Half-day ✪$33.

Port Water Sports, ✆1800 025 935 for details. Parasailing ✪$50, coastal tour $39.

Golf

Supa Putt Golf, ✆1800 025 935 for details. Adult ✪$7, child $5 for 18 holes.

Tours

The Visitor Information Centre has details of many river cruises, boat hire outlets and deep sea fishing charter boats. They can also advise on bush and forest safaris.

Festivals

Port Macquarie has The Carnival of the Pines over the Easter period, and Wauchope has Colonial Week in September.

Outlying Attractions

South West Rocks

The largest seaside resort in the Kempsey Shire is South West Rocks, 32km (20 miles) north-east of Kempsey, near the mouth of the Macleay River.

There are many beaches in the area, and two interesting places to explore: Trial Bay Gaol and Smoky Cape Lighthouse.

Trial Bay Gaol, overlooking Trial Bay, was opened as a prison in 1886, and later during World War I was an internment centre. The gaol is ⏲open 9am- 5pm daily, ✆6566 6168.

Smoky Cape Lighthouse, on the border of Hat Head National Park, is the highest lighthouse on the NSW coast, standing 128m (420 ft) above sea level, and was opened in 1891. Visitors are welcome on ⏲Tuesdays and Thursdays.

Kempsey

Situated 48km (30 miles) north of Port Macquarie, Kempsey straddles the Macleay River and is the heart of a fast growing valley known for its natural beauty and stress-free lifestyle.

Attractions include: The **Macleay River Historical Societies' Museum**, which can be found in the Information Centre complex on the Pacific Highway, South Kempsey, open daily 10am-4pm; The **Kempsey Shire Library and Les Graham Art Collection**, Elbow Street, West Kempsey, open Mon-Fri 10am-6pm, Sat 9am-noon; and **Kempsey Saleyards**, Kemp Street.

There are many bushwalks and drives in the **Macleay Valley**.

The beaches in the Kempsey Shire offer safe, patrolled sections for families. The village of **Stuarts Point** is the focal point for the beaches that stretch north from the mouth of the Macleay River to the Shire's boundary above Middle Head.

The coastal village of **Hat Head** is regarded as one of the top fishing spots on the coast of NSW. Hat Head is situated in the heart of the **Hat Head National Park**.

The Kempsey Visitor Information Centre is on the Pacific Highway, South Kempsey, open Mon-Fri 9am-5pm, weekends 10am-4pm. (02) 6554 8799 or 1800 642 480 or email at ktic@midcoast .com.au

Wauchope

Wauchope is 19km (12 miles) west of Port Macquarie on the Oxley Highway. At the centre of the region's timber industry, this historic town draws visitor mainly to its Timbertown theme park.

The main attraction is **Timber-town**, 6585 1866, an entire village recreated to demonstrate the struggles and achievements of the pioneers. It has a steam train, timber sawing, a bullock team, a woodturner and a general store. Timbertown is open daily from 9am. It is 3km from Wauchope on the Oxley Highway.

Another attraction is the **Big Bull** in Redbank Farm, 50 Redbank Road, 6585 2044, just over the river. The Bull is 14m (46 ft) high, and in the complex there is a working dairy farm, an animal nursery, an educational display, hay rides, a restaurant, and a souvenir shop. It is open daily 9am-5pm.

The Wauchope Information and Neighbourhood Centre is in Shop 3 Roland Plaza, 33 High Street, 6586 4055.

Laurieton

Laurieton is south of Port Macquarie on Ocean Drive, and is part of Camden Haven. It is another popular holiday spot, with a range of accommodation, restaurants and clubs.

This is a great area for fishing, and there are many good beaches to tempt you. The town is overlooked by **North Brother Mountain**, from which there are good views of the town and the coastline. **Kattang Nature Reserve**, a few kilometres east, and **Crowdy Bay National Park**, just south, are two pleasant natural features of the local environment.

Crowdy Bay National Park is located in the northern section of the Manning Valley, and covers some 6000ha (14,820 acres). Access to the park is via the Coralville Road at Moorland, some 35km (22 miles) north of Taree. Picnic and camping areas are available within the park and the main attractions are fishing and surfing. ***Diamond Head*** is the main camping area with barbecues and toilet facilities, however drinking water is not available within the Park.

Boorganna Nature Reserve is on the western edge of the Comboyne Plateau, 7km (4 miles) west of Taree. Access is along the Innes View Road from the Wingham/Comboyne Road. Brochures on both of these parks are available from the Tourist Information Centre in Taree.

The Camden Haven Neighbourhood Information Centre is in 1 Seymour Street, Laurieton, 6559 5676.

Coffs Harbour with Grafton

This region is separated into two sections: The coastal region of Coffs Harbour, and the inland region of Grafton.

Coffs Harbour

Population 22,170
Coffs Harbour is situated on the coast of New South Wales, 578km (359 miles) north of Sydney and 427km (265 miles) south of Brisbane.

Climate

Average temperatures: January max 26C (79F) - min 19C (66F); June max 19C (66F) - min 9C (48F). Average annual rainfall: 1759mm (69 ins); wettest six months October to March.

Characteristics

Coffs Harbour is a popular year-round tourist destination. On one side there are the blue waters of the Pacific Ocean, while the western border area is the Great Dividing Range. The combination of golden sands, high mountains, dense luxuriant rainforests, steep banana plantations, clear rivers and streams make it a superb holiday area.

Coffs Harbour was originally called Korff's Harbour, named after Captain John Korff, who sheltered here in 1847. The harbour, being halfway between Brisbane and Sydney, was an extremely busy port facility for the many vessels plying the coastal trade. It was considered a dangerous port, however, and after a boycott by many ships' captains, the lighthouse was eventually built in 1878.

The surrounding lowlands and rolling hills were once a source of red cedar and other valuable timber when discovered some 150 years ago. The pastoralists followed and the area was given to cattle, dairying, vegetable growing and, of course, banana plantations.

How to Get There

By Air

The following airlines fly regional services into Coffs Harbour: Qantas, ✆13 1313 and Kendell, ✆9670 2677.

By Bus

Interstate coach lines operate daily in Coffs Harbour. Contact Greyhound Pioneer, ✆13 2030, or McCaffertys, ✆13 1499.

By Rail

XPT services operate daily from Sydney and overnight expresses operate from Sydney and Brisbane, ✆13 2232.

By Road

Travelling by the Pacific Highway, it is an 8 hour drive from Sydney, and about 6 hours from Brisbane.

Visitor Information

The Coffs Harbour-Tourism Holiday Coast Information Centre is located at the corner of Rose Avenue & Marcia Street, Coffs Harbour, ✆(02) 6652 1522 or 1300 369 070. It is open 9am-5pm daily. Email them at tourism@ coffscoast.com.au or check out the website at www.coffs.net

Accommodation

Coffs Harbour has resorts, motels, holiday apartments, caravan parks, hotels, cabins/ lodges and hostels. Here is a selection with prices for a double room per night, which should be used as a guide only. The telephone area code is 02.

Aanuka Beach Resort, Firman Drive, Diggers Beach, ✆6652 7555. 49 units, licensed restaurant, swimming pool, spa, sauna, gym, tennis, bbq - ✪$205-400 including breakfast.

Coffs Harbour Motor Inn, 22 Elizabeth Street, ✆6652 6388. 35 units, licensed restaurant, swimming pool, spa, barbecue - ✪$90-130.

Big Windmill Motor Lodge, 168 Pacific Highway, ✆6652 2933. 39 units, licensed restaurant, swimming pool, spa, sauna, gym, barbecue - ✪$80-130.

Premier Motor Inn, Pacific Highway, ✆6652 2044. 32 units, licensed restaurant (closed Sun), swimming pool, barbecue - ✪$160-120.

Coachmens Inn, 93 Park Beach Road, ✆6652 2055. 41 units, pool, spa - ✪$55-100.

Matador Motor Inn, cnr Grafton & Albany St, ✆6652 3166. 16 units, pool - ✪$55-85.

Bananatown Motel, 15 Grafton Street, ✆6652 4411. 13 units, pool, bbq - ✪$50-90.

Caravan Parks

Coffs Village Caravan Park, 215 Pacific Highway, ✆6652 4633. (No pets allowed), 52 sites - powered sites ✪$17 for two, on-site vans $25 for two.

Bananacoast Caravan Park, Pacific Highway, ✆6652 2868. (Dogs allowed by arrangement), 105 sites - powered sites ✪$17-26 for two, cabins $35-105 for two.

Split Solitary Caravan Park, Split Solitary Road, ✆6653 6212. (No pets during holiday period), 125 sites - powered sites ✪$15-20 for two, cabins $40-75 for two.

There is a **Youth Hostel** in 110 Albany Street, ✆6652 6462. It has 15 rooms at ✪$20-22 per person twin share.

Eating Out

Coffs Harbour has many restaurants and fast food outlets, particularly down on the Marina. The restaurants range from many international cuisines to the family type catered for by the local clubs. Many of the motels and hotels have restaurants and bistros, and here is a taste of what else is available.

The Fishermans Katch, 394 High Street, ✆6652 4372. Seafood platters and steak. Open 6am-8pm daily, closed Public Holidays.

Tequila Mexican Restaurant, 224 High Street, ✆6652 1279. Fully licensed open 5.30pm-8pm every day.

Stetsons Steakhouse & Saloon, cnr Pacific Highway & Bray Streets, ✆6651 9166. Open 5.30pm-10pm 7 days, closed Public Holidays.

Sawan Thai Restaurant, 376 High Street, Coffs Jetty, ✆6652 9699. Vegetarian food is a speciality, Open 5.30pm-10.30pm Mon-Sat, closed Sunday and Public Holidays.

Star Anise, 93 Grafton Street, open 6pm-9pm Wed-Sun, 11.30am-2pm Thursday and Friday, closed Monday and Tuesday with selected hours on Public Holidays.

The Dragon, 108 Grafton Street, ✆6652 4187. Cantonese cuisine with a seafood emphasis.

Ocean Oyster & Steak Grill, 394 High Street, ✆6650 0444.

Sands, cnr Park Beach Road & Ocean Parade, ✆6652 2666.

Taruah Thai Restaurant, 360 High Street, ✆6652 5992.

The Village, 97 Park Beach Road, ✆6652 2055.

McDonalds have a branch on the corner of the Pacific Highway and North Boambee Road and one in the High Street Mall. There is a Pizza Hut on the corner of High and Gordon Streets, and you can call them for delivery on ✆13 1166.

Coffs Harbour

Points of Interest

The Big Banana, Pacific Highway, ✆6652 4355 is the landmark of Coffs Harbour, and is 3km north of the town. There you will find an audio-visual theatrette, Aboriginal Dreamtime Cave, historical exhibits, hydroponics glasshouse, banana packing shed, Triffid Forest, Time Tunnel, Future Culture Space Station, Greenhouse Food Fair/Souvenir complex, display gardens, machinery museum/ocean lookout, and a farmers' market.

Pet Porpoise Pool, ✆6652 6133, in Orlando Street, has performing dolphins and sea lions, native fauna, marine animals, live sharks and reef tank, a kiosk and souvenir outlet. It is open daily 9am-5pm. Shows are at 10.30am and 2.15pm.

North Coast Regional Botanic Garden, ✆6648 4188, in Hardacre Street in the centre of town, has 19ha (47 acres) featuring native and exotic plants, open daily.

Within an hour's drive of Coffs Harbour, and covered with magnificent rainforest, is **Dorrigo National Park**, which has many walking trails.

There are seven State Forests in the area. Sealy Lookout is a must when visiting Bruxner Park Flora Reserve, as it offers panoramic views of the city, Pacific coastline and banana-clad hillsides. The **Dorigo National Park and Rainforest Centre** is on the corner of Dome Road and Lyrebird Lane, ✆6657 2309.

Several art and opal galleries are in and around the town. The Tourist Information Centre in Hickory Street, Dorrigo, ✆6657 2486, can provide you with details.

Joy flights over Nambucca Heads, Bellingen, Orara Valley, Woolgoolga and the Solitary Islands, are available (***Skylink Helicopters***, Aviation Drive, ✆6658 0899; ***Wingaway Air***, Airport Drive, ✆6650 0655), as are deep sea fishing trips (***Adriatic Fishing Trips***, Shop 5 International Marina, ✆6651 1277; ***Cougar Cat 12 Fishing Trips***, ✆6651 6715).

Storyland Gardens, ✆6653 1400, 10km south of Coffs Harbour on Lyons Road, Sawtell, has a giant Old Woman's Shoe, surrounded by popular fairytale settings such as Snow White and Little Red Riding Hood. It is open 10am-4pm Thu-Sun and every day during school holidays.

And of course, there are the **beaches**. Coffs Harbour has many, and they range from those with full-blooded rolling surf for boardriders and body surfers, to the more sheltered, lagoon-type that are perfect for toddlers. There are also secluded beaches for nude bathing.

Festivals

The Agricultural Show is held in May.

Facilities

Two golf courses, five lawn bowling clubs, three surf clubs, a yacht club, a deep sea fishing club and racecourse. Tennis, squash, tenpin bowling, croquet and indoor cricket facilities are available. An indoor stadium caters for basketball, badminton, indoor hockey and many other indoor sports.

Outlying Attractions

Woolgoolga

Situated 25km north of Coffs Harbour, Woolgoolga has a large Sikh community and they have built a lavish temple, called Guru Nanak.

The **Raj Mahal Emporium**, ✆6644 1149, an Indian Theme Park on corner of Pullen Street and the Pacific Highway, has Indian artefacts and food.

The **Woolgoolga Art Gallery**, Turon Parade, ✆6654 1064, has a treasure trove of fine art, pottery, batikwork and woodcraft, and is open daily 10am-4pm.

Whitewater rafting on the **Nymboida River** is available for the adventurous.

George's Gold Mine, ✆6654 5355, 782 Moleton Road, Moleton, is open Wed-Sun 10am-5pm, and has inspections of the

Bonville Golf Course

Bayfield gold mine and original equipment. There are picnic and barbecue areas, and food is available.

Valery Trails, 758 Valery Road, Valery, ✆6653 4401, offer escorted trail rides through the Pine Creek State Forest, catering for both experienced and inexperienced riders.

Nambucca Heads

Situated 114km (71 miles) south of Coffs Harbour, Nambucca Heads is another popular holiday resort, and has a wide range of accommodation from premier hotels to flats and caravan parks.

It is a farming and timber district, and there are facilities for boating, lawn bowls, fishing (river, rock, beach and deep sea), golf, surfing and tennis. Attractions include the Nambucca Historical Museum; Mary Boulton's Pioneer Cottage; The Pub with No Beer; Taylor Arm - venue for the Easter Country Music Festival and Fair; the historical Star Hotel; Kew House Toy and Doll Museum; and the Worm Farm, Valla Road, Valla, which has worm picking, packing and racing.

The Nambucca Valley Visitor Information Centre can be found at 4 Pacific Highway. They are ⏲open 9am-5pm daily, and have all the information you will need, ✆(02) 6568 6954 or ✆1800 646 587.

Grafton

Grafton

Population 16,500
Grafton is situated on a bend of the Clarence River, 660km (410 miles) north of Sydney, 320km (199 miles) south of Brisbane, and 160km (99 miles) east of Glen Innes.

Climate

Average temperatures: January max 32C (90F) - min 19C (66F); July max 17C (63F) - min 7C (45F).

Characteristics

Grafton, the Jacaranda City, has tree lined streets and graceful old buildings. The district was originally discovered by the escaped convict Richard Craig in 1831. For a pardon and one hundred pounds, he brought a party of cedar getters to log the huge cedar stands. The stories of the 'red gold' spread, and John Small arrived in 1838 and first occupied land on Woodford Island.

The settlement was established shortly after, and the first sale of town blocks took place in 1851. Governor Fitzroy officially named the town after his grandfather, the Duke of Grafton, and it was proclaimed a city in 1885.

How to Get There

By Bus

Greyhound Pioneer and McCaffertys stop at Grafton on the Sydney/Brisbane routes.

By Rail

There are daily Countrylink services from Sydney to Grafton.

By Road

From Sydney and Brisbane, via the Pacific Highway.

Accommodation

For a holiday with a difference, visitors can hire a houseboat accommodating up to eight adults in comfort, and cruise up and down the Clarence River, stopping at many of the 100 islands. No licence is required to operate local houseboats. For more information contact Clarence River Boats, Clarence Street, Brushgrove, ✆6647 6232.

As regards more conventional accommodation, Grafton has motels and hotels, and South Grafton has motels, hotels and caravan parks. Here is a selection, with prices for a double room per night, which should be used as a guide only. The telephone area code is 02.

Reilley's Hideaway Grafton Farm-stay, 218 Reilly's Lane off Pacific Highway, ✆6642 6008. 3 rooms, cooking facilities, fireplace, playground, table tennis, pool, spa - ✪$110.

Bent Street Motor Inn, 62 Bent Street, ✆6643 4500. 20 units, barbecue, licensed restaurant, car parking, spa, pool - ✪$70-90.

Abbey Motor Inn, 59 Fitzroy Street, ✆6642 6122. 24 units, breakfast room service - ✪$65-70.

Fitzroy Motel, 27 Fitzroy Street, ✆6642 4477. 21 units, spa, pool - ✪$70-105.

Hi-Way Motel, Pacific Highway, ✆6642 1588. 31 units, playground, pool - ✪$55-75.

Roches Family Hotel, 85 Victoria Street, ✆6642 2866. 14 rooms, licensed restaurant, barbecue - ✪$40.

Caravan Parks

The Gateway Village, 598 Sum-merland Way, ✆6642 4225. 90 sites, pool, practice golf, barbecue - powered sites ✪$20 for two, cabins $60-85, on-site vans $40-45 for two.

Grafton Sunset Caravan Park, 302 Gwydir Highway, ✆6642 3824. (Pets allowed by arrangement) 70 sites, barbecue, kiosk, pool - powered sites ✪$15 for two, on-site vans $30-35 for two, cabins $40-45 for two.

Clarence River

Eating Out

Most of the hotels are open for counter lunches and counter teas from Monday to Saturday, and the Bowling Club, in Kemp Street, is open for lunch and dinner Mon-Fri, while the District Services Club in Mary Street, is open for lunch and dinner daily. In South Grafton, the Golf Club is open for dinner Wed-Sat.

Here is a selection of restaurants you might like to try.

New Oriental Chinese Restaurant, 127 Prince St, ✆6642 7888.
Kuppazz Family Restaurant, Shopping World Shop 40, ✆6643 1003.
Lea-Mar's Bistro, 93 Prince St, ✆6643 2290.
Clancys Restaurant & Bistro, Grafton Hotel, 97 Fitzroy St, ✆6643 3411.
Jarmers Restaurant, 85 Victoria St, ✆6642 2866.
KFC, Fiztroy Street, ✆6642 1621.

Grafton

Tourist Information

The Clarence River Tourist Association is on the corner of Spring Street and the Pacific Highway, ✆6642 4277. They can give tips on the best parts and offer you directions on how to access them, and whether road conditions require 4WD at your time of visit.

Points of Interest

Grafton has a bus service operating hourly tours that pass many of the historic buildings and points of interest (no service Sun or after noon Sat), ✆6642 3111. Buses leave Market Square at 20 minutes past the hour. There are also regular bus services to Yamba, Maclean, Ulmarra, Lismore and Glen Innes.

Clarence River Ferries, ✆6646 6423, have a fleet of three passenger ferries with individual capacities up to 160 people, servicing the needs of residents and visitors from Grafton to the river mouth, during special events like the Jacaranda Festival. Every day a minimum of four return trips connect Iluka and Yamba. The 30 minute river crossing is a popular scenic alternative to the lengthy road journey. The services from Yamba are met at Iluka by a courtesy bus provided by Iluka's Sedger's Reef Hotel.

Regular **river cruises** also operate from Yamba and Iluka including a weekly visit to Maclean (Monday) and Harwood Island (Wednesday and Friday). There are plans to have regular river cruises and ferry services to Susan Island from the wharf at the river-end of Prince Street, beginning in 1991.

Susan Island is situated in the Clarence River, with its tip almost opposite Prince Street. The northern end of the island has a rainforest with walking tracks, and the largest fruit bat colony in the southern hemisphere. It is a spectacular sight when the colony departs at dusk each summer evening. The southern section of the island has barbecues, picnic and toilet facilities.

Grafton Regional Art Gallery, 158 Fitzroy Street, occupies the restored Prentice House (1880), and has a variety of exhibitions from many notable artists and crafts people. It is ⌚open 10am-4pm Wed-Sun.

Schaeffer House Museum, 192 Fitzroy Street, is in another fine old homestead, and has exhibits tracing the history of Grafton and the Clarence Valley. ⌚Open 2-4pm, Tues, Thurs & Sun.

Christ Church Cathedral (1884), is designed along Gothic lines with towering arches and a spacious interior. The Cathedral is ⌚open 7am-5.30pm daily.

Saraton Theatre in Prince Street, is a restored traditional picture theatre which also hosts live shows, conventions and community functions.

The **National Parks** of the Clarence Valley are Yuraygir, Bund-jalung, Gibraltar Range and Wash-pool. Yuraygir and Bundjalung are coastal parks, and Gibraltar Range and Washpool to the west offer a variety of scenic drives, camping areas and walking tracks.

Grafton is very proud of its trees, and 7000 of them line the avenues and shade the 24 well-maintained parks. The Visitor Centre has a brochure on trees and parks, but the most popular parks are: Market Square, adjacent to the clock tower in Prince Street; Memorial Park and Boulevarde, river end of Prince Street; South Grafton Boulevarde, Through Street; See Park Arboretum, Pound Street.

Festivals

The Jacaranda Festival was first held in 1935, and is Australia's longest running festival. The Jacaranda Queen is crowned on the last Saturday in October each year, heralding the start of the major festival week. On the first Saturday in November there is a spectacular street parade for the close of the Festival, but not the end of festivities, as people flock for weeks before and after to view the trees and the many exhibitions and events.

Facilities

Horseback trail rides can be taken through the coastal forests; the Grafton racetrack has over 40 meetings a year, with the July Racing Carnival rating as the richest country carnival in the nation; the July Carnival at the nearby greyhound track is also a major event; lawn bowls are catered for at four licensed clubs; the Big River Squash and Fitness Centre, Hoof Street, ✆6642 6633, has a gym, swimming pool, sauna, aerobic classes, masseurs and Tae-kwan-do training; Grafton Squash Centre, 39 Queen Street, ✆6642 2989, welcomes visitors; tennis courts are in Prince Street, ✆6642 5666; the Grafton Olympic Pool in Oliver Street has a waterslide, and there is a heated pool in Armidale Street; Big River Ski Lodge at Seelands caters for skiers and hires out boats, ✆6644 9324; and the Visitor Centre can advise on local sailing clubs.

Outlying Attractions

Ulmarra

Situated 13km (8 miles) north of Grafton, Ulmarra is a fine example of a 19th century river port, and the township is classified by the National Trust. It was chosen in 1986 as the location for the filming of the TV mini series Fields of Fire, a story based on life in a 1929 Queensland cane town.

In the early 1900s, Ulmarra was a bustling town with 4 blacksmiths, a killing factory and bacon works, general stores, hospital, two hotels, two schools and three permanent policemen to maintain law and order. Ulmarra wharf was a major pick-up point for steam and sailing vessels serving Sydney markets. The town thrived, but improved road systems and advancing technology eventually finished Ulmarra as a major river port.

The Commercial Hotel is a magnificent old style country pub on the river bank. Ulmarra boasts numerous antique, arts and crafts, and bric-a-brac shops, and cosy little tearooms.

Maclean

"The Scottish Town in Australia," Maclean, 34km (21 miles) north of Grafton, was first settled by Scottish immigrants, and the town's annual Highland Gathering over the Easter period, and Free Presbyterian Church (the oldest in Australia) are legacies of this past.

During September, the Cane Harvest Festival is celebrated with a Queen Crowning, a street parade, and plenty of fun. A local cane farm can be inspected every Friday, throughout the year.

The Clarence River is one of only two NSW rivers trawled for prawns, and the river fleet works from the Ulmarra ferry to the river mouth using Maclean as its base.

For tourist information look out for places displaying the blue "I" sign, or call in at Scottish Corner souvenir shop in River Street.

Attractions include Maclean Lookout, The Pinnacle Rocks, and the Bicentennial Museum, all in Wharf Street, and a number of historic buildings. Water skiing, sailing and fishing are popular pastimes.

The Lower Clarence Visitors Centre is in Ferry Park, Pacific Highway, ✆6645 4121, email crta1@nor. com.au. It is open 9 - 5 daily.

Yamba

Yamba is the largest coastal resort in the Clarence Valley, and is 14km (9 miles) off the Pacific Highway, and 62km (39 miles) north-east of Grafton. It is primarily a holiday town with motels, caravan parks and hundreds of holiday flats and cottages. In the July school holidays the Family Fishing Festival is held, and tonnes of fish are caught.

Yamba's main beach is patrolled during the summer season and has an adjoining rock pool which is popular throughout the year. Neighbouring beaches are also popular for boardriding, sunbaking and fishing.

South of Yamba is the village of Angourie, famous for its surfing, and natural freshwater swimming at the Blue Pool. Angourie marks the northern limit of the Yuraygir National Park.

A daily passenger ferry service operates between Yamba and Iluka, with a minimum of four return services a day. There are also river cruises on Wednesday and Friday.

Iluka

The town of Iluka is situated on the opposite headland to Yamba, and is connected by the ferry service. Nearby is a rainforest that is World Heritage listed. It has excellent walking tracks, with interpretive signs for the most notable features.

West of Iluka is the world's southernmost coffee plantation, and they have tours of the plantation on weekends and during school holidays. At the plantation there is an intimate coffee house, and an arts and crafts shop.

Wooli

The third largest beach resort in the Clarence Valley is located 45km (28 miles east of Grafton with access from Ulmarra, or from the Pacific Highway 12km (7 miles) south of Grafton at the Airport turnoff. On the way to the village you pass by Lake Hiawatha. Wooli is bounded by the Wooli River to the west and the Pacific Ocean to the east. The river and beach offer many ideal swimming and fishing spots.

Wooli River is probably the most unpolluted river in Australia, as it flows completely through National Park. Party pontoon boats can be hired from Bushland Caravan Park.

Lismore

Population 27,200
Situated between rainforest and sea, Lismore is in northern New South Wales, inland from Ballina on the Bruxner Highway.

Climate

Average temperatures: January max 30C (86F) - min 19C (66F); July max 20C (68F) - min 6C (43F). Average annual rainfall, 1349mm (53 ins); wettest months December-May.

Characteristics

The commercial, cultural and sporting capital of the North Coast region. Lismore is the administrative centre for Federal and State Government departments, as well as being the commercial and retail hub of the region. The surrounding countryside is extremely fertile and all types of agriculture are found in the region. Tropical fruits, such as bananas, avocados, pineapples and macadamia nuts, are widely grown. Dairying is also popular and the hills away from the coast are still timbered. There has been much controversy in past years over logging.

How to Get There

By Air

Hazelton Airlines ✆131713 fly to/from Sydney.

By Bus

Greyhound Pioneer ✆132030, stop at Lismore on Sydney/Brisbane Pacific Highway route.

Kirklands Coaches, ✆1300 367 077, provide daily services to/from Brisbane and nearby regional centres.

Lismore

Accommodation

Here is a selection of accommodation available in Lismore, with prices for a double room per night, which should be used as a guide only. The telephone area code is 02.

Sisleys Inntown Motel, 111 Dawson Street, ✆6621 9888. 8 units, comfortable facilities - ✪$70-100.

Dawson Motor Inn, cnr Dawson & Orion Streets, ✆6621 8100. 19 units, swimming pool - ✪$65-85.

Karinga Motel, 258 Molesworth Street, ✆6621 2787. 31 units, licensed restaurant (Mon-Thurs) - ✪$65-80.

Arcadia Motel, cnr James Road & Ballina Road, Goonellabah (to the east of the city), ✆6624 1999. 10 units, swimming pool - ✪$65.

McDermotts's B&B, cnr Dawson & Magellan Streets, ✆6624 1158. 2 rooms, comfortable facilities - ✪$65-75.

Caravan Parks

Lismore Tourist Caravan Park, Dawson Street, ✆6621 6581. (Pets allowed by discretion), 92 sites, barbecue - powered sites ✪$17 for two, on-site vans $30-35 for two, cabins $40 for two.

Lismore Lake Caravan Park, Bruxner Highway, ✆6621 2585. (Pets on application), 138 sites, pool, barbecue - powered sites ✪$13 for two, cabins $35-45 for two.

Road Runner Caravan Park, Caniaba Road, ✆6621 6705. (No pets allowed), 133 sites, tennis, pool - powered sites ✪$14 for two, cabins $40 for two.

Eating Out

The Gollan Hotel, cnr Woodlark and Keen Streets, serves meals, as do most of the hotels. For tasty and reasonably priced meals, try the Golf Club and the local RSL Club. A few additional suggestions are:

Mandarin Palace Chinese Restaurant, 153 Keen Street, 11.30am-2pm and 5pm-8pm 7 days, closed Public Holidays.

Ho Ho International, 67 Wyrallah Road, ✆6621 5518. Chinese and international cuisine, open 11am-2pm and 5pm-9pm every day ex-cept Tuesdays.

Paupiettes, 56 Ballina Street, ✆6621 6135. Open 6.30pm-9.30pm Tue-Sat only.

Mexican Magic, 6 Carrington Street, ✆6621 8206.

Giorgios Vegetarian Italia, 73 Magellan Street, ✆6622 3177.

The Tempted Palate, 34 Moles-worth Street, ✆6621 6566.

Lismore Seafood Inn, 25 Eggins Lane, ✆6621 3736.

The Loft, 6 Nesbitt Lane, ✆6622 0252.

Bangkok Lismore, 44 Ballina Street, ✆6621 3375.

Thai Lotus Classic, 207 Ballina Street, ✆6622 0062.

If the budget is wearing thin, look for McDonalds on the corner of Laurel Avenue and Brewster Street or call Pizza Hut on ✆13 1166. Otherwise try another of the several take-away establishments in the city, most of which are on Keen, Ballina and Union Streets.

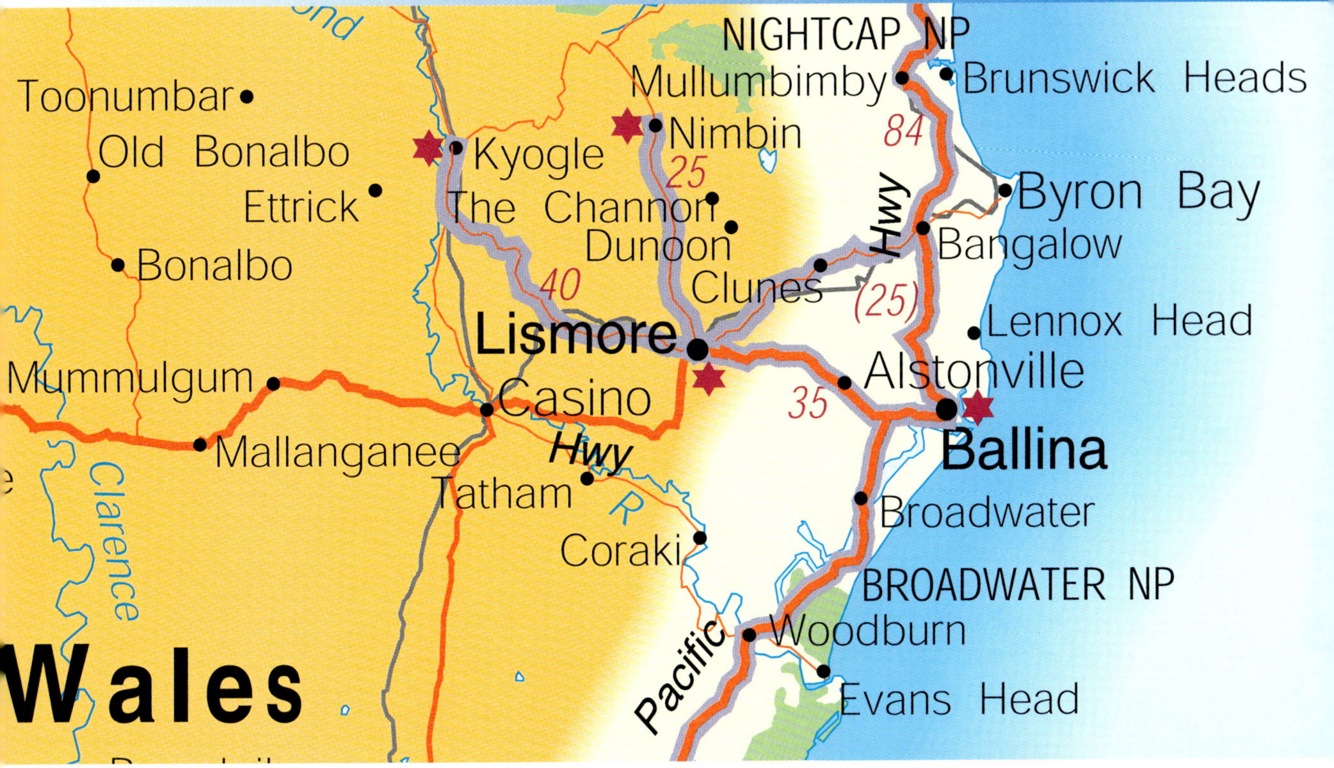

How to Get There - *continued*

By Rail

There is a regular Countrylink service from Sydney to Lismore, ✆13 2232.

By Road

Via the Pacific Highway and the New England Highway from Sydney (787km - 489 miles) and Brisbane (222km - 138 miles).

Visitor Information

The Lismore Visitor Information Centre, cnr Ballina & Molesworth Streets (the main street), ✆(02) 6622 0122 or ✆1300 369 795, has literature, maps, souvenirs and accommodation booking services, and is open 9.30am-4pm Mon- Fri, 10am-3pm weekends and 9.30am-4pm on Public Holidays. The online references for more info are: email tourism@liscity.nsw. gov.au and website www.liscity. nsw.gov.au

Points of Interest

Lismore was the queen of the river towns last century, as it was as far up river as the trading schooners could reach. The red cedar and other rainforest timber logs from 'The Big Scrub' were floated downstream to Lismore.

Cedar Log Memorial - a giant cedar log is displayed in the small park behind the City Hall as a permanent memorial to the first cedar loggers of the Richmond Valley.

Claude Riley Memorial Lookout, 3km north-east along the New Ballina Cutting, offers a fine view of the city.

Robinson's Lookout, also called Girard's Hill Lookout, is 2km south of the city centre. It offers views of the city, the river and the surrounding countryside.

There is a walking track that joins onto **Wilson's walk**, which starts at Albert Park and is 6.5km (4 miles) long. It takes you through Wilson's Park, a rainforest remnant where you can spot local bird life.

The Lismore Visitor and Heritage Centre, ✆6622 0122, established during the Bicentennial Year, features an unusual walk-through, indoors 'rainforest experience'. Also incorporated are 'hands on' displays, models and photographic features of Lismore's history.

Lismore Lake is 2.5km from Lismore on the Casino road. There are gas barbecues and a swimming pool, children's playground and a BMX track. It is popular with water skiers.

Heritage Park, near the Visitors Centre, has toilets and gas barbecues.

The Richmond River Historical Society Museum, 165 Moles-worth Street, ✆6621 9993, contains a fascinating collection of Aboriginal artifacts and pioneer relics, as well as geological specimens.

The Regional Art Gallery, 131 Molesworth Street, ✆6622 2209, houses fine collections of paintings, pottery and ceramics.

An **Aboriginal Bora Ring** adjoins Tucki Tucki Cemetery. The Ring overlooks the Steve King's Plain and the mid-Richmond valley. It is one of several tribal ceremonial grounds in the district, and has been fenced and marked with a description board.

Historic River Cruises aboard MV *Bennelong*, a fully licensed cruise boat, sail regularly from Lismore. For bookings, call into their office in Boat Harbour Road, Ballina, or ✆0414 664 552 (mobile).

At Alphadale, on the eastern edge of the city, Cowlong Road, is **Macadamia Magic**. This is a macadamia nut processing complex where factory inspections are welcome. The tourist annex specialises in macadamia products and provides refreshments and souvenirs daily, ✆6624 2900. It is ⏲open 9am-5pm weekdays and 10am-4pm open weekends.

Festivals

September is the month when it's all happening: The Spring Orchid Show; The Lismore Cup, which is the highlight of the racing calendar in Lismore; The Cedar Guitar Awards; The Spring Greyhound Racing Carnival and the Annual Spring Garden Competition.

The North Coast National Show is held in the third week of October each year.

Facilities

Rolling skating at Summerland Skate Centre, North Lismore; Lismore Grand Prix, South Lismore, is a racing circuit where you are the driver, or where you can enjoy mini-golf.

You can learn to water ski at the Lismore Lake Ski School; The Lismore Bowl is ⏲open daily 9am-midnight for ten-pin bowling.

Lawn bowls, tennis, swimming, squash and golf are all catered for, as well as spectator sports and seasonal activities, such as the Speedway and Karting programmes.

Outlying Attractions

Murwillimbah Region

If you wish to visit the Murwil-lumbah region, drop into the World Heritage Rainforest Visitor Information Centre Murwillumbah, cnr Pacific Highway & Alma Streets, ⏲open Mon-Sat 9am-4.30pm, Sun 9.30am-4pm. They share a web page with Tweed Heads Information at www.tactic.nsw.gov.au, and you can email them here at info@tactic.nsw.gov.au

Mt Warning, 1157m (3796 ft), which towers above the Tweed Valley behind Murwillumbah, dominates the scenery for miles around. It was named by Captain Cook in 1770. The area is a National Park, and a walking track winds its way to the top through rainforest for panoramic views of the Tweed Valley and the coast. Ask at the Information Centre about where to start and the current conditions of the climb.

The Channon

This is a charming village on Terania Creek, 20km (12 miles) north of Lismore.

On the second Sunday of every month, the famous The **Channon Craft Market**, the original country market in the area, is held. Only hand-made articles and produce are sold. There is always a colourful crowd with buskers, street theatre, pony rides and games.

Terania Creek, about which there was so much controversy in the 1970s, is now part of the **Nightcap National Park**, in which there are many walking tracks through tropical rainforest and to Protesters' Falls.

The **Wyymara Protea Plantation**, 8 Cooks Lane, Dalwood, ✆6629 5270, has 2000 protea shrubs in production, with many different varieties of fresh and dried protea flowers.

Nimbin

Situated inland, in the centre of an area where the 'hippy' approach to life is very popular, one could say Nimbin was the birthplace of alternative lifestyle in Australia in the late 1960s. It is 30km from Lismore.

The town has a unique style and character of its own, and unusual local crafts may be purchased at the **Nimbin School of Arts Gallery**, 47 Cullen Street.

Nimbin Rocks, or Needles, are unusual rock formations 3km on the Lismore side of Nimbin. They are a sacred site of the Bundjalung Aboriginal Tribe.

The **Tuntable Falls**, 13km (8 miles) from Nimbin, can only be reached by a three hour return hike along the creek bed, and it is a walk only for the fit and healthy.

The website at www.nimbin. net will give you an idea of the limited facilities the town offers and a taste of the prevailing attitudes of this small rural community. The email address is: thecrew@ nimbin.net.au

Kyogle

Kyogle is a small town 50km (31 miles) inland north-west of Lismore that is known as the Gateway to the Rainforest. From the township it is an easy drive to the spectacular **Border Ranges National Park**. The town has an Information Centre at the Shire Council in Strathedon Street, ✆(02) 6632 1611.

The Channon Craft Market

Brunswick Heads

Going back to the coast, Brunswick Heads is a fairly quiet tourist resort. It is 21km (13 miles) from Byron Bay, and is popular with keen fishermen and families. Apart from the attraction of the beaches, you will find a subtropical **Nature Reserve** located near the Brunswick River. Just north of the town is an alternative route along the coast, passing many popular surfing and fishing beaches, to Kingscliff. When in town, drop into Brunswick Valley Coach and Travel, Park Street, ✆6685 1385, for local information. There is a good website located at www.tropicalnsw/ brunswickheads

Byron Bay

42km (26 miles) from Lismore is idyllic Byron Bay - New South Wales' worst-kept secret. More than 500,000 tourists flock here each year, making it the most visited destination outside Sydney. The city is renowned for its relaxed, peaceful atmosphere.

The focus here is on recreation and relaxation, so most of the town's services fall into one of these categories. Visit or contact the Information Centre to find the interests that most appeal to you.

View from Cape Byron

Cape Byron is the most easterly point of Australia, topped by an extremely powerful lighthouse built in 1901. The Lighthouse is open daily 8am-6.30pm.

For further details, the Byron Bay Visitor Information Centre is located at the Old Railway Cottage, Johnson Street, (02) 6685 8050. It is open 9am-5pm daily. You will find a useful internet reference at the website: www.byronbayvbo.com

Alstonville

An attractive village that boasts a nice little bookshop, Alstonville is 19km (12 miles) from Lismore on the way to the coast.

Near the village is the **Victoria Park Nature Reserve**, a remnant of the 'big scrub' which once covered most of the district.

The **Summerland House With No Steps**, Wardell Road, 6628 0610, is a unique project providing job skills and training for the handicapped. It also has avocados, macadamia nuts, tropical stone fruit, custard apples, lychees and citrus fruits growing in plantations, and on sale, as well as a craft cottage, retail nursery and fruit packing house. Devonshire teas and light lunches are available daily 9-5.

At Bexhill, 10km north-east of Lismore, is an **open-air cathedral**. The pews are fashioned from logs, whilst behind the stone altar and cross are magnificent views of the Corndale Valley.

Ballina

A resort town, Ballina has all the usual tourist facilities. The **Big Prawn** can be seen several kilometres from town. Take the coast road for a more pleasant drive to/from Byron Bay, rather than rejoining the Pacific Highway.

The **Maritime Museum**, Regatta Lane, 6681 1002, records the maritime history of the Richmond River and features the *Las Balsa Raft* which voyaged from South America to Ballina in 1973.

Shaws Bay Hotel, next to the caravan park, 2 Brighton Street, East Ballina, has a beautiful red cedar dining room and staircase which were carved in Spain, open daily 10am-10pm, 6686 2034.

The **Broadwater Sugar Mill**, 19km (12 miles) south of Ballina, has tours during the crushing season (June to December).

The Ballina Visitor Information Centre is on the corner of La Balsa Plaza & River Street. They have a startling range of literature on tourist interests and should be your first point of contact. The centre is open 9am-5pm Mon-Fri, 9am-4pm on weekends. Phone them on (02) 6686 3484 or email them at balinfo@balshire.org.au

Evans Head

A charming coastal town, Evans Head is 55km (34 miles) south-west of Lismore. North of the town is the Broadwater National Park, with unspoiled beaches and heathland that becomes a blaze of colour in spring. On the town's southern edge is the Bundjalung National Park, which is popular for surfing, boating, picnicking and bushwalking.

Blue Mountains

Population 70,800

The City of the Blue Mountains, comprising 26 towns and villages, stretches from Penrith, 53km (33 miles) from Sydney, to Mount Victoria, 122km (76 miles) from Sydney. The drive up to the region's major centre, Katoomba, only takes about an hour and a half, making this scenic area a comfortable distance from Sydney city for day trips or a weekend retreat.

Climate

The area has distinct seasons and is cooler than Sydney all year round. Occasionally snow falls in winter, usually July, but it does not last.

Characteristics

The Blue Mountains derive their name from the perpetual haze draped over them. Miniscule drops of eucalyptus evaporate from the leaves of the dense forest and are struck by the sunlight to produce this effect.

It was not until twenty-five years after the arrival of the First Fleet that the Blue Mountains were crossed in search of grazing land. The intrepid men who performed the feat in 1813 were Blaxland, Wentworth and Lawson, and three mountain towns bear their names.

How to Get There

By Rail

Electric trains depart from Central Station in Sydney every day with stops at Lapstone, Glenbrook, Blaxland, Warrimoo, Valley Heights, Springwood, Faulconbridge, Woodford, Hazelbrook, Lawson, Wentworth Falls, Leura, Katoomba, Medlow Bath, Blackheath and Mt Victoria.

CityRail have special off-peak fares to Katoomba - any train after 9am on weekdays, or any time at the weekend, with return before 4am the next morning, for ✪$11.80 adult. For further information ✆(02) 4782 1902.

Blue Mountains

By Bus

AAT Kings, ✆9666 3899, Newmans, ✆1300 300 036, and Australian Pacific Tours, ✆9247 7222, have daily tours from Sydney Day Tour Terminal, Circular Quay West at 9am. Try also Fantastic Aussie Tours, ✆9938 5714 (Sydney) or ✆4782 1366 (Katoomba.

By Road

From Sydney, via Parramatta Road, the F4 Freeway and the Great Western Highway. From the west, the Great Western Highway.

Visitor Information

Echo Point Information Centre, ✆1300 653 408 and Glenbrook Visitor Information Centre, Great Western Highway, Glenbrook, ✆1300 653 408, are open Mon-Fri 9am-5pm, Sat-Sun 8.30am-4.30pm.

Contact them by email on info@bluemountainstourism.org.au. The official website of Blue Mountains Tourism, ✆1300 653 408, is www.bluemountainstourism.org.au but another one to see is www.bluemts.com.au

Local Transport

Bus

Pearce Omnibus, ✆4751 1077, have services between Faulcon-bridge, Penrith; Springwood, Winmalee; Blaxland, Mt Riverview.

Katoomba Woodford Bus Company, ✆4782 4213, operate services between Katoomba, Leura and Wentworth Falls; Bullaburra and Lawson; Hazelbrook and Wood-ford; Katoomba Falls, Scenic Railway and Skyway. (No service on public holidays)

Katoomba Leura Bus Service, ✆4782 3333 links Leura, Katoomba, Echo Point, North Katoomba, Blackheath, Medlow Bath and Mt Victoria. (No service Saturday afternoon, Sunday or public holidays)

Car Hire

Thrifty, 80 Megalong Street, Leura, ✆4784 2888.

Taxi

Taxis Katoomba, ✆4782 1311; Springwood Taxis, ✆4751 1444; Blue Mountains Taxi Cabs, ✆4759 3000; Lawson Taxis, ✆4759 3000.

Accommodation

Here is a selection of accommodation, with prices for a double room per night, which should be used as a guide only. GST is included. The telephone area code is 02.

Katoomba

Alpine Motor Inn, cnr Great Western Highway & Orient Street, ✆4782 2011. 20 units, 4 suites, licensed restaurant, indoor heated swimming pool, sauna - ✪$200-255.

Mountain Heritage, cnr Lovel & Apex Streets, ✆4782 2155. 41 units, licensed restaurant, playground, swimming pool - ✪$180-420.

Katoomba Town Centre Motel, 218-220 Katoomba Street, ✆4782 1266. 18 units, spa - ✪$80-230.

The Cecil Traditional Blue Mountains Guest House, 108 Katoomba Street, ✆4782 1411. 23 rooms, unlicensed restaurant, barbecue, spa, playground tennis - B&B ✪$140-180.

Echo Point Motor Inn, Echo Point Road, ✆4782 2088. 37 units, licensed restaurant - ✪$70-130.

3 Sisters Motel, 348 Katoomba Street, ✆4782 2911. 20 units, unlicensed restaurant - ✪$65-120.

Leura

Peppers Fairmont Resort, 1 Sublime Point Road, ✆4782 5222. 210 rooms, 20 suites (private facilities), licensed restaurant, swimming pool, spa, sauna, gym, tennis, squash - ✪$240-340.

Mercure Resort Blue Mountains, Fitzroy Street, ✆4784 1331. 80 units, 9 suites, licensed restaurant, swimming pool, spa, sauna, gym, tennis, squash, putting green - ✪$130-170.

Medlow Bath

Hydro Majestic Hotel, Great Western Highway, ✆4788 1002. 63 rooms (private facilities), modern Art Deco and classic Edwardian style rooms available, very famous heritage hotel, licensed restaurant, swimming pool, tennis, spa (selected rooms) - ✪$220-1350.

Chalet Blue Mountains, 46 Portland Road, ✆4788 1122. 8 rooms, unlicensed restaurant, tennis, playground - ✪$130-150.

Mt Victoria

Mount Victoria Motor Inn, Station Street, ✆4787 1320. 12 units - ✪$95-160.

The Hotel Imperial, cnr Great Western Highway & Station Street, ✆4787 1233. 23 rooms, licensed restaurant - ✪$75-275 (a range of room standards offered).

Jenolan Caves

Caves House, ✆(02) 6359 3304. 50 rooms, licensed restaurant, playground, tennis, pool, barbecue - B&B ✪$80-200 a double; hotel section, 28 units - ✪$100-105 including breakfast.

Blackheath

Blackheath Motor Inn, 281 Great Western Highway, ✆4787 8788. 18 units, spa - ✪$90-135.

High Mountains Motor Inn, 193 Great Western Highway, ✆4787 8216. 21 units, unlicensed restaurant, swimming pool - ✪$70-120.

Caravan Parks

Katoomba Falls Caravan Park, Katoomba Falls Road, ✆4782 1835. (No pets), 68 sites, barbecue - powered sites ✪$25-30 for two, cabins $60-84 for two.

Leura Village Caravan Park, cnr Great Western Highway & The Mall, ✆4784 1552 (no pets) - powered sites ✪$13 for two, on-site vans $31-33 for two.

Blackheath Caravan Park, Prince Edward Street, ✆4787 8101. (No pets), 74 sites, - powered sites ✪$20-22 for two, cabins $38-55 for two.

Eating Out

The Swiss Cottage Restaurant, 132 Lurline Street, Katoomba, ✆4782 2281.

Undoubtedly one of the best restaurants in the Blue Mountains, *The Swiss Cottage* offers excellent meals in a warm atmosphere. The steaks and fish are superb, the soup is thick and rich, and, for dessert, the melted-Lindt-chocolate-soaked pudding is unbeatable (look for 'Death By Chocolate' on the menu). Your lively host Monique will make you feel welcome and keep you chuckling as she serves up each course.

Grand View, 174 Great Western Highway, Wentworth Falls, ✆4757 1001.
Fairmont Resort, 1 Sublime Point Road, Leura, ✆4782 5222.
Hydro Majestic Hotel, Great Western Highway, Medlow Bath, ✆4788 1002.
The Imperial, Station Street, Mt Victoria, ✆ 4787 1788.

Guest Houses serving good meals include:
Felton Woods Manor, cnr Lurline Street & Merriwa Streets, Katoomba, ✆4782 2055.
Clarendon, 68 Lurline Street, Katoomba, ✆4782 1322.
Mountain Heritage, cnr Apex & Lovel Streets, Katoomba, ✆4782 2155.
Cecil, 108 Katoomba Street, ✆4782 1411.
St Mounts, 194 Great Western Highway, Blackheath, ✆4787 6111.
The Victoria & Albert, 19 Station Street, Mt Victoria, ✆4787 1241.

For a touch of nostalgia make sure you visit the National Trust classified ***Paragon Cafe*** at 65 Katoomba Street, Katoomba, ✆4782 2928, which is fully licensed and is the home of the famous Paragon Chocolates.

Points of Interest

Penrith

Situated on the Nepean River, less than an hour's drive from Sydney, Penrith is one of the most rapidly growing regions in Australia. The biggest tourist attraction is **Panthers Leagues Club**, set in 81ha (200 acres), where bona fide visitors are most welcome. It is located in Mulgoa Road, ✆4720 5555.

Other major attractions Penrith offers are the **Nepean Belle Paddlewheeler** (✆4733 1274), the **Museum of Fire** (✆4731 3000), **Warragamba Dam** and **Wonderland Sydney** (✆9830 9100). For more information on these and other places contact the Tourist Information Centre in the carpark at Panthers, Mulgoa Road, ✆4732 7671.

Lower Blue Mountains

Lapstone-Blaxland

Lapstone Zig-Zag Walking Track begins behind the RAAF base at Glenbrook, and follows the original railway cuttings with views of the arches of Knapsack Viaduct.

Blue Mountains National Park, Glenbrook Area, has bushwalking, picnicking and camping. Information and advice plus publications are available from the Visitors Information Centre, Great Western Highway, Glenbrook, ✆1300 653 408.

Lennox Bridge, Mitchell's Pass Road, Glenbrook, was built in 1833 and is the oldest bridge on Australia's mainland. The bridge is well sign-posted from the Great Western Highway.

Wascoe Siding, 15 Grahame Street, Blaxland, ✆4739 9701, has a miniature railway and picnic area, and is open on the first Sunday of each month, except January.

Springwood

The **Local History Centre** and a **Community Art Gallery** are in Braemar, an early Federation home classified by the National Trust, as are the Frazer Memorial Presbyterian Church and Spring-wood Railway Station.

In the cemetery is the grave of Sir Henry Parkes, the Father of Federation.

Faulconbridge

Norman Lindsay Gallery and Museum, Chapman Parade, ✆4751 1067, is the home of this famous Australian artist and writer. There are displays of his paintings, etchings, ship models and family mementos, and a special Magic Pudding room. The house is set in delightful gardens with dozens of statues, some of which are also 'delightful'. There is a shop and a good coffee shop. ⏲Open Fri-Sun and public holidays 10am-4pm.

Central Blue Mountains

Bull's Camp, Great Western Highway, Linden, was used as a camp for convicts working on the road across the Blue Mountains. It is now a good picnic spot.

Selwood Science & Puzzles, 41 Railway Parade, Hazelbrook, ✆4758 6235, is a mid-Victorian house which has been classified by the National Trust. It is ⏲open Thurs-Mon 9am-5pm, and has a fine collection of art and science features.

Wentworth Falls

Yester Grange, Yester Road, ✆4757 1110, is a 19th century house with a collection of 19th century water colours, Victoriana and ceramics. The house is set in bush and parkland and Devonshire teas and light lunches are available. ⏲Open Wed-Fri 10am-4pm, Sat-Sun and public holidays 10am-5pm.

Wentworth Falls Lake, Sinclair Crescent, is a pleasant picnic spot with a playground and tame ducks. Row boats are available for hire.

Upper Blue Mountains

Leura

Sublime Point, at the end of Sublime Point Road, has great views of the Three Sisters and the Jamison Valley.

The Everglades Gardens, 37 Everglades Avenue, ✆4784 1938, is classified by the National Trust as one of the Great Gardens of Australia. ⏲open daily 10am-5pm during spring and summer, and closing an hour earlier during the colder seasons. Admission is ✪$5 adults and $1 children.

Leuralla, 36 Olympian Parade, ✆4784 1169, is an historic art deco mansion with a collection of 19th century Australian art and a Memorial Museum to Dr H.V. Evatt, first President of the United Nations Organisation. There is also a toy and railway museum.

Gordons Falls Reserve is a pleasant picnic area with playground and toilets, and from it there is a walk to the Pool of Siloam and Lyrebird Dell.

Leura Cascades on Cliff Drive is another picnic area, and there are a number of bushwalks that start from this point, with the Round Walk taking about 40 minutes.

Blue Mountains

Katoomba

The best way to see the attractions of Katoomba is to follow **Cliff Drive**. Along the drive there are many lookouts, all signposted, the most famous of which is undoubtedly **Echo Point**, from where there are the best views of **The Three Sisters**, Mennhi, Wimlah and Gunnedoo. These rock formations are very important in Aboriginal legend, and are floodlit at night. From the point you can also see the Ruined Castle and Mount Solitary, and it is possible to pick out many animal shapes on the mountains on the other side of the valley.

From Echo Point the **Giant Stairway** of almost 1000 steps leads to the floor of the Jamison Valley and the Federal Pass, and the Prince Henry Cliff Walk leads left towards Leura or right towards the Scenic Railway Complex.

The Point has picnic facilities, a restaurant and a takeaway food outlet.

Katoomba Falls Reserve is another picnic spot because the cascades, and several walking tracks begin behind the kiosk.

The Scenic Railway and Skyway on Cliff Drive, ✆4782 2699, offer a ride down to the Jamison Valley, which is not for the faint-hearted, or a ride over the valley in the Skyway. The complex also has the cafeteria-style restaurant, a fun parlour and a souvenir shop, and is open daily 9am-5pm. Fares are $5 for adults and $2 for children.

Also on Cliff Drive is **Cahill's Lookout**, another picnic spot, this time with views of escarpment and valley, and of Boar's Head Rock. The Drive ends at the Great Western Highway, at Katoomba Holiday Caravan Park.

Explorers' Tree, on the highway 2km west of Katoomba, commemorates the crossing of the Blue Mountains by Blaxland, Went-worth and Lawson. From behind the tree a Katoomba to Jenolan Caves walk begins, which takes 2-3 days. More information is available from the Tourist Information Centres.

Blackheath

Evans Lookout, Evans Lookout Road, offers superb views of the Grose Valley.

Govett's Leap, Govett's Leap Road, also has views of Grose Valley and of Bridal Veil Falls, the longest single drop fall in the Mountains.

National Parks & Wildlife Service Heritage Centre, Govett's Leap Road, ✆4787 8877, has an exhibition on natural features of the Blue Mountains, and nearby Fairfax Heritage Track is suitable for disabled people.

Blue Mounts Rhododendron Garden, Bacchante Street, is set in native bushland. It is open 9-5 and admission by donation. There are easy walking tracks and picnic facilities.

From **Anvil Rock** and Wind-eroded Cave, Hat Hill Road, Black-heath, you can get good views of the Grose Valley.

Mount Victoria

A visit to the village of Mt Victoria is like taking a step back in time, with buildings of sandstone and iron lace, and others of colonial weatherboard housing antiques, crafts and tearooms.

The Mounts Area

Rich volcanic soils and high rainfall produce the lush vegetation for which the Mounts are renowned. A beautiful area with famous gardens, lookouts and walks.

Cathedral of Ferns, Mount Wilson, is a beautiful rainforest with nearby picnic area.

Mount Tomah Botanic Garden, Bells Line Road, ✆4567 2154, was a Bicentennial project of the Royal Botanic Gardens, Sydney. The gardens are open 10am-4pm March to September, and until 5pm during the other months.

Festivals

Lawson Festival - March;
Wentworth Falls Autumn Festival - April;
Yulefest - June/July;
Springtime in the Blue Mountains - September thru November;
Leura Gardens Festival - October;
Leura Village Fair - October;
Blackheath Rhododendron Festival - Nov;
Glenbrook Festival - November.

For dates and attractions for these festivals it's best to contact Glenbrook Visitors Centre.

Facilities

Lawn bowls, bush walking, golf, horse riding, scenic drives, swimming pool, tennis, cinemas, squash, art galleries and craft shops.

Outlying Attractions

Hartley Historic Site, Hartley, 6355 2117 includes the old Courthouse, churches and inns. The site consists of a relatively small cluster of mid-nineteenth century buildings preserved by the NSW National Parks and Wildlife Service. Hartley is about 35km (22 miles) west of Katoomba.

Zig-Zag Railway

Situated about 7km east of Lithgow, the Railway is an engineering feat. It is a system of tunnels, cuttings and stone viaducts built 1866-69 to overcome the steep descent from the Blue Mountains to the Western Plains beyond. There are picnic areas, and rides are available on an old world steam train. Trains run daily and the cost of a return journey is $13 adults, $6.50 children.

Jenolan Caves

Probably the best-known limestone caves in NSW, the Jenolan Caves were discovered in the 1830s when the victim of a bushranger tracked his attacker to this hideout. The entrance to the caves is in a narrow gorge accessed through the Grand Arch, about 24m (79 ft) high. The view from Carlotta Arch, which overlooks the Blue Lake, is superb. Nine of the twenty-two caves are open for inspection, and guided tours are available. Phone the Jenolan Caves Reserve Trust on, 6359 3311 for more information.

Caves House, 6359 3322, right at the caves complex, is a charming hotel, with a restaurant, bar and accommodation. There are several bush walks in the area, and daily tours are run from Sydney and Katoomba.

Above: Katoomba Scenic Skyway, *Inset:* Katoomba Village

Bathurst

Population 26,500
Bathurst is situated on the fertile western slopes of the Great Dividing Range, 208km (129 miles) west of Sydney.

Climate

Average temperatures: January max 27C (81F) - min 13C (55F); July 11C (52F) - min -1C (30.2F). Average annual rainfall: 629mm (25 ins); drizzle rain in winter and storms in summer.

Characteristics

Bathurst is Australia's oldest inland settlement and the centre of a large pastoral district with many historic, distinctive buildings. When gold was discovered in the surrounding hills, many towns such as Hill End, Sofala and Hargraves sprung up. Most have now either disappeared or become ghost towns.

How to Get There

By Bus

Greyhound Pioneer all have daily services to Bathurst from Sydney.

By Rail

There is a Countrylink service from Sydney to Bathurst and Orange.

By Road

From Sydney, either via the Great Western Highway, or via the Kurrajong Road through Bilpin and Bell to Lithgow.

From Melbourne, via the Hume Highway to Seymour and then the Goulburn Valley Highway to Tocumwal, then the Newell Highway to West Wyalong.

From Adelaide, via the Sturt Highway through Renmark and Mildura to Hay, then via the Mid Western Highway to West Wyalong; or via the Barrier Highway through Broken Hill to Nyngan and then via the Mitchell Highway.From Brisbane, via the

Cunningham Highway to Warwick and Goondiwindi, then via the Newell Highway through Moree to Dubbo; or via the New England Highway from Warwick to Tam-worth then the Oxley Highway to Dubbo, then the Mitchell Highway.

Accommodation

Here is a selection of accommodation with prices for a double room per night, which is a guide only. The area code is 02.

James Cook International Motor Inn, cnr Mid Western & Great Western Highways, 6332 1800. 50 units, licensed restaurant, pool, bbq - $110-135.

Sundowner Chain Motor Inn, 19 Charlotte Street, 6331 2211. 37 units, licensed restaurant (closed Sunday), pool - $85-175.

Coachman's Inn Motel, cnr Great Western Highway & Oberon Road, 6331 4855. 26 units, restaurant (closed Sunday) - $95.

Ben Chifley Motor Inn, 272 Stewart Street, 6331 5055. 28 units, licensed restaurant, pool - $105.

Bathurst Motor Inn, 87 Durham Street, 6631 3568. 53 units, licensed restaurant, swimming pool, spa, gym, room service - $55-150.

Park Hotel, cnr George & Keppel Streets, 6331 3399. 19 rooms (private facilities), licensed bistro - B&B $70.

Caravan Park

Easts Bathurst Caravan Park, Sydney Road, 6331 8286. (No pets) 145 sites, pool, tennis - powered sites $18 for two, cabins $50-85 for two.

Eating Out

Many of the motels have restaurants, either licensed or BYO, and the licensed clubs have dining rooms or restaurants/bistros. There are also the usual takeaway food outlets, and the Tourist Office will have a complete list.

Tourist Information

The Bathurst Visitor Information Centre is at 28 William Street, Bathurst. They have a website, www.bathurst.nsw.gov.au, and email: visitors@ bathurst.nsw.gov.au

Points of Interest

The Visitor Centre has trained guides available to provide a commentary on historic buildings in Bathurst for tour groups, and makes brochures available to individuals.

The **Victorian Renaissance Court House**, with its double-storey portico and large octagonal central dome, faces Kings Square. It has two wings and the verandahed wing was built as a telegraph office. The Historical Museum is in the East Wing, and is open Mon-Fri 9am-4.30pm, Sat-Sun 10am-4pm.

The **Bathurst Regional Art Gallery**, 70 Keppel Street, is open Tues-Sat 10am-5pm, Sat-Sun 2-5pm.

Abercrombie House, built in the 1870s and classified by the National Trust, is open for inspection on Sundays at 3pm, except in winter.

Ben Chifley's Cottage, the home of the former Prime Minister, is open Tues-Sat 2-4pm, and Sunday 10am-noon.

Old Government Cottage, behind no. 1 George Street, is where Macquarie stayed during his farewell visit to Bathurst in 1821. It is open Sundays 1.30-3.30pm.

Miss Traill's House, 321 Russell Street, is also a National Trust property and is open Tues-Sat 1pm-3pm and Sun 10am-3pm.

The **Holy Trinity Church** at Kelso was completed in 1835 and is the oldest consecrated Anglican Church in Australia.

St Michael and St John's Catholic Cathedral was completed in 1861. St Stanislaus' College has taken pupils since 1873, and is Australia's oldest Catholic Boarding School.

Ohkuma Japanese Garden is on the corner of Stanley and George Streets. Okhkuma is the sister-city of Bathurst, and this garden was laid out in 1998 as a symbol of the link.

Macquarie River Bicentennial Park is a popular spot for a picnic.

The 35 bells of the Carillon in **Kings Parade** plays every day at noon and 1pm. Also located within the park are three war monuments which commemorate the sacrifice of men from the Bathurst district.

Outside the Visitor Centre is the **Victors' Walk**, where brass plaques have been embedded in checker-board concrete to commemorate winners of the Bathurst 1000.

At Mt Panorama is the Motor Racing Circuit which is used for the annual Bathurst 1000 motor race. Experience the excitement, disappointment and enjoyment that is motor racing in Bathurst at the **National Motor Racing Museum**, which is on Murray Corner and is open daily 9am-4.30pm. It has a selection of memorabilia associated with the big race, collected over the years, from cars and trophies to souvenirs.

Located on Mt Panorama is the **Sir Joseph Banks Nature Park**, which has koalas, kangaroos and wallabies in a 41ha (101 acres) park, open daily 10am-4pm.

The **Bathurst Sheep and Cattle Drome**, Rossmore Park, Limekilns Road, Kelso, is only an eight minute drive from the centre of town. There visitors can milk a cow or sit back in air-conditioned comfort and enjoy an 80 minute show of sheep shearing and wool classing. If the weather is fine, there will be a sheep dog in action. The newest addition to the Sheep and Cattle Drome is their Golf Practice Driving Range, open daily.

Bathurst Rotalactor is a modern rotary dairy that milks over 300 cows, situated in the picturesque Dunkeld Valley. There is a large, well-appointed, indoor viewing area, a cafe specialising in dairy products, and many educational displays on various aspects of the dairy industry. To get there, take the Blayney Road for 7km, then turn right for Dunkeld.

Festivals

The Bathurst 1000 Motor Race is held during the October long weekend (first Monday in October), with activities organised during the week leading up to the Race.

Facilities

There is an olympic swimming pool and water slide. Bathurst also has all the usual sporting facilities you would expect in a large town, including lawn bowls, golf course, tennis courts and squash courts.

Outlying Attractions

Orange

Situated 55km (34 miles) from Bathurst, Orange is a larger town than Bathurst, and the area produces 10% of Australia's apples, as well as cherries and other stone fruit, on the rich volcanic soil slopes of Mt Canobolas. The upper slopes of the extinct volcano are a flora and fauna reserve with picnic areas and walking trails. There is a lake in the crater, and canoeing, sailing and fishing are popular.

The Ophir gold find gave the early settlement a firm foundation, and it has grown into the largest town in the district. Bowen Terrace is a perfect and rare example of its period, with a row of ironwork-decorated houses. Endsleigh House, built in 1858, is thought to be the oldest house. The golf club is housed in the 1876 Duntryleague mansion.

A.J. (Banjo) Paterson, perhaps Australia's most popular poet and writer, was born along the Ophir Road in 1864 and an obelisk marks the spot. It is inscribed with a verse from Clancy of the Overflow.

Orange is the headquarters of the Ministry of Agriculture, and has a large agricultural college. The Orange Visitor Information Centre is on corner of Byng and Peisley Streets, 63938226, tourism@orange.nsw.gov.au. The website is www.orange.nsw .gov.au

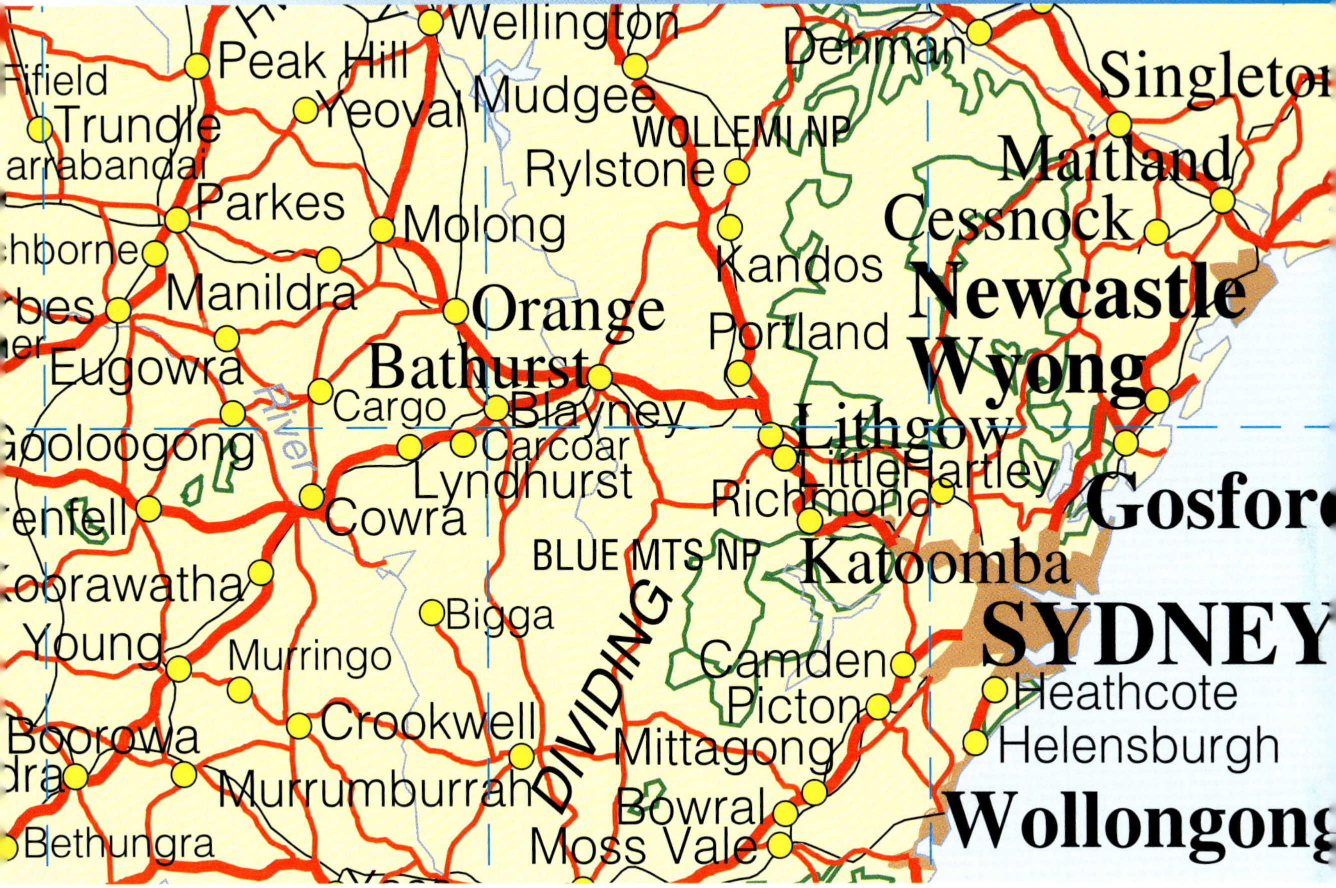

Ophir

Gold was first discovered in Australia in 1951 at Ophir, approximately 40km (25 miles) from Orange. Today the area is a reserve, and trails lead to old tunnels, sluices and other relics among the hills. The reserve is, naturally enough, popular with fossickers.

Abercrombie Caves

On the Goulburn Road, 72km (45 miles) from Bathurst, is one of the smaller but most spectacular limestone cave systems in Australia. The reserve has a camping/caravan park with picnic facilities, and cave inspection times and tours vary. For more information phone 6368 8603, visit www.jenolancaves.org.au or send email abercrombie@jenolancaves.org.au

Sofala

Set amongst the steep hills of Turon Valley, Sofala's one of the old gold rush towns. It has a quaint store and faded old-time buildings.

The Royal Hotel is the only hotel remaining of the forty which were operating during the gold rush era.

Hill End

The Parks and Wildlife Service have declared Hill End an historic site, and they publish an excellent information sheet 'Exploring Hill End Historic Site' which has a map on one side and an excellent walking tour on the other. Only a small community remains today. Miners dug up 701,000 ounces of gold here. Panning and fossicking are still popular, and gold pans may be hired in town. Hill End is 84km (52 miles) from Bathurst.

Mudgee

Situated 69km (43 miles) north of Hill End, Mudgee is the second oldest town west of the Blue Mountains, and was laid out in 1838. A score of handsome buildings, classified by the National Trust, dot the town, the oldest being the Catholic Presbytery, built in 1852. The church, St Mary's, was commenced five years later, and has an exceptional iron screen and stencilled decorations.

The Court House, St John the Baptist's Church, the Police Station and Post Office were all built in the early 1860s. The Colonial Inn Museum, Market Street, is open Sat 2-5pm, Sun, school and public holidays 10-5pm.

Mudgee is renowned for its honey, and visitors are able to watch honey processing at two factories.

There are also many wineries in the district, and all have cellar door sales. Mudgee is well known for its fine wines, and is gaining fame for its beautiful rose gardens. There is a Days of Wine and Roses Festival each year in September/October.

Mudgee Gulgong Tourism is at 84 Market Street, 6372 1020, email tourist@mudgee.nsw. gov.au. It is open 9am-5pm Mon-Fri, 9am-3.30pm Sat and 9.30am-2pm Sundays.

Gulgong

Gulgong, 29km (18 miles) from Mudgee was, until the advent of plastic currency, the 'Town on the Ten Dollar Note'.

It has narrow streets which wind between quaint clapboard and iron buildings, complete with verandahs and iron lace. The Pioneers' Museum, in Medley Street, covers .4ha (1 acre) and includes an astonishing array of Australiana. The Henry Lawson Art Gallery is open during school holidays. The Phonograph Parlour, 69 Lee Street, has recorded sound equipment dating back to 1889. Gold is still

Dubbo

Population 33,700

Dubbo is situated in mid-western New South Wales on the Macquarie River, at the junction of the Newell and Mitchell Highways. The city is 416km (258 miles) from Sydney; 862km (536 miles) from Brisbane; 818km (508 miles) from Melbourne; and 1207km (750 miles) from Adelaide.

Climate

Average temperatures: January max 32C (90F) - min 18C (64F); July max 15C (59F) - min 3C (37F). Average annual rainfall - 584mm (23 ins); height above sea level - 262m (859 ft); average number of rainy days per year - 74.

Characteristics

Dubbo is known as the Hub of the West. It is a prosperous service centre for the fertile farmlands around it.

How to Get There

By Bus

Pioneer and Greyhound stop at Dubbo on their Melbourne/Brisbane/Gold Coast runs.

By Rail

There a Countrylink service from Sydney to Dubbo.

By Road

From Adelaide, via the Sturt Highway to Mildura, and then the Mid Western or the Barrier and Mitchell Highways.

From Brisbane, via the Cunningham Highway to Goon-diwindi, and then the Newell Highway.

From Melbourne, via the Hume Highway to Seymour, the Goulburn Valley Highway to Tocumwal, and then the Newell Highway.From Sydney, via the Great Western Highway to Bathurst, and then the Mitchell Highway.

Dubbo

Accommodation

Here is a selection with prices for a double room per night, which should be used as a guide only. The telephone area code is 02.

Ashwood Country Club Motel, Whylandra Street, ✆6881 8700. 39 units, licensed restaurant, pool, spa, tennis, bbq - ✪$90-130.

Cascades Motor Inn, 147 Cobra Street, ✆6882 3888. 36 units, licensed restaurant, swimming pool, barbecue - ✪$85-95.

Australian Heristage Motor Inn, cnr Cobra and Brisbane Streets, ✆6884 1188. 22 units, licensed restaurant, bistro, pool - ✪$105-145.

Blue Gum Motor Inn, 109 Cobra Street, ✆6882 0900. 24 units, pool, barbecue - ✪$75-85.

Country Comfort Dubbo, Newell Highway, ✆6882 4777. 60 units, licensed restaurant, swimming pool, spa, tennis, bbq - ✪$90-150.

All Seasons Motor Lodge, 78 Whylandra Street, ✆6882 6377. 19 units, licensed restaurant, pool, spa, sauna - ✪$70-75.

Forest Lodge Motor Inn, Myall Street, ✆6882 6500. 15 units, licensed restaurant (closed Sun & Mon), swimming pool, bbq - ✪$75-90.

Matilda Motor Inn, 231 Darling Street, ✆6882 3944. 38 units, licensed restaurant, swimming pool - ✪$60-80.

Castlereagh Hotel, cnr Brisbane & Talbragar Streets, ✆6882 4877. 13 rooms (some with private facilities), licensed restaurant (Mon-Thurs) - B&B ✪$55-70.

Caravan Parks

Dubbo City Caravan Park, Whylandra Street, West Dubbo, ✆6882 4820. (Pets allowed) 128 sites, facilities, pool - powered sites ✪$18 for two, on-site vans $28 for two.

Poplars Caravan Park, Lower Bultje Street, ✆6882 4067. (Pets allowed) 69 sites - powered sites ✪$12 for two, on-site vans $26 for two.

Windmill Caravan Park, cnr Mitchell Highway & Sheraton Road, ✆6882 4583. (Pets allowed on application) 78 sites, pool, barbecue, playground - powered sites ✪$14 for two, on-site vans $25 for two.

Midstate Motor Park, 21 Bourke Street, ✆6882 1155. 53 sites, barbecue, golf, pool - ✪$16 for two, on-site vans $35 for two.

Eating Out

As mentioned in the Accommodation section, several of the motels and hotels have restaurants. Here are some others you might try.

The Dubbo RSL Club, Wingewarra Street, ✆6882 4411, welcomes visitors.

Jules Crepes Restaurant, 195 Macquarie Street, ✆6882 9300, is fully licensed, and serves a wide variety of crepes in an old world atmosphere. It is open Mon-Sat noon-2.30pm, 6.30pm onwards.

Hing Wah, 143 Talbragar St, ✆6882 4401.

Darbar Indian Restaurant, 215 Macquarie St, ✆6884 4338.

Rose Garden Thai Restaurant, 208 Brisbane St, ✆6882 8322.

Blue Lagoon, 81 Cobra St, ✆6882 4444.

Golden Dragon Restaurant, 36 Victoria St, ✆6882 6663.

Settlers Restaurant, Newell Hwy, West Dubbo, ✆6882 4777.

Safari Lounge Restaurant, 78 Whylandra St, ✆6882 1600.

McDonalds is at 22-24 Cobra Street.

Tourist Information

The Dubbo Visitors Information Centre is on the corner of Macquarie and Erskine Streets, ✆6884 1422, email tourism@dubbo.nsw.gov.au. It is open daily 9am-5pm, but closed Christmas Day.

Points of Interest

The city is best seen by following the signposted **Tourist Drive**, which starts at the Civic Centre, Darling Street.

Heritage Walk commences at the Museum and takes in many historic buildings around the city.

The **Old Dubbo Gaol**, ✆6882 8122, in Macquarie Street between the State and Commonwealth Banks, is open daily 9am-5pm, and has many items of interest including animated robots, and the original gallows.

The **Museum**, 234 Macquarie Street, includes a village square with 14 shop exhibitions. It is open daily 9am-5pm.

Dubbo Regional Art Gallery in Darling Street, ✆6881 4342, has changing exhibitions every four to six weeks, and you can book in advance for tours by trained guides. The Gallery is open Mon, Wed, Thurs, Fri 11am-4.30pm, Sat-Sun 10am-noon, 1-4pm.

Western Plains Zoo, Obley Road (6km south of the city), ✆6882 5888, is Dubbo's main tourist attraction, and entry is daily 9am-4pm, but visitors are welcome to remain until 5pm. The Zoo, opened in 1977, is a sister zoo to Sydney's Taronga Park. It is administered by the Zoological Parks Board of New South Wales, and is Australia's only official open range zoo. Its 300ha (741 acres) of open bushland and landscaped exhibits are home to more than 2000 animals. Visitors can drive their own cars around the 6km sealed road in the Zoo, or hire a bike or mini moke, or fitness fanatics can walk. There are several picnic areas en route, as well as free gas barbecue

facilities, or you can lunch at the licensed bistro, open noon-2pm, or grab a bite to eat from the fast food outlet.

The **Dubbo Military Museum**, Newell Highway, ✆6884 5550, has a whole range of WW2 military equipment in an open air setting. The museum is ⏲open daily 10am-4.30pm.

Yarrabar Pottery and Gallery, Peakhill Road, ✆6884 2455, has a potter in action, and can make functional and decorative pottery to your requirements. The Gallery is ⏲open daily 9am-5pm.

Facilities

Golf, lawn bowls, tennis, fishing, sauna, cinema, swimming pool, ice skating rink, ten pin bowling, slot car racing and horse racing. Paddle boats, canoeing and water skiing on the Macquarie River.

On the second Sunday of the month, Markets are held in the Showground, 10am-1pm, and hundreds of stall holders sell everything from plants and toys to furniture.

Festivals

The Orana Country Music Festival is usually held during the Easter period. The Dubbo Agricultural Show is held in May.

There are events held every month in Dubbo, and the Visitor Information Centre has all the details.

Outlying Attractions

Peak Hill

Located 71km (44 miles) south-west of Dubbo, on Roose Road, Peak Hill, is the site of an open cut gold mine, ✆6869 1733. It consists of two holes of enormous depth. When you view the mine from the lookouts, it is hard to realise that these holes were originally gouged out by hand. The walls of the holes reflect an array of colours, due to the presence of iron, calcium, magnesium and other trace elements. To get to the lookouts, turn right at the Ex-Services Club and follow the signs.

Peak Hill Tourist Information is at105 Caswell St, ✆6869 1981.

Parkes

Parkes is 121km (75 miles) south-west of Dubbo, and is the major centre of the Lachlan Valley, servicing the towns of Peak Hill, Alectown, Bogan Gate, Trundle and Tullamore.

Parkes has a town population of 10,100, and Parkes Visitor Information Centre is on the Newell Highway, ✆6862 4365 or email ✉tourism@parkes.nsw.gov.au They are ⏲open 9am-5pm Mon-Fri, 10am-4pm Sat-Sun.

The main attraction in the area is the Radio Telescope, and to get there travel north on the Newell Highway for 20km (12 miles), turn off the highway and follow Telescope Road for 6km (4 miles), then follow the signs. The Visitors Centre is ⏲open daily 8.30am-4.15pm, ✆6861 1776, and you shouldn't miss the audio-visual show entitled "The Invisible Universe", which is screened daily from 8.30am, with the last show at 3.30pm. There is a moderate admission fee.

For those who love statistics: The radiotelescope is neither a tracking station for Earth-orbiting satellites, nor a communications station. It's for astronomy. It was built in a very quiet radio interference zone, near a large service town, close to Divisional headquarters in Sydney, and in a location with a low recorded average wind speed. The telescope was opened on October 31, 1961. The dish and drive mechanism weigh about 1,000 tonnes. The dish is 64m (210 ft) in diameter and 0.4ha (1 acre) in area. There are about 20 full-time staff, not all astronomers. Only 4 live on site, the rest live in and around Parkes. When the dish is pointing vertical to the ze-

nith, the astronomers are not observing. The telescope is normally operational 24 hours a day, seven days a week.

Other attractions in Parkes include: Henry Parkes Historical Museum, 316 Clarinda Street, ✆622 815; Motor Museum - Craft Corner, cnr Bogan & Dalton Streets; BHP Gold Mine, 6km south-west of Parkes; Pioneer Park, a collection of agricultural machinery and road transport; Bushman's Hill Development, the restoration of the Bushman's gold mine adjacent to the Visitor Centre; and Mugincoble, a Wheat Terminal with inspections arranged by the Tourist Centre.

Forbes

35km (22 miles) south-west of Parkes on the Newell Highway, is Forbes, which has many well attended parks and gardens and historic buildings. Forbes Railway Arts and Tourist Centre, Union St, can be contacted on ✆6852 4155.

Forbes is Ben Hall country. The famous bushranger was part of the notorious Gardiner Gang who carried out a gold escort robbery at nearby Eugowra. He met his death in a hail of bullets at the age of 28 and is buried in the Forbes Cemetery. The Forbes Museum, in an old Music Hall which once formed part of the Osborn Hotel, houses an interesting collection of relics of the bushrangers, and outside of Forbes a plaque marks the spot where Ben Hall was killed.

Other interesting graves in the old cemetery are those of Kate Foster, sister of Ned Kelly, and Rebecca Shield, grand-niece of Captain Cook.

The Lachlan Vintage Village, ✆6852 2655, is one kilometre from Forbes on the Newell Highway, and visitors can relive the past of an old gold town with exhibits dating from 1860 to 1900. Many of the early buildings and commercial businesses of the area have been reconstructed in a central part of the 81ha (200 acres) village to provide the visitor with a view of a country town from yesteryear. The complex also contains: the Lachlan Diggings, built on the site of the Forbes goldfield, where you can try your luck panning for gold in the creek; the Farming Museum, an 1860s farm complete with equipment, animals and the historic 'Nelungaloo' homestead with original furniture; Ben Hall's cottage; the home of the famous Australian poet, Henry Lawson; and the Trigalana Woolshed, the entry building which houses the Blackridge Restaurant and a souvenir shop.

Forbes also has three wineries, two of which have distilleries. For inspections and cellar door sales enquire at the Tourist Centre.

Wellington

Situated on the Mitchell Highway, 50km (31 miles) south-east of Dubbo, Wellington is famous for the Wellington Caves, 8km (5 miles) south of the town. There are tours of the caves every hour 9am-4pm, except 1pm, ✆6845 1733, and accommodation is available in nearby *Caves Caravan Park*, ✆6845 2970.

The Wellington Tourist Information Centre is at Cameron Park, ✆6845 1733, and they have information on attractions in the town, which include a clock museum, a winery, and arts and crafts galleries. You can email them at wellvic@australis.aunz.com and they are open 9am-5pm daily except Christmas Day.

The Burrendong Dam is 32km (20 miles) upstream from Wellington, and there you can waterski, sail, swim, fish, or relax in the sun. Burrendong's arboretum covers an area of nearly 160ha (395 acres), set aside for the cultivation and preservation of plant life native to Australia. Mookerawa, another section of the Burrendong State Recreation Park, and Burrendong offer great facilities for visitors who love to camp.

Gilgandra

The town of Gilgandra is on the Newell Highway, 66km (41 miles) north of Dubbo, on the western side of the Warrumbungles. It was known originally as the town of windmills, and is home to one of the country's best privately owned observatories. The Gilgandra Visitor Information Centre is on the Newell Highway, ✆6847 2045 email gilinfo@tpg.com.au It is open 9am-5pm daily, closed Christmas Day. Drop in here for information on the attractions in the town, and available accommodation.

Coonabarabran

Situated 95km (59 miles) north-east of Gilgandra, Coonabarabran has a population of around 4000. The town name means 'Inquisitive Person' and the Visitors Centre is on the Newell Highway at the southern end of town, ✆6842 144, or you can email coonavic@lisp.com.au, open daily 9am-5pm. They have enough information to satisfy any inquisitive person on accommodation and attractions, which include Miniland and Museum, and Crystal Kingdom.

The main attraction, however, is the Anglo-Australian Observatory, in Siding Spring, whose visitor's gallery allows visitors to view some of the workings of this immense piece of equipment. On the site there is also a fascinating permanent exhibition, 'Exploring the Universe', which should not be missed. The Observatory is 28km (17 miles) west of the town, and is open daily from 9am-4pm, ✆6842 6291.

35km (22 miles) from town is the Warrumbungle National Park, covering 21,004ha (51,880 acres) and containing magnificent scenery and prolific fauna and flora. The Park has spires and domes that are remnants of violent volcanic activity some 13 million years ago, and they are a spectacular sight. Food is not available in the park, and pets are prohibited. For further information ✆1300 361 967 or visit www.npws.nsw.gov.au

Between the Warrumbungle Mountains and the Namoi River is the Pilliga Forest and Nature Reserve, a vast flat area covering approximately 5400 sq km (2084 sq miles) of natural wild forest and scrublands known as the Pilliga Scrub.

The town of Baradine is the heart of the Pilliga, and there you can visit the Baradine Forest Centre, Lachlan Street, ✆6843 1607, and find out details of the many forest drives, and the location of the numerous sandstone caves.

Broken Hill

Population 24,466
Broken Hill lies in the Barrier Ranges in outback New South Wales, near the South Australian border. It is a long way from anywhere - 1170km (727 miles) from Sydney; 882km (548 miles) from Melbourne; 510km (317 miles) from Adelaide.

Climate

The city is 304m (997 ft) above sea level, and has an average rainfall of 235mm (9.25 ins) which is spread fairly evenly throughout the year with the greatest fall usually in June. As a rule the temperature only climbs above 38C (100F) eight or nine time a year. Maximum summer temperatures are generally in the low 30s (around 85F), but this causes little discomfort due to the low humidity. The nights are cold throughout the year. The winter months of May, June and July can be quite cold during the day as well.

Characteristics

Broken Hill is first and foremost a mining town, and in earlier days the dust problem appeared insurmountable, but due to a regeneration scheme started in 1930s, this problem has been largely overcome, at least as far as local storms are concerned. It has one of the richest silver and lead deposits in the world. Recently its popularity in the tourist market has grown.

Tourist Information

The Broken Hill Visitor Information Centre is on the corner of Blende and Bromide Streets, ✆(08) 8087 6077, email tourist@pcpro.net.au. It is open 8.30am - 5pm daily.

Broken Hill

Eating Out

Broken Hill has plenty of restaurants, cafes, clubs and hotels serving meals. Here are some you might like to try.

Pagoda Chinese Restaurant, 357 Cobalt Street, ✆8087 3679.

Oceania Chinese Restaurant, 423 Argent Street, ✆8087 3695.

Silver City Workingmen's Club, 402 Argent Street, ✆8087 5337.

The Haven Restaurant, 577 Argent St, ✆8088 2888.

Betina's, 271 Kaolin St, ✆8088 2999.

Accommodation

Here is a selection of accommodation with prices for a double room per night, which should be used as a guide only. The telephone area code is 08.

Broken Hill Overlander Motor Inn, 142 Iodide Street, ✆8087 7013. 12 units, heated swimming pool, spa, sauna, barbecue - ✪$85-105.

Daydream Motel, 77 Argent Street, ✆8088 3033. 12 units, swimming pool, barbecue - ✪$65.

Charles Rasp Motor Inn, 158 Oxide Street, ✆8088 1988. 20 units, swimming pool, spa, barbecue - ✪$95-110.

Miners Lamp Motor Inn, 357 Cobalt Street, ✆8088 4122. 32 units, licensed restaurant, swimming pool, barbecue - ✪$90-100.

Silver Spade Hotel/Motel, 151 Argent Street, ✆8087 7021. 14 units, licensed restaurant, swimming pool, barbecue - ✪$60-65.

Sturt Motel, 153 Rakow Street, ✆8087 3558. 19 units, swimming pool - ✪$55-60.

Caravan Parks

Broken Hill City Caravan Park, Rakow Street, ✆8087 3841. (Pets allowed in a restricted area) 173 sites, barbecue, heated pool - powered sites ✪$18 for two, on-site vans $32 for two.

Lake View Broken Hill Caravan Park, 1 Mann Street, ✆8088 2250. (Pets allowed under strict control) 137 sites, pool - powered sites ✪$20 for two, on-site vans $30 for two.

Broken Hill

How to Get There

By Bus

Pioneer have a Sydney/Adelaide service via Broken Hill.

Greyhound have a service from/to Melbourne.

Stateliner have a service from Adelaide.

By Rail

The Indian Pacific (Sydney/Perth) and The Alice (Sydney/Alice Springs) stop at Broken Hill.

By Car

From Sydney, via the Great Western Highway to Orange, the Mitchell Highway to Nyngan, then the Barrier Highway.

From Melbourne, via the Calder Highway to Mildura, then the Silver City Highway.

From Adelaide, via National Route 32.

Points of Interest

Broken Hill has two **Tourist Drives** - the Silver Arrow tour 1 and 2, and maps are available from the Tourist Centre.

Walking Tours depart from the Information Centre Mon-Fri and Sun at 10am, and are of approximately one and half hour's duration.

The **Sundown Nature Trail**, situated in the rocky Sundown Hills on the northern edge of the city Common, winds through the countryside for 2.8km (2 miles) and affords an opportunity to examine the sparse vegetation up close. It takes about one and a half hours, and is at its best just before sunset or just after sunrise.

Interesting and informative inspections of the surface workings of **North Mine** are conducted every afternoon Mon-Fri, and the Information Centre has details. Note that solid footwear must be worn.

Underground tours are available Mon-Fri 10.30am and Sat 2pm, ✆8088 1604, but children under 8 are not admitted. The Daydream Mine, ✆8088 5682, near Silverton, 45 minutes away, also has underground tours with no age limit.

For tours of the **Royal Flying Doctor Base**, enquire on ✆8080 1777. The School of the Air is open weekdays, and bookings for this are handled by the Information Centre.

At the **Whites Mineral Art and Mining Museum**, 1 Allendale Street ✆8087 2878, you can see life size replicas of current and old-time mining procedures.

The **Railway Mineral and Train Museum**, Blende Street, ✆8088 4660, has a large display of old railway machinery.

Broken Hill has more than twenty-one Art Galleries open for public viewing. Here are a few names and addresses:

The Broken Hill City Art Gallery, cnr Chloride and Blende Streets, ✆8088 5491, ⏲open Mon-Sat 9am-4pm, guided tours Tues-Sat 11.30am.

Pro Hart Gallery, ✆8087 2441, 108 Wyman Street, ⏲open Mon-Sat 9.30am-5pm.

Hoppy Hopgood Gallery, 589 Fisher Street, ⏲open daily from 9am.

Facilities

Car Hire: Avis, ✆8087 7532; Budget, ✆8087 9151; and Hertz, ✆8087 2719.
Taxi services: Yellow Radio Cabs, ✆13 1008.
There are two laundromats, 3 Council run libraries, 3 swimming pools (one heated), golf, horse riding, lawn bowls, indoor cricket, squash and tennis.

The Royal Automobile Association of South Australia has an office at 261 Argent Street, ✆8088 4999.

Outlying Attractions

Menindee

Situated 110km (68 miles) south-east of Broken Hill, there is a series of natural lakes stretching 50km (31 miles) north and 35km (22 miles) south of the town of Menindee, and areas have been developed for caravan parks, weekend cottages, speedboats, water skiing, sailing, safe swimming and good fishing.

The Kinchega National Park, on the western bank of the Darling River adjacent to Menindee, is a significant example of one of the major landscape categories of the arid and semi-arid regions of New South Wales.

The Menindee Regional Tourist Association is in the Railway Station, Maiden St, ✆8091 4274.

Silverton

On a sealed road 25km (16 miles) north-west of Broken Hill, is Silverton, once a thriving community of over 3000, but now a ghost town where many films have been shot, eg A Town Like Alice, Mad Max II and Razorback, and several commercials and documentaries.

The Sturt National Park begins just north of Tibooburra, which is 337km (209 miles) north of Broken Hill, and reaches to the spot where the New South Wales, Queensland and South Australian borders meet. At the three-state corner the dingo fence can be seen. It is part of the 'longest fence in the world'.

White Cliffs

The well-known opal field and township of White Cliffs is 295km (183 miles) north-east of Broken Hill. There you can try your luck at fossicking, see the superb opalised Plesiosaur skeleton, and the dugouts where many of the residents live. Facilities include a hotel, motel, general store and cafe. Fossicker's Licences are available from the Tourist Information Centre in Karara Road, ✆8091 6611.

Tamworth

Population 34,500
Tamworth is situated at the junction of the New England and Oxley Highways, on the banks of the Peel River. It is 411km (255 miles) from Sydney; 1152km (715 miles) from Melbourne; 1,446km (898 miles) from Adelaide; 589km (366 miles) from Brisbane.

Climate

Average temperatures: January max 30C (88F) - min 17C (63F); July max 16C (61F) - min 4C (39F). The town is 389 metres (1276 ft) above sea level and has an average rainfall of 650mm (25in). Occasional snow falls in winter on the hilltops around Nundle (60km [37miles]) to the south.

How to Get There

By Rail

An air conditioned Countrylink service operates daily to Tamworth. The Countrylink connects in Tamworth with a fleet of luxury coaches which travel over a large area of north-west NSW.

By Bus

Tamworth is on the main Brisbane/Sydney, Brisbane/Melbourne and Brisbane/Adelaide routes which are covered daily by Greyhound Pioneer and McCafferty's.

By Road

Tamworth is approximately 5.5 hours drive from Sydney and 6.5 hours from Brisbane along National Highway 15 - the New England Highway. The city also has highway links to the Gold Coast, Melbourne, Port Macquarie and Adelaide.

Tamworth

Characteristics

As well as being famous as the Australasian Country Music Capital, Tamworth was also the first city in the country to install electric street lighting. The city is in the heart of the biggest gemstone fossicking region of NSW, and is surrounded by picturesque countryside.

Tourist Information

The Tamworth Visitor Information Centre is on the corner of Peel and Murray Streets, ✆02 6755 4300 or contact by email: tourism@tamworth.nsw.gov.au. Their opening hours are 8.30am-4.30pm Mon-Fri, 9am-5pm on weekends.

Eating Out

There are licensed clubs which provide lunch and dinner, and have activities and live entertainment for guests. Visitors are always welcome. There are a number of fully licensed restaurants mainly associated with the major hotels, and many fast food outlets such as McDonald's and the local cafes.

83 Restaurant, 199 Marius St, ✆6766 2383.

Valentino's Italian Restaurant, 2 Byrnes Ave, ✆6766 4246.

Empress Chinese Restaurant, 455a Peel St, ✆6766 1616.

Bangkok Thai Restaurant, North-gate Shopping Centre Shop, 18 Peel St, ✆6761 3098.

Deepka Indian Restaurant, 23 Brisbane St, ✆6766 1771.

Tamworth

Accommodation

Ask for a room away from the highway as trucks travelling at night can ruin your sleep. Here is a selection with prices for a double room per night, which should be used as a guide only. The telephone area code is 02.

Powerhouse Boutique Hotel, New England Highway, ✆6766 7000. 81 units, licensed restaurants, pool, sauna, spa, gym - ✪$115-125.

Tamwell Motel, 121 Johnston Street, ✆6766 2800. 16 units, unlicensed restaurant (closed weekends), secure parking - ✪$95-100.

Abraham Lincoln, 343 Armidale Road, ✆6766 1233. 15 units, pool, barbecue - ✪$75-80.

Alandale Flag Inn, New England Highway, ✆6765 7922. 25 units, licensed restaurant, pool, spa, half-court tennis - ✪$85-100.

Thunderbird Hotel, 999 Armidale Road (3km north of Tamworth)✆67609200 web: www.warner1@optusnet.com.au, 22 good sized units, with great facilities and air conditioning. Units are away from the highway so traffic noise is not a problem. Games room, swimming pool - ✪$59.00, Good hearty breakfast costs $10.00 - served to your room. Great value for Money, and Michael and Cheryl Parker are helpful and cheerful hosts.

Roydon's Motel, cnr New England Highway & Church Street, ✆6765 7355. 12 units, basic facilities - ✪$55-60.

Southgate Inn, cnr. Kathleen & Kent Streets, ✆6765 7999. 6 rooms (private facilities), unlicensed restaurant - ✪$60-65.

Tamworth Hotel, Marius Street, ✆6766 2923. 11 rooms, licensed restaurant - ✪$40.

Caravan Parks

City Lights Caravan Park, New England Highway, ✆6765 7664. (Pets allowed) 102 sites, pool, playground, bbq- powered sites ✪$16-25 for two, on-site vans $30-45.

Austin Caravan Park, 581 Armidale Road, ✆6766 2380. (Pets allowed on application) 104 sites, barbecue, pool, good facilities - powered sites ✪$19 for two, cabins $35-75.

Points of Interest

The Department of Lands has created a **Heritage Walk** and a **Nature Walk** in Tamworth. Maps of both walks are available from the Visitor Information Centre in Kable Avenue.

The **Powerstation Museum** in Peel Street celebrates Tamworth's centenary as Australia's first city with electric street lighting, and features working steam-powered electricity-generating equipment.

Calala Cottage in Denison Street was constructed in 1875 as the home of Tamworth's first Mayor, and today forms part of the local Historical Society complex.

Munro's Mill in Peel Street opened in 1863. Built from handmade bricks and hand-forged nails, it was the first commercial flour mill in New England. Today, it is an antique shop.

The **Country Collection**, ✆6765 2688, on the New England Highway offers an interesting combination of attractions including the Rock, Gem and Mineral Collection, a wax museum filled with legends of country music, and Britten's Boutique Brewery which produces a series of Tamworth ales.

Endeavour Drive, at the top of Brisbane Street, takes you to Oxley Park, a peaceful sanctuary for kangaroos and other native wildlife, with full amenities, picnic and barbecue facilities.

Bicentennial Park, in Kable Avenue, is a peaceful 'people's place' of parkland, pathways, fountains, pergolas, restaurant and a central pool. The pool is ringed by granite etched with depictions of the district's history and wildlife.

Tamworth City Gallery, ✆6755 4459, in Marius Street has a silver collection on permanent display. It also houses travelling exhibitions and is the site for the National Fibre Exhibition.

Festivals

The Australasian Country Music Festival is held over ten days each January. The festival normally has over 600 concerts and events.

The Tamworth Arts in Action Festival is held biennially in October. It includes concerts, homecrafts displays, opera and live theatre.

Facilities

Excellent sporting facilities are available in Tamworth for just about every type of sport. At Lake Keepit you can water ski, canoe, fish, sail and bushwalk. There are also facilities for gliding (Keepit Soaring Club). The hilltop countryside around Tamworth is best appreciated on horseback. Four Wheel Drive enthusiasts will find the surounding back roads challenging.

Outlying Attractions

Manilla

On the Namoi River, it is known for Dutton's Meadery in Barraba Street, where you can taste their honey-based alcoholic drink, which is reputedly mans' oldest liquor.

Kootingal

Pyramid Planetarium on the New England Highway features a working model of the solar system.

Moonbi

Braecroft Cottage Gallery, Braefarm Road is the home of the ceramic artist Fred Hillier and his range of ceramic figurines and Australian bush buildings.

Nundle

If you want to try your luck fossicking then try the 'Hills of Gold' area, after visiting Hanging Rock, and asking one of the locals for advice. The Nundle historical Museum is in Jenkins Street, ✆6769 3292.

Armidale

Population 22,000

Armidale is situated in the New England Tablelands, part of the Great Dividing Range which stretches from around Newcastle to the Queensland Border. The city is surrounded by National Parks - Oxley Wild Rivers National Park, New England National Park, Cathedral Rock National Park and Beautiful Gorge Country. Distance from Sydney 563km (35 miles), Melbourne 1268km (788 miles), Brisbane 464km (288 miles), Adelaide 1636km (1017 miles).

Climate

Average temperatures: January max 26C (79F) - min 14C (57F); June max 14C (57F) - min 2C (36F). Average annual rainfall is 795mm (31 ins). Situated 1000m (3281 ft) above sea level. Armidale has definite seasons, and occasional snowfalls in winter.

Characteristics

The principal town of the area, it is an education centre with over 8 high schools and other institutions, and it is the site of New England University. The surrounding district produces fine merino wool, wheat and fruit.

How to Get There

By Bus

Border Coaches, Bus Australia, Trans City and McCaffertys have services to Armidale from Sydney and Brisbane.

By Rail

There is a daily Countrylink service from Sydney to Tamworth, with a connecting coach to Armidale.

Armidale

By Road

From Sydney, via the New England Highway from Newcastle. From Melbourne, via the Princes or Hume Highways to Sydney; or via the Newell Highway to Tamworth and then the New England Highway. From Brisbane, via the Pacific Highway and then either Route 78 from Coffs Harbour; the Gwydir Highway from Grafton; the Oxley Highway from Port Macquarie; or the Bruxner Highway from Ballina via the New England Highway through Tenterfield.

Accommodation

Here is a selection with prices for a double room per night, which should be used as a guide only. The telephone area code is (02).

Armidale Recency Hallmark Inn, 208 Dangar Street, ✆6772 9800. 40 units, licensed restaurant, pool, spa, sauna - ✪$110-120.

Deer Park Motor Inn, 72-74 Glen Innes Road, ✆6772 9999. 24 units, licensed restaurant (closed Sun), pool, spa, sauna- ✪$100-130.

Alluna Motel, 180 Dangar Street, ✆6772 6226. 20 units, restaurant, pool - ✪$65-75.

Acacia Motor Inn, 192 Miller Street, ✆6772 7733. 15 units, spa, bbq, parking - ✪$60-75.

Armidale Rose Villa Motel, New England Highway, ✆6772 3872. 10 units, undercover parking, barbecue - ✪$50-75.

Armidale Acres Motel, New England Highway, ✆6771 1281. 11 units (some with private facilities), pool, tennis, bbq - ✪$55-60.

Caravan Parks

Pembroke Tourist and Leisure Park, 39 Waterfall Way, ✆6772 6470. (Pets allowed on leash) pool, barbecue, tennis, excellent facilities - powered sites ✪$20-25 for two, on-site vans $30-40 for two.

Highlander Van Village, 76 Glen Innes Road, ✆6772 4768. (Dogs allowed on leash) pool, barbecue, playground - powered sites ✪$16-18 for two, on-site vans $35 for two.

Eating Out

There are many places to eat in the main street, and the licensed clubs welcome visitors.

Armidale Cattleman's Motor Inn, 31 Marsh Street, ✆6772 7788, has an a la carte menu, and you can select your wine from the public wine racks.

Moore Park Motor Inn, New England Highway, ✆6772 2358, also has a licensed restaurant and cocktail bar which is open 7 days.

Ming Court Restaurant, 11 Beardy St, ✆6772 9363.

Squires Cottage Restaurant, 86 Barney St, ✆6772 8511

Minio's Restaurant, 201a Brown St (Cnr Markham St), ✆6771 4555.

Lizabeth's, 208 Dangar St, ✆6772 9800.

Mandarin Restaurant, 213 Beardy St, ✆6772 6535.

Tourist Information

Armidale Visitor Information Centre is at 82 Marsh Street, ✆(02) 6772 4655 or email armvisit@ northnet.com.au Opening hours are 9am-5pm Mon to Fri, 9am-4pm Sat, 10am-4pm Sun. It is closed on public holidays.

Points of Interest

Central Park is attractive in all seasons, and contains a tourist directory, rotunda, a memorial fountain and picnic facilities.

There is a signposted **Tourist Drive** which takes in the main attractions.

University of New England, off Queen Elizabeth Drive, 5km north of town, west of centre, ✆6773 3333, has 5 faculties and is open for inspection daily 9am-5pm. Booloominbah, an historic house, is the Administrative Centre. It also has a deer and kangaroo park.

The **Folk Museum**, cnr Rusden & Faulkner

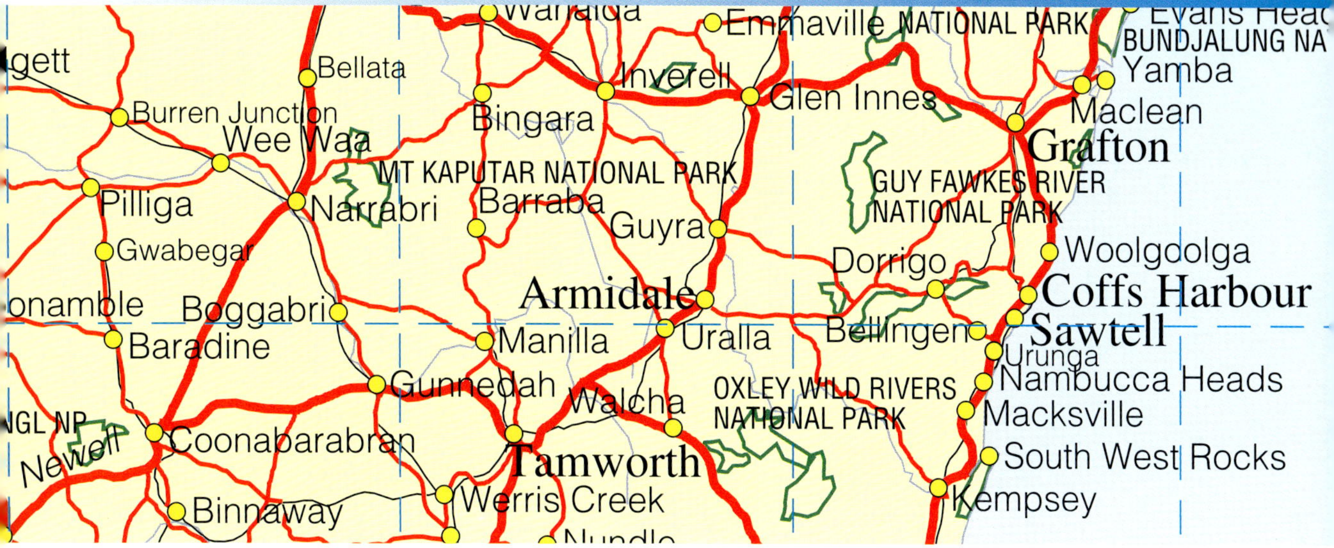

Streets, ✆6770 3536, is classified by the National Trust and has displays of early transport, lighting, handicrafts, and more, ⊙open daily 1-4pm.

The **New England Regional Art Museum**, Kentucky Street, ✆6772 5255, houses the famous Hinton, Armidale City and Coventry Collections, ⊙open Mon-Sat 10am-5pm, Sun 1-5pm. Other museums include the CB Newling Campus Educational Museum in Kentucky Street, the Museum of Printery, also in Kentucky Street, and the Museum of Antiquities in Queen Elizabeath & Madgwick Drive.

The **The Berry Best Cafe & Bakehouse** on the New England Highway towards the airport, is the largest hydroponic berry farm in Australia, ✆6772 5974. They specialise in pies and strudels, and are ⊙open daily 8.30am-6pm.

From **Apex Lookout** you can obtain a view of the whole city.

St Mary's Roman Catholic Cathedral, Dangar Street near Central Park, is built in Gothic Revival style and has a fine spire, marble sanctuary and Flemish bondwork, ⊙open 7am-6pm daily. Nearby is **St Peter's Anglican Cathedral** (cnr Dangar & Rusden Streets), which has an Ecclesiastical Museum with exhibits relating not only to the church itself, but also to Armidale in general.

Festivals

Woolexpo is held annual in March, and the Arts Festival, lasting about a week, is held biennially in October.

Facilities

Lawn bowls, trout fishing, golf, squash, swimming pool and tennis.

Outlying Attractions

Dangar's Falls

The Falls and Lagoon, 22km (14 miles) south of Armidale, feature a large rock pool and many species of birds. Dumaresq Dam, 8km from town, has a boat ramp (only non-powered boats permitted) and swimming.

Ebor Falls

These are 74km (46 miles) to the east, and it is a delightful picnic spot. The falls are divided into two with a total drop of 115m (377 ft).

Armidale

North of Armidale

Statue of Captain Thunderbolt

Hillgrove

An old ghost town about 27km (17 miles) east of Armidale, Hillgrove has been carefully restored to serve as an uncanny reminder of its vibrant and colourful past.

Wollomombi Falls

The highest falls in Australia, Wollomombi Falls have a drop of 460m (1509 ft).

For rockhounds and gem fossickers: The area has numerous little pockets which contain sapphires, zircons, topaz, diamonds, gold, silver, tin, jelly beans, quartz, smokey quartz, grass stone, agate, rhodorite, tourmaline, petrified wood, and almost anything else you can think of. Inverell, to the north-west, is one of the more popular fossicking towns.

Uralla

A little less than 20 kilometres south of Armidale, the town is famous in local folklore for being the resting place of the bushranger Captain Thunderbolt. In the 1860s he committed many robberies throughout the Liverpool Ranges (including Blandford) and the New England region. The town dates from 1855 when it became a centre for the rich pastoral district and a thoroughfare to gold diggings further afield. It has many historic buildings, a couple of pubs and boasts a good-sized second hand bookshop.

Lightning Ridge

Population 6,000 (est.)
Lightning Ridge is situated 770km (478 miles) north-west of Sydney and about 60km (37 miles) from the Queensland border.

Climate

The area has long hot summers and short cold winters, with summer temperatures dropping as much as 20C (68F) degrees at night.

Characteristics

An old fashioned, carefree, 'tomorrow will do if it can't be done today' atmosphere, which is treasured and preserved by local residents as a valuable way of life. The only place in the world where a wet pudding can be seen (the operation which is used to separate opal nobbies from the clay in which they are found). This area is world famous for its black and blue opals and that is why it has merited inclusion in this guide. It attracts many tourists.

How to Get There

By Rail & Coach

Trains and buses run from Sydney via Dubbo every day.

By Car

From Sydney travel along the Mitchell Highway to Gilgandra, and then north along the Castlereagh Highway. The road is bitumen sealed right into the town itself.

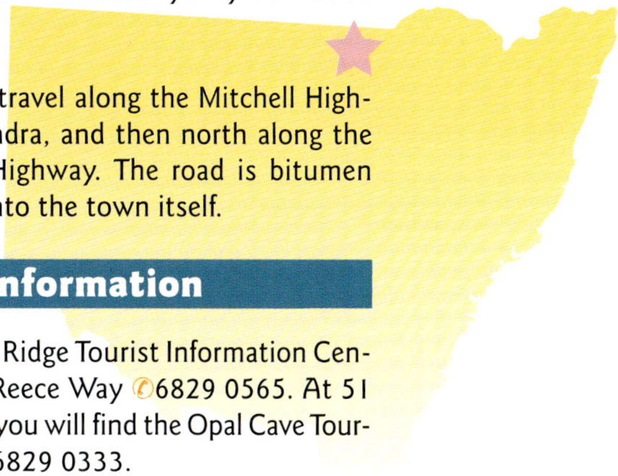

Tourist Information

The Lightning Ridge Tourist Information Centre is in Fred Reece Way ✆6829 0565. At 51 Morilla Street you will find the Opal Cave Tourist Centre, ✆6829 0333.

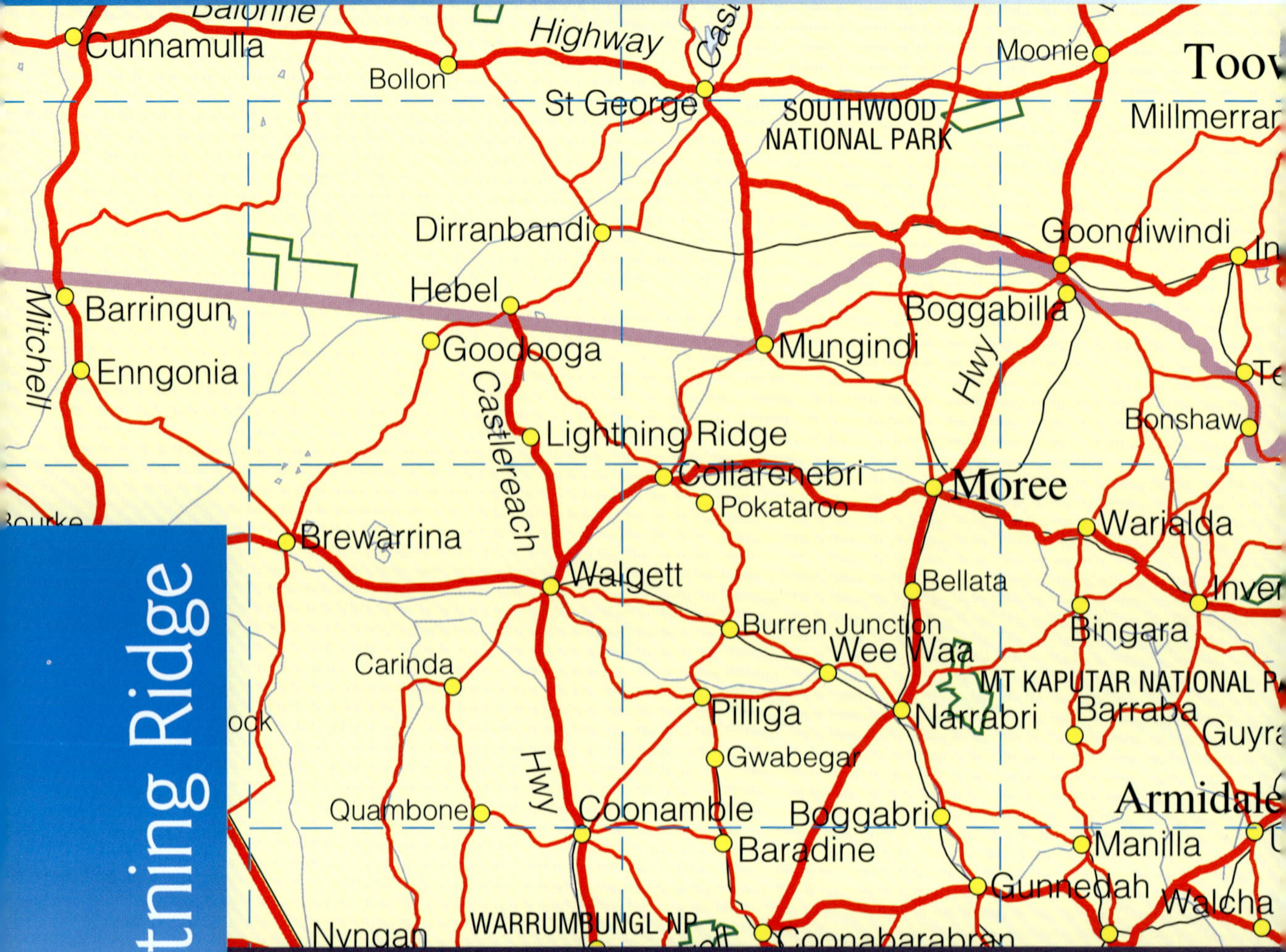

Lightning Ridge

Accommodation

The standard of accommodation is comfortable. Prices included here are for a double room per night, which should be used as a guide only. The telephone area code is 02.

Black Opal Motel, Opal Street, ✆6829 0518. 11 units, basic facilities - ✪$70.

Lightning Ridge Motor Village, Onyx Street, ✆6829 0304. 41 units, licensed restaurant, barbecue - ✪$70.

Wallangulla Motel, cnr Morilla & Agate Streets, ✆6829 0542. 42 units, basic facilities - ✪$55-85.

Caravan Parks

Crocodile Caravan & Camping Park, Morilla St, ✆6829 0437. (Pets allowed on a leash) 30 sites, barbecue, pool - powered sites ✪$14 for two, cabins $45-55 for two.

Lightning Ridge Caravan Park, Harlequin Street, ✆6829 0532. (Pets allowed on leash) 84 sites, barbecue, basic facilities - powered sites ✪$14 for two, on-site vans $35 for two.

Lightning Ridge Motel Hotel, Onyx Street, ✆6829 0304. (Pets allowed on a leash) 47 sites, licensed restaurant, barbecue, pool - powered sites ✪$11 for two, cabins $40-50.

Eating Out

Take aways or eat-in:
Miners Mate, Lot 4 Opal St, ✆6829 2725 - Chinese & Thai, open 7 days, licensed.
Nobby's Restaurant, Onyx St, ✆6829 0611.
Wong's Restaurant, 14 Opal St, ✆6829 2330.
Diggers Rest Bistro & Takeaway, Opal St, ✆6829 2410.

Points of Interest

Visitors can explore the mining fields and fossick for opal. At the **Big Opal Bazaar**, 3 Mile Road, you can see opals being cut, and at **Spectrum Mines**, Bald Hill Road, ✆6829 0581, there is a film show and underground display.

At the **Bush Museum**, Hatters Flat, ✆6829 0016, there is memorabilia from the early mining days. At the **Drive-in Mine**, 13 Gem Street, old and new techniques used in mining for opals are displayed and the **Walk-in Mine**, 1 Bald Hill Field, has underground tours.

Other attractions include **Kangaroo Hill Wildlife Park**, ✆6829 0155, the **Bottle House Mining Museum**, ✆6829 0618, the **Bird of Paradise Art Gallery**, ✆6829 0538, and the **Lightning Ridge Bore Baths** in Pandora Street.

Festivals

The Great Goat Race is held during Easter and the Opal Festival during the NSW September school holidays.

Facilities

The town has artesian baths, a children's park with a BMX track, a drive-in theatre, horse riding facilities, tennis courts, bowling club, golf course and a pistol club.

Outlying Attractions

Walgett

This town is near the junction of the Namoi and Barwon rivers and a little over 100km (62 miles) from Lightning Ridge. It is surrounded by pastoral properties stretching far in each direction. Irrigation has opened up large new areas to cotton, sorghum, maize and other crops. There is good fishing in the area.

Bourke

A town with its own folklore, Bourke is approximately 300km (186 miles) south-west of Lightning Ridge, 946km (588 miles) south-west of Brisbane, and 781km (485 miles) north-west of Sydney. It has been included in this section as it is even further from anywhere else. Its population varies but is generally in excess of 5,000 people with a large proportion being Aboriginal.

The town is 110m (361 ft) above sea level and has an annual rainfall of 325mm (13 ins). The area produces wool and beef, and in recent years cotton and other irrigated crops have been grown. A cotton gin operates in the area.

Bourke is situated on the upper banks of the Darling River, and its Post Office still flies the pennant indicating it is a port, from the days when boats would travel up and down the Darling transporting goods and produce. Now the wharves are broken up and hang in mid-air, a symbol of another era, whilst over the years the river has silted up making such transport impossible.

The town is considered to be the last before the vast empty centre. Just about everyone uses the expression "out the back of Bourke" when they want to describe the loneliness and emptiness of the centre of Australia.

The Bourke Visitor Information Centre is in Anson Street, ✆6872 2280 or email tourinfo@lisp. com.au Opening hours are daily 9am-5pm.

Southern Highlands

Population 30,000

The Southern Highlands are south of Sydney, and the district includes, amongst others, the towns of Bowral, Mittagong, Moss Vale, Berrima, Bundanoon, Robertson and Kangaroo Valley.

Climate

Average temperatures: January max 25C (77F) - min 18C (64F); July max 10C (50F) - min -2C (28F). Average annual rainfall varies from 760mm (30 ins) in the north and west to 1140mm (45 ins) at Moss Vale and 1950mm (77 ins) at Robertson.

Characteristics

The rich, the famous and the powerful have long valued the Highlands as a rural retreat. The Governor of New South Wales used the Highlands as a 'holiday home' as early as 1868 when the Earl of Belmore rented Throsby Park. Later Hillview at Sutton Forest became a permanent vice-regal country residence, thus sealing the popularity of the area with the well-to-do citizens of Sydney. Many fine homes of the period remain. More recently, the Highlands have become a centre for artists and craft-workers, who find inspiration for their work in the quiet of the country and the beauty of their surroundings.

How to Get There

By Bus

All the major interstate bus companies stop in the Southern Highlands on their Sydney/Canberra/Melbourne routes.

There are regular bus services between Moss Vale and Canberra, and a daily service between Moss Vale and Nowra.

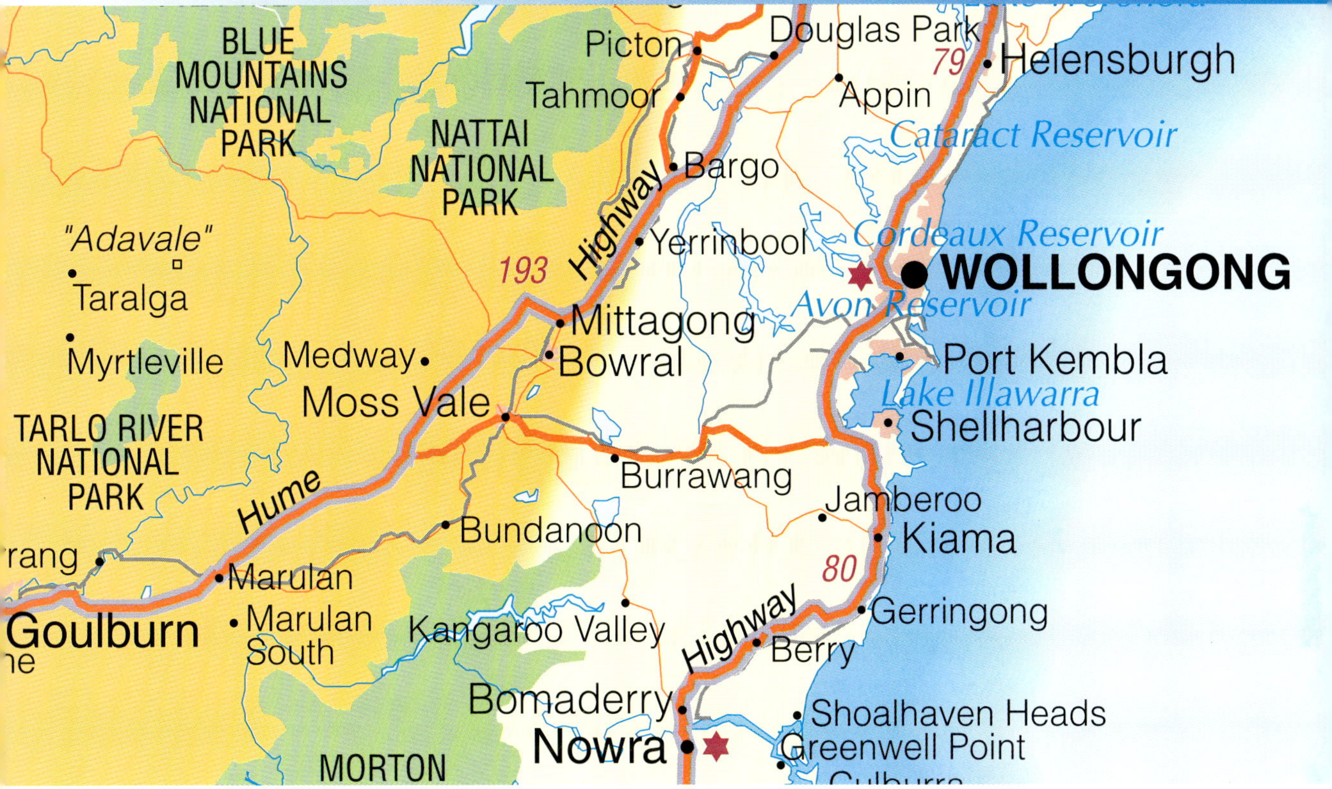

By Rail

There are daily services from Sydney and Canberra.

By Road

From Sydney, via the F5 Freeway from Liverpool, or the old Hume Highway - 1.5 hours. Or, via the Freeway to Wollongong, then the Illawarra Highway over Macquarie Pass, through Robertson, to Bowral - 2 hours. From Canberra, via the Hume Highway through Goulburn - 2 hours. From Nowra, via Kangaroo Valley and Fitzroy Falls - 1 hour.

Tourist Information

The Southern Highlands Visitor Information Centre is at 62 -70 Main Street, Mittagong, (02) 4871 2888. You can email them at wingtour@wsc.nsw.gov.au The opening hours are 8am-5.30pm daily. There is a comprehensive website at www.southern-highlands.com.au

Points of Interest

Mittagong

The area was one of the first settled by Europeans when the government allowed settlement south of the Cowpastures (now Camden). In 1821, William Chalker, principal overseer of government stock at the Cowpastures, was granted 200 acres of land on the Old South Road as a reward for service, and although he died before the grant was surveyed, his widow took up the grant, and his descendants still live in the area. In fact, in 1988 the family erected a cairn on the Old South Road to mark the site of the original grant, and from there you can get a good view of Mittagong and the surrounding countryside.

Many gracious sandstone buildings were constructed in the town in the 1860s, not only public buildings, but small cottages, and

Accommodation

Here is a selection of the available accommodation in each town, with prices for a double room per night, which should be used as a guide only. The telephone area codes are after the town names.

Mittagong

Mittagong Motel, 7 Old Hume Highway, ✆4871 1277. 28 units, unlicensed restaurant - ✪$55-90.

Poplars Motel, Hume Highway, ✆4889 4239. 15 units, licensed restaurant, bbq - ✪$75-105.

Grand Country Lodge, Main Street, ✆4871 3277. 23 units, undercover parking, room service - ✪$85-135.

Melrose Motel, Old Hume Highway, ✆4871 1511. 16 units, barbecue - ✪$75-95.

Mittagong Caravan Park, Hume Highway, ✆4871 1574. 71 sites, basic facilities - powered sites ✪$18 for two, on-site vans $35.

Bowral

The Briars Country Lodge, Moss Vale Road, ✆4868 3566. 30 units, licensed restaurant, swimming pool, tennis - ✪$165-220.

Boronia Lodge Apartment Hotel, Boronia Street, ✆4861 1860. 8 apartments, undercover parking, comfortable rooms- ✪$85-135.

Golf View Lodge, Boronia Street, ✆4861 2777. 28 units, pool, bbq, tennis - $90-135.

Port O'Call Motor Inn, cnr Bong Bong & Bundaroo Streets, ✆4861 1779. 20 units, licensed restaurant, good facilities - ✪$55-105.

Craigieburn Family Resort (guest house), Centennial Road, ✆48611977. 63 rooms (private facilities), fireplace, pool, tennis, golf - ✪$195.

Links House Country Guesthouse, 17 Links Road, ✆4861 1408. 15 rooms, tennis, fireplace - B&B ✪$135-330.

Moss Vale

Bong Bong Motel, 238 Argyle Street, ✆4868 1033. 10 units, comfortable rooms - ✪$75-90.

Golf Ball Motel, cnr Arthur & Spring Streets, ✆4868 1511. 19 units, licensed restaurant (closed Sun-Mon), barbecue - ✪$60-85.

Lynton B&B, 618 Argyle Street, ✆4868 2552. 3 rooms - B&B ✪$110-180 .

Moss Vale Village Park, Willow Drive, ✆4868 1099. (Pets allowed under supervision) 114 sites, excellent facilities - powered sites ✪$15 for two, on-site vans $35 for two.

Berrima

Berrima Bakehouse Motel, cnr Wingecarribee Street & Hume Highway, ✆4877 1381. 19 units, swimming pool, barbecue - ✪$85-180.

Walden Wood, Old Mandemar Road, ✆4877 1164. 2 rooms, comfortable rooms - ✪$110-165.

Robertson

Robertson Country Motel, Illawarra Highway, ✆4885 1444. 6 units, basic facilities - ✪$60-85.

Ranelagh House (private hotel), Illawarra Highway, ✆4885 1111. 42 rooms (some with private facilities), unlicensed restaurant, pool - DB&B ✪$105-155 per person.

Bundanoon

Bundanoon Holiday Resort (motel), Anzac Parade, ✆4883 6068. 21 units, swimming pool, barbecue, tennis - ✪$75-100.

Morton National Park, Church Street, ✆4887 7270. (No pets allowed) - no power, advance site reservations only - ✪$10-18 for two.

Kangaroo Valley

Pioneer Motel Kangaroo Valley, 152 Moss Vale Road, ✆4465 1877. 23 units, licensed restaurant, fireplace, gym, heated swimming pool - ✪$95-185.

Big Bell Farm, 1666 Kangaroo Valley Road, ✆4465 1628. 2 cabins, comfortable facilities - ✪$70-90.

Kanagroo Valley Glenmack Caravan Park, Main Road, ✆4465 1372. (No pets allowed) 108 sites, bbq, tennis, mini-golf - powered sites ✪$18-20 for two, cabins $50-75 for two.

Kangaroo Valley Tourist Park, Moss Vale Road, ✆4465 1310. (No dogs allowed) 60 sites, canoeing, playground, bbq - powered sites ✪$17 for two, cabins $45-95 for two.

Eating Out

Following are some restaurants you might like to try in the various towns.

Mittagong

Lion Rampant, cnr Victoria Street & Hume Highway, ✆4872 2980 - Bistro - open Wed-Sun 6-8.30pm, counter lunches noon-2pm.

Lesters Restaurant of Mittagong, 16 Bowral Road, ✆4871 2696 - licensed, Italian - open Wed-Mon 5-10pm, plus Sun noon-2.30pm.

1890 Restaurant & Cafe, 84 Hume Highway, ✆4871 1871 - licensed, French a la carte - open Mon-Sat 6-9.30pm, Fri-Sun noon-2.30pm.

Mittagong Chinese Restaurant, 91 Hume Hwy, ✆4871 1704.

B C's Italian Restaurante, 79 Hume Hwy, ✆4872 1777.

The Blue Cockerel Bistro, 95 Hume Hwy, ✆4872 1677.

Thonburi Thai Restaurant, Beaumont Gardens Shp 1/ Bowral Rd, ✆4872 1511.

Bowral

House of Lowe, 236 Bong Bong Street, ✆4861 2308 - licensed, Chinese and seafood - open daily for dinner from 5pm, and for lunch Wed-Sun noon-2pm.

Toshis Japanese Restaurant, Bong Bong Street, ✆4861 4274.

Shanghai Restaurant, 265 Bong Bong Street, ✆4861 1774.

Prego Trattoria Pizzeria, 412 Bong Bong Street, ✆4862 5009.

Da Giacomo Cafe Restaurant, 275 Bong Bong Street, ✆4862 2996.

Jack Style Thai Restaurant, Boolwey & Station Street , ✆4862 1905.

Station Street Restaurant, 48 Station Street, ✆4861 7171.

Moss Vale

Chow's Hong Kong Restaurant, 443 Argyle Street, ✆4868 2208 - licensed, Chinese - open for lunch 11.30am-2.30pm, dinner Sun-Wed 5-9.30pm, Thurs 5-10.30pm, Fri-Sat 5-11pm.

Seafood Affair, 515 Argyle Street, ✆4868 1726 - open Mon-Sat for dinner, Tues-Sat for lunch.

Cedar's Lebanese Restaurant, 490 -494 Argyle Street, ✆4869 4600.

Peking Restaurant, Moss Vale Mall, ✆4868 2366.

Argyle St Bistro, Argyle Street, ~4868 1599.

Sattahip Thai Restaurant, Shop 2/ 249 Argyle Street, ✆4869 1891.

Berrima

Journeyman Bistro, Old Hume Highway, ✆4877 1911 - licensed, specialise in flare-grill - open 7 days for lunch and dinner.

Victoria Inn, Jellore Street, ✆4877 1475 - licensed, gourmet a la carte - open for dinner Wed-Sat, lunch Sun.

Old Breens Restaurant, Hume Hwy, ✆4877 1977.

Robertson

Robertson Country Motel, Illawarra Highway, ✆4885 1444 - BYO, country style cuisine - open 7 days 6.30-8.30pm, bookings essential.

Ranelagh House, Illawarra Highway, ✆4885 1111 - BYO, country style cooking - open 7 days for lunch and dinner (except when house closed for conferences).

Bundanoon

Highlander Restaurant, Anzac Parade, ✆4883 6242 - licensed, a la carte with German influence - open Wed-Sun from 6.30pm, Sun noon-2pm.

Tree Tops Guest House, 101 Railway Parade, ✆4883 6372 - BYO, International and Indian cuisine - open for dinner Fri-Sat.

Bundanoon Chinese Restaurant, 21 Railway Avenue, ✆4883 6368.

Kangaroo Valley

Restaurant Deville, Moss Vale Road, ✆4465 1314 - licensed, char grill, blackboard menu - open Wed-Sun 10am-3pm, Fri-Sat from 7pm.

Points of Interest - *continued*

many of these can be found in the side streets between the Hume Highway and Lake Alexandra.

The town has many specialty craft outlets, that display and sell the works of both local and outside artists, including such items as tapestry, stained glass, woodwork, pottery and weaving.

The Southern Highlands Visitor Information Centre is in Main Street.

Mount Gibraltar

The mount (863m - 2831 ft) is known locally as The Gib and its lookouts can be reached by following Oxley Drive from Bowral or Mittagong, or there are fire trails and foot tracks for dedicated bushwalkers. The Tourist Information Offices have details of all the lookouts, and maps of the various tracks.

Moss Vale

The town of Moss Vale stands on part of the original grant made to the district's first European settler, Charles Throsby, who played an important part in the exploration of New South Wales, opening up not only the Southern Highlands, but also the South Coast, Goulburn and Canberra regions. His nephew, also named Charles, came to the district and established Throsby Park as a respected grazing property.

The site is open by arrangement and guided yours are available, contact The National Parks and Wildlife Service ©4887 7270 for information and bookings.

Scenic attractions in the area include Belmore and Fitzroy Falls, and Morton National Park, with its 55km (34 miles) of river frontages and virgin bushland.

Fitzroy Falls

The falls are within 100m of the car park and visitor information centre in Morton National Park, one of the largest National Parks in New South Wales, covering an area of over 154,000ha (380,380 acres). The Falls cascade 82m (269 ft) to the valley below.

Berrima

Situated 14km (9 miles) south of Mittagong on the Hume Highway, Berrima is considered the best remaining example of a small Australian town of the 1830s. The town was founded in 1829 by Sir Thomas Mitchell, the Surveyor-General of New South Wales, and in its heyday was an affluent community with a population of over 500. Many of the original buildings have been restored, and former hotels now trade as craft shops, galleries and restaurants.

Surveyor General Inn, 1835, the oldest continuously licensed inn in Australia still trading within its original walls; Superintendent's House, built in the 1880s as the Governor's House for the Gaol;

Bowral

Bowral was originally part of a property granted to the explorer John Oxley, and in 1859, 200 acres of his estate were subdivided by members of his family to coincide with the news of the coming of the railway. The village was first known as Wingecarribee (now the name of the Shire), then Burradoo, and finally in 1867, Bowral. The town was the site of the first store in the district, but development was slow until the opening of the railway. From 1870 onwards, the village grew rapidly, and by 1890 was considered a fashionable resort where Sydneysiders could retreat from the heat of summer.

Now, with a population of 8,500, the town is a blend of historic buildings, quaint old residential cottages and commercial premises. There is a uniformity to the architecture, and a number of mature deciduous trees form a backdrop for magnificent public and private gardens. Bendooley Street is subject to a Heritage Commission protection order, to prevent it from being altered.

The Bradman Museum, ©4862 1247, is in St Jude Street, overlooking the Bradman Oval, and opposite his former home (52 Shepherd Street, which is a private residence), ⏲open daily 10am-4pm. Admission is ✪$7.50 adults, $3.50 children and $20 for families. A website with

everything you want to know about The Don is: www.bradman.org.au.

Robertson

The town was named in honour of John Robertson who was responsible for the Land Act of 1861 under which land was thrown open for selection before survey. The Robertson Nature Reserve, located 300m south of the township, is easily accessible and is an important conservation area, containing about 5ha (12 acres) of the Yarrawa Brush vegetation which, prior to European settlement, covered about 2500ha (6175 acres) around what is now Robertson township. Up until the 1950s, farmers in the area were still clearing the native timber, and the casual visitor must wonder what made them persevere against such overwhelming odds.

Today the Robertson area is one of the most beautiful to be found anywhere, with its rolling red soil country and rugged bushland.

Bundanoon

The town of Bundanoon has been a holiday spot for decades, but still manages to retain a quiet village atmosphere. It is a bushwalker's paradise, with walks going to Glow Worm Glen, Fern Glen, Fairy Bower Falls, and the Amphitheatre, amongst other places. The Southern Highlands Visitor Information Centre has all the details on durations of walks, and fitness required.

In April, Bundanoon goes Scottish in more than name alone, with the popular annual "Brigadoon" festival. The entertainment is as you'd expect, the day filled with the unmistakable tune of bagpipes, traditional dancing and a host of highland games.

Kangaroo Valley

Kangaroo Valley is situated on a plateau between the Highlands and the coast, and is easily accessible. The Kangaroo River winds through the valley, and is crossed by the Hampden Suspension Bridge, built in 1898 of castellated stone by convict labour. The bridge is named after Viscount Hampden, Governor of New South Wales at that time. The river under the bridge is popular for swimming and canoeing. Barbecue and toilet facilities are provided. Adjacent to the bridge is the Pioneer Settlement Museum. The museum is open 9-5.

Historic Barrengarry Store and Post Office is found 1km north of the Suspension Bridge. They were established in 1880 and retain the old-world charm of a pioneer general store that sells almost everything.

The Kangaroo Valley village has many coffee shops, craft shops and specialty stores, while the river offers many spots for picnicking, swimming, bushwalking and canoeing.

Bendeela Pondage and Pumping Station is 7km (4 miles) west of the Main Road, on Bendeela Road. Here water is pumped 127 (417 ft) vertically to a reservoir above Fitzroy Falls. A picnic area, barbecues and toilets are provided.

Kangaroo Valley can also be reached easily from Nowra.

Festivals

January - Bowral Horse Show.
February - Mittagong Dahlia Festival and Fun Run. Kangaroo Valley Show.
March - Robertson Show. Moss Vale Show.
Easter - Berrima Art Society Exhibition. Musica Viva (biennial).
April - Brigadoon Day, Bundanoon.
August - Bowral Horse Show.
September - Tulip Time Festival, Bowral. Bowral Fun Run.
October - Tulip Time Festival, *(pictured left)* Bowral. Berrima District Art Society Exhibition.
December - Moss Vale Summer Gymkhana.

Goulburn

Population 21,300
Goulburn, 638m (2093 ft) above sea level, is 197km (122 miles) south-west of Sydney and 94km (58 miles) north-east of Canberra.

Climate

Average temperatures: January max 26C (79F) - min 12C (54F); June max 12C (54F) - min 0.5C (32.5F). Average annual rainfall: 671mm (26 ins).

Characteristics

Goulburn is Australia's oldest inland city dating back to the earliest days of the colony. Many of the buildings in the town have beautiful cast iron lace work. Wheat was grown in the locality as early as the 1820s, and today primary industry is still important. Goulburn is also an administrative centre for several State Government Departments. It was the last town of the British Empire to become a city by virtue of the Royal Letters Patent in 1863. Goulburn is home to 'Rambo' the 14m (46 ft) high ram at the Big Merino complex.

How to Get There

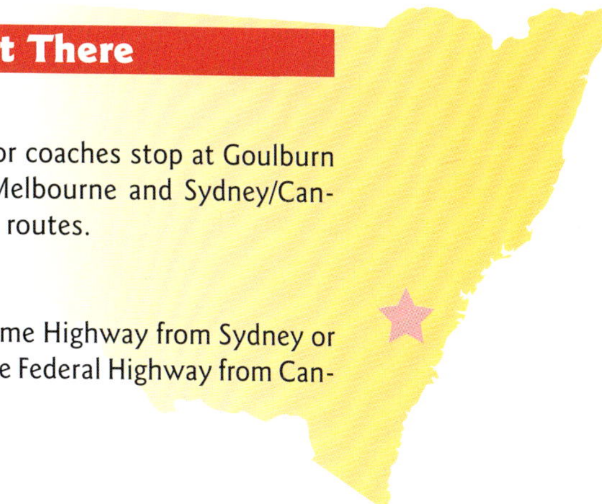

By Bus

Most of the major coaches stop at Goulburn on the Sydney/Melbourne and Sydney/Canberra/Melbourne routes.

By Car

Travel via the Hume Highway from Sydney or Melbourne, or the Federal Highway from Canberra.

Goulburn

Accommodation

Places to stay in Goulburn are excellent and varied. Here is a selection, with prices for a double room per night, which should be used as a guide only. The phone area code is 02.

Posthouse Motor Lodge, 1 Lagoon Street, ✆4821 5666. 38 units, licensed restaurant, swimming pool - ✪$85-105.

Lilac City Motor Inn, 126 Lagoon Street, ✆4821 5000. 28 units, licensed restaurant - ✪$75-90.

Clinton Lodge, 80 Clinton Street, ✆4821 4488. 22 units, comfortable facilities - B&B ✪$75-80.

Parkhaven Motel, 60 Lagoon Street, ✆4821 4455. 15 units - ✪$65.

Hillview Motel, 2 Cowper Street, ✆4821 3130. 20 units, basic facilities - ✪$45-50.

Alpine Heritage Motel, 248 Sloane Street, ✆4821 2930. 45 units, unlicensed restaurant - ✪$45-75.

Caravan Parks

Governors Hill Carapark, 77 Sydney Road, ✆1800 227 373. (No dogs) 60 sites, good facilties, barbecue - powered sites ✪$19-21 for two, on-site vans $35 for two.

Goulburn South Caravan Park, Hume Street, ✆4821 3233. (Pets allowed under supervision) 112 sites, basic facilties - powered sites ✪$17 for two, on-site vans $40-60 for two.

Eating Out

Goulburn has restaurants, coffee bars, family style cafes and licensed clubs, so whatever your budget you will find something to suit. Here are a few you might like to try:

Goulburn Italian Pizza Restaurant, 147 Auburn Street, ✆4821 5998.

Billabong Station Restaurant, cnr Hume Hwy & Lansdowne Street, ✆4822 8014.

Khun Lek Thai Restaurant, 150 Auburn Street, ✆4821 2025.

Riley's Restaurant, 148 Sloane Street, ✆4822 747.

Blue Plate Restaurant, Lagoon St, ✆4821 5666.

Hung Win Chinese Restaurant, 277 Auburn Street, ✆4821 8933.

McDonalds has two locations, one in North Goulburn on the corner of the Hume Highway and Common Street, the other in South Goulburn on the Old Hume Highway.

Goulburn Court House

Tourist Information

The Goulburn Visitor Information Centre, 201 Sloane Street, ✆(02) 48 23 4492, is ⏲open 9am-5pm every day except Christmas Day. The website is www.igoulburn.com and you can email visitor@goulburn. nsw.gov.au

Points of Interest

A **walking tour** of Historic Goulburn and a walking tour of the Wollondilly River are available to the traveller - brochures may be obtained from the Goulburn Visitors Centre.

Some of the historic buildings are open to the public, including the Court House, St Clair, St Saviours Cathedral and Riversdale.

Other attractions include the **Big Merino Complex**, on the corner of the Hume Highway and Lans-downe Street, ✆4822 8013, which has a craft centre, educational area, lookout and restaurant.

The Goulburn Yurtworks, ✆4821 5931, is the only producer of Yurts in Australia (yurts are roundhouses based on Mongolian tents).

The Rocky Hill War Memorial dominates the town and is Goulburn's landmark.

The Black Stag Deer Park, Gorman Road, ✆4821 4386, has fallow red deer as well as Australian wildlife.

The Goulburn Rail Heritage Centre, in Braidwood Road, features many pieces of industrial steam machinery, and is open the first weekend of every month.

The Goulburn Regional Art Gallery is in the Civic Centre, on the corner of Bourke and Church Streets, ✆4823 4443.

Gulsons Craft Village, located at the historic Gulsons brickworks, Common Street, features many quality craft shops.

More information on these and other attractions may be obtained from the *Goulburn and District Visitors Guide* - available from the Goulburn Visitors Centre.

Festivals

The Lilac City Festival is held during the October long weekend.

The Argyle County Fair is held in November each year.

Carnivale, which is part of the NSW Government sponsored festival, is held in September each year.

Goulburn also stages an annual show and rodeo.

Facilities

There are many sporting facilities available in Goulburn, including squash courts, tennis courts, indoor cricket and sports centre, ten pin bowling centre, swimming pool and water slide. Lawn bowls, golf, darts, and fishing are also catered for. Contact the Visitor Information Centre for all the details.

Outlying Attractions

The Bungonia State Recreation Area

Situated approximately 35km (22 miles) south-east of Goulburn, the Bungonia is the largest State Recreation Area in New South Wales. Bushwalking, caving, climbing, canoeing, and spectacular lookouts are all available there.

Pejar Dam Aquatic Recreation Reserve

25km (15 miles) north-west on the Crookwell Road, the reserve is one of the best trout fishing areas in the south-east region. Only non-powered boats are permitted, and there is sailing, windsurfing and canoeing.

Wombeyan Caves

The caves are 77km (48 miles) north-east of Goulburn, and there are five cave tours. Many pleasant hours may also be spent strolling through the beautiful bushland reserve surrounding the caves. The road to the caves is very winding, so it is best to have the attitude that this excursion is a full day, and take your time. The Wombeyan Caves Visitors Centre and Caravan Park can be contacted on ✆4843 5976.

Snowy Mountains

The Snowy Mountains are in the south-east corner of New South Wales, and the highest peak is Mt Kosciusko, 2230m (7316 ft). The mountains are home to the ski fields of New South Wales, and they conjure up visions of fashionable skiers hurtling down ski slopes before sipping their apres-ski drinks, but that is only one facet of the Mountains. One of Australia's engineering marvels is also here: the Snowy Mountains Hydro Electric Scheme, which captures the water from the melting snow destined for the coast, and redirects it through mountain channels to the interior.

The mountains are a carpet of wildflowers in summer and there are numerous trails for bushwalkers. The many lakes and rivers are an aquatic paradise for those wishing to get away from it all. Lake Jindabyne (three times the size of Sydney Harbour) is ablaze with sailboard and catamaran sails, and the lakes and rivers abound with trout.

Cooma

Population 8,500
Cooma is where the Snowy Mountains begin, and is near the New South Wales-Victorian Border. Distance from Canberra 114km (71 miles); from Sydney 420km (261 miles); from Thredbo 97km (60 miles); from Charlotte Pass 105km (65 miles); from Perisher 98km (61 miles); from Adaminiby 52km (32 miles); from Mt Selwyn 99km (62 miles).

Climate

Cooma is 810m (2657 ft) above sea level. Average temperatures: January max 26C (79F) - min 11C (52F); July max 9C (48F) - min 1C (30F). Annual rainfall 450mm (17 ins).

Snowy Mountains

Characteristics

If you are travelling to the snow by train or air, Cooma will be your port of call. It is a pleasant town and offers transport to Jindabyne and the snowfields.

Tourist Information

The Cooma Visitor Information Centre, 119 Sharpe Street, ✆(02) 6450 1742, is open 9am-5pm daily. Email them at cvc@snowy.net.au or visit the website, www.snowymountains.com.au

How to Get There

By Road

Greyhound Pioneer have services from Sydney and Canberra.
Snowliner Coaches, ✆6452 1584, provide services from Bega and Canberra.

By Rail

There is a train service from Sydney via Canberra daily, with connections to Melbourne from Goulburn.

By Road

From Sydney via the Hume Highway, 420km (216 miles), or via Bega, 542km (336 miles). From Melbourne via the coast 730km (454 miles), or the Alpine Way 664km (400 miles).

Accommodation

Cooma has motels, hotels and caravan parks. Here is a selection with prices for a double room per night, which should be used as a guide only. The telephone area code is 02.

Kinross Inn - Cooma, 15 Sharp Street, ✆6452 3577. 17 units, barbecue, undercover parking, indoor heated pool - $70-110.

Alkira Motel, 213 Sharp Street, ✆6452 3633. 13 units, undercover parking, bbq- $65-110.

Cooma Motor Lodge, 6 Sharp Street, ✆6452 1888. 44 units, licensed restaurant, sauna, room service - $60-150.

High Country Motel, 12 Chapman Street, ✆6452 1277. 40 units, licensed restaurant, swimming pool, recreation room - $60-80.

Hawaii Motel, 192 Sharp Street, ✆6452 1211. 23 units, unlicensed restaurant - $50-60.

Alpine Country Guest House, 32 Massie Street, ✆6452 1414. 13 rooms (private facilities), unlicensed restaurant - $30-60.

Caravan Parks

Snowtels Caravan & Camping Park, Snowy Mountains Highway, ✆6452 1828. (Pets allowed under supervision and by arrangement) 134 sites, good facilities, tennis, ski hire - powered sites $20 for two, cabins $40-90 for two, on-site vans $35-55 for two.

Eating Out

Many of the motels and hotels have licensed and BYO restaurants, and the licensed clubs offer good family meals. There are several takeaway food outlets.

Grand Court Chinese Restaurant, Snowstop Village, Sharp Street, ✆6452 4525.

Cooma Truckstop Restaurant, 1 Polo Flat Road, ✆6452 5550.

Bahn Thai Noodle Restaurant, 178 Sharp Street, ✆6452 4277.

McDonald's is in Sharp Street.

Snowy River, Cooma

Points of Interest

Tourist Drive markers signpost an easy drive through and around Cooma, taking in the town's many points of interest. The first marker is at Centennial Park near the Visitors' Centre, and from there it goes past Cooma Creek, Lions Lookout, the Murrumbidgee Water Filtration Plant, Snowy Mountains Authority Information Centre, the Snowy Memorial, Festival Pool, Nannygoat Hill, Cooma Cenotaph, Cooma Prison, Lambie Street, Raglan Gallery, Mt Gladstone, Alpenthaler Park, Southern Cloud Park, Christ Church, the Lookout, Polo Falt, and back to the Centre.

The **Snowy Mountains Hydro Electric Authority Information Centre**, Monaro Highway, 1800 623 776, open Mon-Fri 8am-4.30pm, Sat 8am-noon, has displays and models of the Snowy Mountains Scheme, and a film show, Mon-Fri at 11am and 3pm. Visit www.snowyhydro.com.au for more details. **Snowy Mountain Scheme Tours** to Adaminaby, Old Adaminaby, Providence Portal, Kiandra, Cab-ramurra, and Tumut underground Power Station, can be organised through the information centre.

For those who are energetic, there is the **Lambie Town Walk**, which passes through residential and natural areas of scenic and historic interest in Cooma. One part of the walk is through the town area (5km) and the bushland section is also 5km, and takes approximately 2.5 hours.

Llama World, Snowy Mountains Highway, 19km (12 miles) from Cooma, has llamas and alpacas, a tractor ride through their paddocks, rides in llama-drawn sulkies, and the Inca Gallery, which sells souvenirs, South American and llama products including yarn, fleece and made-up garments. Open Fri-Mon (weather permitting), 6452 4593.

Festivals

Man from Snowy River Marathon in October each year.

Facilities

Bowling club, golf course, horse riding, swimming pool (heated), snooker, squash, tennis courts, gliding, ski hire shops, car hire depots and taxis.

Snowy Mountains

Outlying Attractions

Adaminaby

The town of Adaminaby is 51km (32 miles) from Cooma, and is the home of The World's Largest Trout. The town was moved to its present site in 1956-57 to allow for the filling of Lake Eucumbene. Facilities include boating, fishing, sailing, snow skiing, tennis and water skiing.

Yarrangobilly Caves

The caves are just before the town of Yarrangobilly, and 6.5km (4 miles) off the Snowy Mountains Highway. They were carved out of the limestone by the Yarrangobilly River around 440 million years ago, and are a strange landscape of rugged bluffs and disappearing streams. Beyond the half light of the cave entrance is an underworld of unrivalled beauty.

The self-guiding Glory Hole Cave is open daily, 10am-4pm. Guided inspections of either the North Glory, Jersey or Jillabenan Caves are conducted at 1pm each non-holiday week day. Additional tours are scheduled during weekends and school holidays. There are plenty of walking tracks in the area, and the Yarrangobilly Caves Visitor Information Centre, (02) 6454 9597, has brochures and information, and is open 7 days a week, 9am-4.30pm, 8.30am to 5.30pm in the peak season. Yarrangobilly is a day use area only, and camping is available at Yarrangobilly Village or Three Mile Dam.

Jindabyne

Population 1600

Situated 40km (25 miles) from Cooma, Jindabyne is the closest centre to the ski fields. Many people choose to stay in the town and drive to the fields each day. In summer time, Lake Jindabyne is the attraction for staying here.

Accommodation

Here is a selection of the accommodation available, with winter prices for a double room per night, which should be used as a guide only. Never go to Jindabyne in the winter thinking you will be able to pick up accommodation without booking, it is too cold to sleep in the bus station. The area code is 02.

Lake Jindabyne Motel Hotel, Kosciusko Road, 6456 2203. 39 units, licensed restaurant, bistro, indoor heated swimming pool, spa, sauna, barbecue- $75-200.

Horizons Snowy Mountains, Kosciusko Road, 6456 2562. 109 apartments, licensed restaurant, bistro, indoor heated pool, fireplace, undercover parking, spa, sauna - $105-405.

Banjo Paterson Inn, Kosciusko Road, 6456 2372. 22 units (private facilities), licensed restaurant - $65-750.

Alpine Resort Motel, 22 Nettin Circuit, 6456 2522. 29 units, good faciliites, unlicensed restaurant, bbq, spa - $100-300.

Lakeview Plaza Motel, 2 Snowy River Avenue, 6456 2134. 13 units, licensed restaurant, bar, spa - $65-200.

Chesa St Moritz, Lot 10 Alpensee Weg, 6456 1856. 1 unit, basic facilities - $65-190.

Yowi Lodge, 67 Gippsland Street, 562 547 - 14 units, unlicensed restaurant, swimming pool, spa, sauna - B&B $60-170.

Caravan Park

Snowline Caravan Park, cnr Kosciusko Road & Alpine Way, 6456 2099. (No pets allowed) 178 sites, excellent faciltities, sauna, spa, cafe, barbecue, tennis - powered sites $20-25 for two, cabins $40-205 for two.

Jindabyne Holiday Park, Kosciusko Road, 6456 2249. 200 sites, basic facilities - powered sites $20-26 for two, cabins $55-130 for two, on-site vans $40-90 for two.

Jindabyne

Eating Out

It is well known that cold weather makes every one hungry, so there is no shortage of eating places in this neck of the woods:

Pom's Balcony Bistro, upper level Petamin Plaza (Town Centre), ✆6456 2144 - fully licensed, steak and seafood, open daily 6pm

Chit Thai Restaurant, Snowline Caravan Park, cnr Kosciusko Rd and Alpine Way), ✆6456 2052.

Brumby Bar & Bistro, Kosciusko Road, ✆6456 2526.

Bacco Italian Restaurant, Nuggets Crossing, Shop 10, Kosciuszko Road, ✆6456 1420.

Gringo's Mexican Restaurant, Aspen Chalet, Kosciusko Road, ✆6457 2229.

Restaurant 14, Town Centre, Shop 14, Kosciuszko Road, ✆6457 2660.

Il Lago Restaurant, Nuggetts Crossing Centre, Shop 19a, Kosciusko Road, ✆6456 1171.

Tourist Information

The Snowy Region Visitor Information Centre is in Kosciuszko Road, ✆(02) 6450 5600. Their opening hours are 8am-6pm in the winter holidays and Easter, 8.30am-5pm the rest of the year. They can be contacted by email at srvc@ npws.nsw.gov.au or you might like to visit the website at www.kos .com.au for a preliminary look.

Ski and Equipment Hire

Ampol Jindabyne, Kosciusko Road, ✆6456 1177; BP Lakeside, Kosciusko Road, ✆6456 1959; Arlberg Ski Centre, Jindabyne Road, Berridale, ✆6456 3177; Jindabyne Sports Store, Shop 12, Town Centre, ✆6456 2216; Snowy Mountains Sports, Petamin Plaza, ✆6456 2530; Thredbo Sports, Nuggetts Crossing, ✆6459 4119; Wilderness Sports, Nuggets Crossing, ✆6456 2966.

Ski Fields

Mt Selwyn (1614m - 5295 ft)

The lowest field, Mt Selwyn is very popular with families and school groups. There is no accommodation at Mt Selwyn.

Ski lifts: 1 Double Chair, 4 T-Bars, 2 Pomas, 1 Platter and 4 Beginner Ropes and 1 Toboggan Lift.

Ski slopes: beginners 40%, intermediates 48%, advanced 12%.

Facilities/services: ticket office, ski school, ski hire, information centre, ski patrol, ski and souvenir shop, licensed cafeteria, resort booking centre.

Prices: half day ✪$35 adult, $20 child; full day $46 adult, $23 child; lift & lesson package $68 adult $45 child.

Information: www.selwynsnow .com.au, snowinfo@selwynsnow .com.au or ✆64549 488.

Perisher Blue

Includes Perisher/Smiggins (2034m - 6673 ft), Mt Blue Cow (1980m - 6496 ft) and Guthega (1932m - 6339 ft) - an extensive 1250 hectares of skifields.

Accommodation: The Stables, ✆6457 5755; Sundeck Hotel, ✆6457 5054; Swagman Chalet, ✆6457 5275.

Ski lifts: 4 Double Chairs, 6 Quad Chairs, 2 Triple Chairs, 22 T Bars, 4 J Bars, 11 others, 3 Ski carpet, Skitube

Ski slopes: beginners 22%, intermediates 60%, advanced 18%.

Facilities/services: ticket office, ski school, ski hire, information centre, resort booking centre, ski patrol, childminding, ski shops, Skitube train station, oversnow transport to lodges, bars, bistros, restaurants, coffee shops, takeaway food outlets (including on-

Perisher Valley

slope), banks, post office, newsagents, chemist, supermarket, bottle shop, photographic services, medical services, souvenirs, lockers, ski-storage.

Transport: Skitube Trains depart frequently as required in peak times during winter. Below snowline on Alpine Way, so no chains required.

Bullock's Flat Terminal (Alpine Way) - free car parking for 3,000 cars and 250 buses. Ticket office for combined Perisher Blue and Skitube tickets. Ski hire, information centre, National Parks and Wildlife Service sales and information, souvenir and ski accessories shop, takeaway food outlet.

Perisher Valley Terminal: ticket office for Perisher/Smiggins and Mt Blue Cow plus train tickets. Ski minding and locker service, coffee shop, licensed bistro, ski equipment and accessories, children's clothing shop, gift shop, takeaway snack bar, full Medical Centre and Police Office, oversnow transport to Perisher Valley lodges.

Prices: check current prices at the time of your visit on the updated website.

Information and prices: www.perisherblue.com.au, 1300 655 822.

Thredbo (2037m - 6683 ft)

Accommodation: Thredbo Alpine, 6459 4200; Snowgoose Lodge, 6457 6349; The River Inn, 6457 6505.

Ski lifts: 2 high-speed quad detachable chairlifts, 1 beginner quad chairlift, 3 double chairlifts, 7 T-bars, 2 rope tows.

Ski slopes: beginners 16%, intermediates 67%, advanced 17%.

Facilities/services: ticket office, ski school, ski hire, information huts, resort booking centre, ski patrol, ski shops, bars, bistros, restaurants (including on-slope), coffee shop, takeaway food outlets (including on-slope),

bank, post office, newsagent, chemist, supermarket, bottle shop, photographic services, medical services, souvenirs, overnight ski storage.

Prices: full day ✪$75 adult, $41 child; lift & lesson $100 adult, $67 child; group lessons $40. Check current prices at the time of your visit.

Information: www.thredbo.com .au, ✆6459 4100.

Charlotte Pass

Accommodation: Kosciusko Chalet, ✆1800 026 369; Arlberg Ski Lodge, ✆9453 2057; Snowbird Ski Resort, ✆1300 651 653. The ski lifts are virtually on the front doorstep.

Ski lifts: 1 triple chairlift, 1 T-bar, 2 poma lifts, 1 rope tow.

Transport: Charlotte Pass is the most isolated resort with access by oversnow transport (snowcats) from Perisher Valley. The journey takes about 35 minutes. If travelling by car, you have to park at the Skitube Terminal at Bullocks Flat and travel on the tube to Perisher. The snowcat part of the trip costs ✪$28 adults, $19 children each way.

Prices: full day ✪$75 adult, $48 child; half day $60 adult, $35 child. Check current prices at the time of your visit.

Information: www.charlottepass .com.au, ✆1800 026 369.

Wagga Wagga

Population 42,900

The city of Wagga Wagga is situated on the banks of the Murrumbidgee River, 459km (285 miles) south-west of Sydney.

Climate

Average temperatures: January max 35C (95F) - min 18C (64F); July max 14C (57F) - min 5C (41F). Average annual rainfall: 669mm (26 ins).

Characteristics

The area was first settled by the largest Aboriginal tribe in New South Wales - the Wiradjuri. It is from their language that the city gets its name, Wagga (Wahga or Wahgam) means 'crow' and the repetition of the word expresses the plural.

In 1829, the land was explored by Captain Charles Sturt while he was on his famous expedition discovering the Murrumbidgee and Murray River systems. Settlement followed and Wagga Wagga was proclaimed a town in 1849. It became a city in 1948, and is the largest provincial city in New South Wales.

How to Get There

By Bus

Greyhound Pioneer have services daily from/to Sydney, Adelaide and Canberra.

By Rail

The Sydney-Melbourne and Melbourne-Sydney Countrylink stops at Wagga Wagga, daily.

By Road

From Sydney, via the Hume and Sturt Highways, 493km (306 miles).

From Canberra, via Barton, Hume and Sturt Highways, 248km (154 miles).

From Melbourne, via Hume to Albury, then via Olympic Way - Culcairn/Henty/The Rock, 443km (275 miles).

Wagga Wagga

Accommodation

Wagga Wagga has plenty of places to stay for a town its size. Here is a selection with prices for a double room per night, which should be used as a guide only. The telephone area code is 02.

Pavilion Motor Inn, 22 Kincaid Street, ✆6921 6411. 45 units, licensed restaurant, indoor heated swimming pool - ✪$130-190.

Heritage Motor Inn, 244 Edward Street, ✆6921 4099. 22 units, sauna, pool, bbq - ✪$95-120.

Carriage House Motor Inn, Sturt Highway, ✆6922 7374. 37 units, licensed restaurant, pool, spa, sauna, tennis, bbq - ✪$120-170.

Townhouse International, Morgan Street, ✆6922 7374. 42 units, licensed restaurant, swimming pool - ✪$80-250.

Allonville Motel, Sturt Highway, Gumly Gumly, ✆6922 7269 - 29 units, licensed restaurant, swimming pool, bbq - ✪$51.

City Park Motel, 1 Tarcutta Street, ✆6921 4301. 26 units, barbecue - ✪$70-80.

Palm & Pawn Motor Inn, Hampden Avenue, ✆6921 6688. 25 units, licensed restaurant, tennis, barbecue- ✪$60.

Caravan Parks

Horseshoe Motor Village, 23 Horseshoe Road, ✆6921 6033. (Pets allowed by arrangement) 44 sites, good facilities, pool - powered sites ✪$15 for two, cabins $45-50 for two.

Easts Van Park Riverview, 93 Hammond Avenue, ✆6921 4287. (No pets allowed) 100 sites, good facilities - powered sites ✪$20 for two, on-site vans $45 for two.

Airport Caravan Park, Sturt Highway, Forest Hill, ✆6922 7271. (Pets allowed under control) 14 sites, basic facilities, barbecue, playground - powered sites ✪$14 for two.

Tourist Information

The Visitors Information Centre is in Tarcutta Street ✆(02) 6926 9621. They have a website at www. tourismwaggawagga.com.au and you can email them at visitors@ wagga.nsw.gov.au

The centre is open daily 9am-5pm.

Eating Out

As with any city of its size, Wagga Wagga has a good selection of restaurants and takeaway food outlets. Here are some you might like to try.

Barter's Restaurant, 143 Fitz-maurice Street, ✆6921 1922 licensed, traditional and nouvelle cuisine, seven nights a week.

Capers Restaurant, at the Country Comfort, cnr Morgan & Tarcutta Streets, ✆6911 6444. Reasonable, for the whole family

Montezumas Mexican Restaurant, 85 Bayliss Street, ✆6921 4428 - licensed - open Wed-Fri noon-2pm, Tues-Sun from 6pm.

Golden Season Family Restaurant, 31 Forsyth Street, ✆6921 1177.

Other restaurants worth considering:

Locksley Steak House, 137 Peter Street, ✆6921 4886 - licensed, also serves seafood, chicken, etc - open Wed-Fri noon-2pm, Tues-Sat 6pm-midnight.

Indian Tavern Tandoori Restaurant, 176 Baylis Street, ✆6921 3121.

Capers Restaurant, Morgan Street, ✆6921 6444.

Olivers, 8 Day Street, ✆6921 3646.

The Rivergum Restaurant, Sturt Highway, ✆6922 7256.

La Porchetta Pizza Restaurant, 161 Baylis Street, ✆6921 5122.

McDonalds and Pizza Hut are in Edward Street, and KFC is on the corner of Edward and Baylis Streets, and in Fitzmaurice Street.

Points of Interest

The Visitor Information Centre has maps of three **historic walks** through the city which were put together by the National Trust.

The Centre also has copies of the 28km (17 miles) **Red Arrow Tour**, which takes about an hour, and the Wollundry Loop, 10km (6 miles) following Wollundry Lagoon and the river bank.

In 1999 an impressive new **Civic Centre** was opened. It contains the regional art gallery, the Museum of the Riverina and the national art glass

gallery. The city is proud of its civic centrepiece, and it is worth stopping in to have a look.

The **Wagga Wagga Regional Art Gallery**, on the corner of Bayliss and Morrow Streets, has changing exhibitions of international, national and regional art. It is open Mon, Wed-Sat 11am-5pm, Sun 2-5pm, 6926 9610.

The **Wagga Wagga and District Historical Museum** in Willan's Hill, 6925 2934, is open weekends, public holidays and school holidays, and Tues-Wed from 2pm.

The **Botanic Gardens**, 6923 5499, are set in 8.9ha (22 acres) on Willans Hill, and have many garden displays such as the Tree Chapel, which is a popular spot for weddings. Also in the Gardens are the Camellia, Cactus, Succulent and **Shakespearian Gardens,** and an Outdoor Music Bowl which has seating for 3,000 people. A model railway runs through the gardens and features a station and booking office. The train runs on the 1st and 3rd Sundays of the month.

Wagga Wagga City Library is in Gurwood Street, and is the headquarters of a regional library. The service caters for 89,000 people in seven council areas - Coolamon, Cootamundra, Gundagai, Lockhart, Temora and Tumut. It is open Mon-Fri 9am-8pm, Sat 9am-noon.

Sunday Markets are held from 8am-noon in Woolworth's Car Park.

Visitors are welcome to drive through the grounds of the **Charles Sturt University** - Riverina, and visit the College Winery, in Boorooma Street, North Wagga, which is open Mon-Fri 10am-4pm, Sat 11am-4pm, for wine tastings and sales.

Aurora Clydesdale Stud & Pioneer Farm, Cameron's Road, 9km past Collingullie, towards Nar-randera, has antique machinery, a pioneer's hut and Clydesdales in action. There is also a large collection of birds and animals, 6928 2215 for information and times.

Murray Cod Hatcheries and Fauna Park on the Sturt Highway, 6922 7360, is home to Big Murray, a 52kg (115 lb) Murray Cod, who measures 1.37m (4.5 ft). The park also has Crab Eating Macaquehs (monkeys) from South East Asia, native snakes, camels, wombats, koalas, kangaroos, native fish and many native birds. There is a gift shop selling pottery, paintings and souvenirs, and a snack bar. Barbecues and playground equipment are set in the picnic area, and the complex is open daily 8.30am-5.30pm.

Kapooka Military Camp invites visitors to view the parades held each Monday at 11am. The camp is the base for the Army's 1st Recruit Training Battalion. The Ka-pooka Band performs during the parades, and holds a series of Music at Midday concerts in Wagga Wagga city. You can join a Green Arrow Tour of the base by reporting to the guard room at the main entrance. The camp is 10km (6 miles) west of Wagga on the Olympic Way.

Facilities

Lawn bowls, croquet, fishing, golf, greyhound racing, horse racing, trotting, sailing, water skiing, sailing, swimming, boating and tennis. The city has 4 licensed Clubs with dining facilities and poker machines.

Festivals

The Gumi Festival is held on the last Saturday in February each year. Gumi is pidgin for 'rubber', and the Gumi Race consists of hundreds of craft made from inner tubes floating down the 11km course on the Murrumbidgee River.

The Wagga Wagga Agricultural Show is held over the October long weekend (the first Monday in October sets the long weekend date).

Outlying Attractions

Lockhart

Proceed south from Wagga Wagga along the Olympic Way to The Rock, then turn left. Lockhart is 42km (26 miles) further on. The Rock (the town), originally named Kingston, is located 6km east of craggy outcrops which rise more than 360m (1181 ft) above the surrounding districts. The peak of the Rock Hill Nature Reserve is the only place in Australia where the Senecio wildflower is found. The Yerong Nature Trail within the Reserve takes about 3 hours to complete, and is worth the effort. The 3km track is gentle on the lower slopes, but fairly steep at the higher levels.

The centre of the town has been classified by the National Trust. Also classified is the Old Urangeline Woolshed. Contact the Tourist Information Centre in Wagga Wagga, ✆6926 9621, for details.

The Lockhart Museum, in 45 Urana Street, ✆6920 5674, contains many fine memories of the district's pioneering past.

Approximately 16km (10 miles) north of Lockhart is Galore Hill Recreation Reserve. The reserve comprises 510ha (1260 acres) of natural bushland, and Galore Hill rises 215m (705 ft) above the surrounding countryside.

Coolamon Shire

The shire includes the townships of Coolamon, Ardlethan, Ganmain, Beckom, Grong Grong, Matong and Marrar, and is the agricultural centre of the Riverina.

Ganmain, situated between Junee and Narrandera, is the centre of the chaff industry of Australia. Pioneer Park houses the haystack-styled museum.

Coolamon is 39km (24 miles) north-west of Wagga Wagga, and has many old world antique shops. The Coolamon Golf Club, ✆6927 3178, welcomes visitors to play a round on the sand green course, and visit their Chinese restaurant.

Junee

The town of Junee is built to an unusual plan with the railway running down the middle of the central business district. The railway has been important to the town as is shown by the impressive railway station, built in 1883.

Monte Cristo, a homestead in traditional Georgian design, is 🕓open daily 10am-4pm, and is a museum of Victorian furniture and antiques.

Temora

Temora, a centre Harness Racing (Paleface Adios, the famous pacer, and winner of the Inter Dominion, was born here), was established after the 1880 gold rush when the famous Mother Shipton nugget weighing 258 ounces was found. The decline of gold saw the town become a major wheat growing district.

The Temora Rural Museum, ✆6977 1291, is 🕓open daily 2-5pm, and is a .8ha (2 acres) complex with agricultural machinery, antique tractors and engines, a pioneer cottage with lifestyles of yesterday, and a rock and mineral display.

The Temora Visitor Information Centre is at 294 -296 Hoskins Street, ✆6977 1511.

Cootamundra

The town of Cootamundra, with a population of 6,600, is the home of the Cootamundra Wattle (Acacia Baileyana) and the birthplace of the late Sir Donald Bradman, Australia's famous cricketer. The cottage where he was born is privately owned but may be viewed from the street (89 Adams Street).

The focal point of the township is the Bicentennial Post Office Plaza, which incorporates the historical post office building and clock tower, and the old Peppercorn tree.

Pioneer Park, on the southern outskirts, commands extensive views of the town and district.

Bethungra Rail Spiral is 23km (14 miles) southwest of Cootamundra. The line spirals around Bethungra Hill, crossing itself and the south line while traversing some of the deepest rail cuttings in Australia.

The Cootamundra Tourist Information Centre, Hovell Street, ✆(02) 6942 4212.

Gundagai

The famous Dog on the Tucker Box is, as every Australian knows, 5 miles (8km) from (north of) Gundagai, on the western side of the Hume Highway. Opposite the memorial to Mateship between man and dog, are copper representations of the Dog, and Dad, Dave, Mum and Mabel at Snake Gully, the characters of Steele Rudd.

The Gundagai Visitor Information Centre, 294 Sheridan Street, ✆(02) 69 44 1341, is 🕒open daily Mon-Fri 8am-5pm, Sat-Sun 9am-5pm. You can contact them by email at ztc1@gundagaishire.nsw.gov.au. The Centre houses the Rusconi Marble Masterpiece, a cathedral in miniature containing 20,948 pieces of NSW marble, built by Mr Frank Rusconi in his spare time over a period of 28 years. The Centre also has a gemstone collection, flood inundation maps and flood scenes of Gundagai.

The walking tour, devised by the Tourist Centre, takes in: the Dr Gabriel Gallery; the Court House built in 1859, where Moonlight the Bushranger was tried; the Gundagai Historic Museum; the Old Flour Mill constructed in 1849; and the two bridges, Railway Bridge, 1901, and Prince Alfred Bridge, 1866, the longest timber viaduct in Australia.

Dad and Dave Sculptures, Gundagai

The Tourist Centre also has details of the Mount Parnassus Walking Tour, and can arrange coach tours and canoe tours of the Murrum-bidgee and Tumut Rivers.

On the Hume Highway is the Tucker Box Tourist Centre, ✆(02) 6944 1450, which serves as an alternative information source.

Tumut

In 1824, Explorers Hume and Hovell crossed the Tumut River slightly south of the site of present day Tumut. The local natives called the area Doomat or Tumott, which meant "quiet resting place by the river".

In the early days, Tumut was squatter country, By 1870, the number of hotels had grown to 18. Dairy farming was the main industry then, but today, timber is big business, particularly softwood like Pinus Radiata, with 52,520ha (130,000 acres) being grown within 25km (16 miles) of Tumut.

Tumut is now a town of around 6,000 people, and the Festival of the Falling Leaf is held there every year in April-May. There are street parades, band recitals, Plaza Night and a Family Fun Day at the Sports Club.

Tumut is 128km (80 miles) west of Canberra, about midway between Sydney and Melbourne, and is the gateway to the giant Snowy Mountains Scheme. The town is surrounded very picturesque countryside, and the rivers and mountain streams within easy access are stocked with trout.

There are regular air and rail services to Tumut, the road access is very good, and the climate averages between 35C (95F) in summer to a low of 5C (41F). The Visitor Information Centre is at the Old Butter Factory, 5 Adelong Road, ✆(02) 6947 7025.

The Yarrangobilly Caves, which are covered in the Snowy Mountains section, are 77km (48 miles) south of Tumut.

Griffith

Located 196km north west of Wagga Wagga, Griffith is worth considering for a day trip or overnight stay. It is part of the Riverina district, its soil made rich and fertile by the irrigation scheme bringing water all the way from the Snowy Mountains. Wine, fruits, vegetables, rice, and poultry products are grown and cultivated here.

There are a number of interesting attrations, including the extensive Pioneer Park museum, the Regional Art Gallery, Catania Fruit Farm, and the natural wonders of Lake Wyangan and Cocoparra National Park.

Griffith Visitor Information Centre, cnr Banna & Jondaryan Avenues, ✆6962 4145 or ✆1800 681 141. You can email them at griffithvc@griffith.nsw.gov.au

Hay

Located on the Murrumbidgee River halfway between Adelaide and Sydney amidst a vast plain, this town with its wide tree-lined streets has become known in recent years for the **Shear Outback museum**. Showcasing the stories, artefacts, technology and culture of the Australian shearing industry, the facility comprises an iconic 'purpose built' interpretative centre and an historic woolshed relocated from the banks of the Murray River. The museum is ✆open 9am to 5pm with extended hours for the cafÈ and special exhibitions: 5pm to 8.30pm. Shearing demonstrations are held from 10:30am, 1:00pm and 3:30pm though these times may vary depending on weather conditions and visitor numbers. Adults $15, Concession $10, Children (under 12) $8, Family $35. Group bookings are available upon application. The buiding won an Australian Architecture award and is worth a visit. Other attractions in Hay include the **Old Hay Gaol**, **Historic Bishop's Lodge**, a restored iron homestead built for the Anglican Bishops of the Riverina in 1889 and famous for its gardens of heritage roses; The Sunbeam' Cobb & Co Coach, the imposing Court House and Railway Station, and Wetlands.

Albury-Wodonga

Population 68,000
The twin cities of Albury-Wodonga sit astride the magnificent Murray River, touching the edges of the Upper Murray, North-East Victoria, the Riverina, the South-West Slopes of NSW and the Murray Valley. Distance from Sydney 592km (368 miles), from Canberra 195km (121 miles), and from Melbourne 300km (186 miles).

Characteristics

Hume and Hovell carved their names in trees beside the Murray in 1824 and Hovell's still stands today. In 1836, Robert Brown arrived and constructed a punt to cross the river, built an inn, and the settlement was born. In 1974 Albury-Wodonga was designated the national growth centre.

Climate

Average temperatures: January max 32C (90F) - min 15C (55F); June max 14C (57F) - min 2C (36F). Average annual rainfall: 796mm (31 ins) - wettest month August. Elevation - 195m (640 ft) above sea level.

How to Get There

By Bus
Greyhound Pioneer travel to/from Melbourne, Sydney, Canberra and Brisbane.

By Rail
Albury-Wodonga is three hours by train from Melbourne on the Sydney/Melbourne route.

By Road
From Sydney and Melbourne via the Hume Highway; from Mildura along the Murray Valley Highway; from Brisbane via the Newell Highway and the Riverina Highway.

Albury-Wodonga

Accommodation

The twin towns have 50 quality hotels and motels and 7 caravan parks. Here is a selection with prices for a double room per night, which should be used as a guide only. The telephone area code is 02.

Country Comfort Albury, Dean Street, ✆6021 5366. 140 rooms, licensed restaurant, heated swimming pool, spa, sauna - ✪$130.

Sundowner Chain Motor Inns, Hovell Tree, cnr Hume Highway and Hovell Streets, ✆6041 2666. 40 units, licensed restaurant, swimming pool, spa, sauna, gym, undercover parking - ✪$115-205.

Elm Court Motel, 435 Townsend Street, ✆6021 8077. 31 units, indoor heated swimming pool, spa, barbecue - ✪$80-85.

Matador Motor Inn, 617 Young Street, ✆6021 1877. 60 units, licensed restaurant, indoor heated swimming pool, spa, gym, sauna, barbecue - ✪$85-100.

Commodore, 515 Kiewa Street, ✆6021 3344. 40 units, licensed restaurant (closed Sunday) - ✪$80-85.

Sodens Australia Hotel/Motel, cnr David & Wilson Street, ✆6021 2400. 50 units, licensed restaurant, barbecue - ✪$40-45.

Caravan Parks

Trek-31 Tourist Park, cnr Wagga Road & Catherine Crescent, ✆6025 4051. (No pets allowed) 119 sites, excellent facilities, pool, barbecue - powered sites ✪$19-22 for two, cabins $45-75 for two.

Albury Central Tourist Park, North Street, ✆6021 8420. (Pets allowed under control) 127 sites, barbecue, tennis, playground, pool - powered sites ✪$16 for two, cabins $45-55 for two.

Tourist Information

Tourist Albury Wodonga Gateway Information Centre, is in Lincoln Causeway, ✆6041 3875, freecall ✆1800 800 743.

Eating Out

Albury-Wodonga offers a diverse range of cuisine styles from fine dining to fast service takeaway. Here are a few you might like to try.

Santino's Licensed Family Bistro, 14 City Walk, Dean Street, ✆6041 1997 - caters for all seven days and nights.

Il Sogno Restaurant, 639 Dean Street, ✆6023 4585 - proclaim themselves 'The Flavour of Italy'.

Puti Vegetarian Restaurant, 1083 Mate Street, ✆6025 0086 - takeaway available.

One Six Eight, 1081 Mate Street, ✆6025 9816 - Chinese cuisine.

Gourmet Inn Restaurant, 473b Dean Street, ✆6021 4321.

Thai Grand Palace Restaurant, 592 Kiewa Street, ✆6041 1238.

Indian Tandoori Restaurant, 449a Dean Street, ✆6041 4705.

Beefeater's Bistro, 324 Wodonga Place, ✆6041 1711.

Points of Interest

The most famous attraction is, of course, the Murray River, which flows on to enter the Southern Ocean through Lake Alexandrina in South Australia, 2500km (1553 miles) from its source. The total Murray system, including the Darling and Murrumbidgee rivers and their tributaries, drains a seventh of the total area of Australia. The Murray supplies 49% of SA's domestic and industrial requirements, and almost all the water for irrigation.

In 1838, Robert Brown built a rough punt at the Crossing Place, followed by an accommodation house for travellers. This established a tradition for the district, and Albury-Wodonga today has more 'accommodation houses' than any other Australian country centre.

Albury-Wodonga's river queen, the ***PS Cumberoona*** operates daily from October through to May, depending on water flow and water level, which depends on the release of irrigation water from Lake Hume.

Other attractions are: **Kinross Woolshed**, which hosts bush dances and jazz nights; **Frog Hollow**, complete with a maze, minature golf and Mr F. Frog; **Hume Weir Trout Farm**, the largest trout farm in the area; and the restored **Cobb & Co** coaches that provide an alternative method of transport.

15km (9 miles) north of Albury is the original **Ettamogah Pub**. As their ad says, "the Ettamogah Mob needed a good excuse to work up a thirst...so we built a town around our Pub", and the end result is a complex which will keep every member of the family occupied for hours. The Pub, ✆6026 2366, is open daily 9am-midnight, and the Winery is open Mon-Fri 9am-5pm, Sat 10am-5pm, Sun 9am-4pm.

At **Albury Pottery**, Lincoln Causeway, Wodonga, ✆6041 6835, you can take a self-guiding tour and watch the potters at work - open daily. If it's culture you seek, the **Albury Regional Art Centre**, 546 Dean Street, Albury, the **Museum**, 66 South Street, Wodonga, the **Pioneer Museum** in Urana Street, Jindera, and the **Albury Botanical Gardens** will get you off to a good start.

Albury's licensed **Clubs** provide meals, entertainment and, of course, poker machines. Thousands of people from Victoria travel to Albury to try and win the big one at the "pokies".

For **aquatic sport**, head for Lake Hume, only 12km (7 miles) upstream from town. It has 320km (199 miles) of shoreline. If you intend to fish, make sure you have both a NSW and Victorian Fishing Licence. The Wyamah ferry links NSW with Victoria, and is operated by friendly folk. At Dora Dora there is a 130-year-old hotel which is more like an entertainment centre than a pub.

There is a lovely **Riverbank Walk** at Albury (Travel Centre has leaflets). The 7.5km (5 miles) trails from Nail Can Hill go along the river, over Monument Hill and past old gold diggings.

A visit to the **Flying Fruit Fly Circus** is a must - for booking and details, ✆6021 7044.

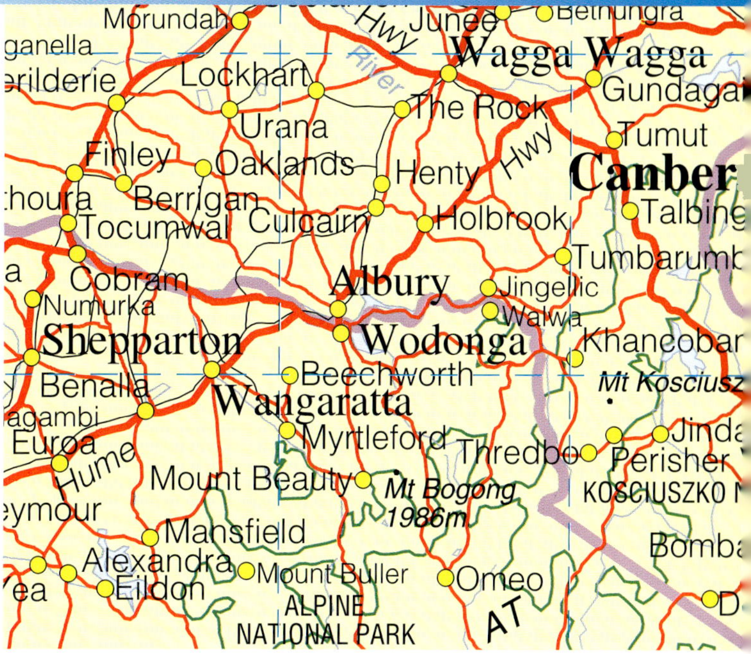

Facilities

The area has 14 licensed lawn bowls clubs. Canoes can be hired, and water skiing tuition is available on Lake Hume. Regular horse racing meetings are held in Albury/Wodonga. Other facilities include golf, tennis, fishing (cod, perch and trout) and swimming (pool and river).

Festivals

Winery Walkabout is held over the long weekend in June. and the Golden Horseshoe Festival is held at Easter.

Outlying Attractions

Howlong

A typical Murray River township, Howlong is 26km (16 miles) west of Albury on the Riverina Highway. The town gets its name, which means 'beginning of the plain', from the Howlong run, a property of 20,000ha (49,400 acres) fronting the river.

Corowa

Corowa is 56km (35 miles) west of Albury, and its wide main street extends to the Murray River's banks. The Tourist Information Centre is in Sanger Street, ✆6033 3221. They are open 9am-5pm daily and can be emailed at corowa.tourinfo@albury.net.au. Additional information is available on the internet at www.corowa. nsw.gov.au

Corowa is known as the birthplace of Australian federation. The first Border Federation League was established in Corowa in January, 1893. The historic conference of the various border leagues was held in July of that year, and together they continued to agitate until the referendum of 1898, when the decision in favour of federation was carried.

Anyone interested in Australian history should visit Corowa's Federation Museum in Queen Street, ✆6033 1568.

Mulwala

The town of Mulwala is 40km (25 miles) west of Corowa, and is renowned for its year-round mild climate. Nearby Lake Mulwala offers swimming, sailing and cruising.

Mulwala is often linked with Yarrawonga, on the other side of the river, and the Tourist Information is there on the corner of Irvine & Blemore Streets, ✆5744 1989 or ✆1800 062 260. There is a website at www.yarrawongamulwalainfo.com and email is ymt@cnl.com.au

Jindera

Only about 20km (12 miles) north-west of Albury, Jindera has a Pioneer Museum that is rated a world-class attraction. It is housed in an old store and home that belonged to the pioneering Wagner family, and the store is stocked with authentic goods of the 19th century. It is open daily 10am-4.30pm, ✆6026 3622.

The Jindera district was settled in the 1860s by German migrants, the township was gazetted in 1869, and a century later a cairn was erected to honour these pioneering families.

Albury-Wodonga

Culcairn

Culcairn is 53km (33 miles) north of Albury-Wodonga, in the heart of 'Morgan' country. Other towns in the area are Henty, Walla, Jindera, Gerogery, Cookardinia, Morven and Walbundrie.

Bushranger Dan Morgan began his criminal career at Round Hill at Culcairn in June, 1864. Events surrounding the incident can be read at a site overlooking Round Hill, about 3km east on the Holbrook Road.

A life-sized effigy of Dan Morgan is displayed in the Billabong Art and Crafts Centre's 'Mad Dog Morgan' art cellar. The effigy was made for the movie of the same name, filmed in the district in 1975, and the first Australian film to win an award at the Cannes Film Festival.

Holbrook

The Tourist Information Office is in the Woolpack Inn Museum, ✆(02) 60 36 2131, email woolpack @dragnet.com.au, open daily 9.30am-4.30pm. Behind the museum is an enclosed area with a vast array of horse-drawn vehicles and farming equipment. The museum also has a section devoted to the exploits of Cdr Norman Holbrook, after whom the town was named. In December, 1914, British submarine commander Lt Norman Holbrook guided a B11 submarine below a minefield to torpedo an enemy Turkish battleship, the Messudiya. The submarine was immediately attacked by destroyers and on-shore forts, and during the trip back through the minefields Holbrook and his crew were forced to stay submerged for nine hours, an incredible feat for a 1914 submarine.

At this time the town was called Germanton, but the wave of anti-German feelings caused by World War I had the citizens searching for a new name. The news of the extraordinary bravery exhibited by the British submarine crew ended their search, and the town became Holbrook.

Wollongong

Population 219,800
Wollongong is situated on the coast of New South Wales, 80km (50 miles) from Sydney, and 238km (148 miles) from Canberra.

Climate

Average temperatures: January max 26C (79F) - min 18C (64F); July max 17C (63F) - min 9C (48F). Average annual rainfall: 1275mm (50 ins).

Characteristics

Wollongong is the seventh largest city in Australia, and the gateway to the Illawarra and Southern Highlands region. To its north, cosy mining villages dot the coastline and the Illawarra coastal plain is narrowest, as rocky sea cliffs reach right to the pounding waves.

In the seaside village of Thirroul, D.H. Lawrence wrote *Kangaroo*, and from Stanwell Park, aviator Lawrence Hargraves tested his kites.

How to Get There

By Rail

Electric trains run regularly between Sydney's Central Station and Wollongong, connecting with on-going services to Port Kembla and south to Bomaderry on Nowra's northern outskirts, ✆13 2232.

By Bus

Greyhound Pioneer, ✆13 2030, and McCaffertys, ✆13 1499, stop at Wollongong daily on their Sydney/Melbourne via the Princes Highway services.

By Road

From Sydney, via the Princes Highway to Waterfall and then the F6, or continue along the highway and turn off at the Stanwell Park signpost for a spectacular drive along the coast.

Another interesting route is via the National Park to Stanwell Park - turn off just past Sutherland.

Wollongong

Accommodation

The Illawarra coast boasts a comprehensive range of accommodation from caravan parks on many of the beaches and lakesides, to an international style resort hotel, leisure village, quality motels, hotels, holiday units and superb convention facilities. Here is a selection with prices for a double room per night, which should be used as a guide only. The telephone area code is 02.

Novotel Northbeach, 2 Cliff Road, ©4226 3555. 203 rooms, 17 suites, licensed restaurants, swimming pool, spa, sauna, gym, tennis, bicycling - ✪$230-360.

City Pacific Boutique Hotel, 112 Burelli Street, ©4229 7444. 61 rooms, licensed restaurant, swimming pool - ✪$75-250.

Boat Harbour Motel, 7 Campbell Street, ©4228 9166. 42 units, licensed restaurant (closed Sun and public holidays) - ✪$115-140.

Golden Pacific North Beach, 16 Pleasant Avenue, North Wollongong, ©4226 3000. 20 units, 2 suites - ✪$95-180.

Downtown Motel, 76 Crown Street, ©4229 8344. 31 units, licensed restaurant (closed Sun) - ✪$75-100.

Beach Park Motor Inn, 10 Pleasant Avenue, North Wollongong, ©4226 1577. 16 units, barbecue - ✪$60-170.

Caravan Parks

Corrimal Beach Tourist Park, Lake Parade, Corrimal, ©4285 5688. 397 sites, barbecue - unpowered sites ✪$15-25 for two, cabins $60-165 for two.

Windang Beach Tourist Park, Fern Street, ©4297 3166. (No pets) 259 sites, barbecue - unpowered sites ✪$15-25 for two, cabins $60-165 for two, bungalows $40-70 for two.

Bulli Beach Tourist Park, 1 Farrell Road, ©4285 5677. (No pets allowed), 269 sites - powered sites ✪$20-25 for two, cabins $60-165 for two.

Eating Out

Wollongong's cosmopolitan community offers you a wide choice of superb restaurants, snack bars and coffee lounges. Here are some you might like to try.

Fuji Yama Tepan Restaurant, 35 Flinders Street, ©4226 2609, specialise in Japanese barbecues.

Charcoal Tavern, 18 Regent Street, ©4229 7298. Modern Australian, seafood and steaks.

Nam, 4 Kenny Street, ©4228 3646. Vietnamese and Chinese food.

Beach House Seafood Restaurant, 16 Cliff Road, ©4228 5410.

Anchorage, cnr Campbell & Wilson Streets, ©4228 9166. A-la-carte menu, beach views.

Branches, Blackbutt Motel, Shellharbour Road, Shellharbour, ©4297 1323. Italian and seafood.

Zita's, 147-149 Corrimal Street, ©4227 1110. French, Italian, German cuisine, local seafood.

King's, 26 Flinders Street, North Wollongong, ©4228 6976. Chinese cuisine.

Amigos, 116 Keira Street, ©4229 8181. Mexican selection.

Bangkok Orchid Thai, Shop 1, 119 Corrimal Street, ©4229 6620.

Mammas Pizza Roma, 56 Crown Street, ©4229 9166.

Tandoori Village Indian Restaurant, Shop 2, 120 Corrimal Street, ©4225 7876.

During business hours a good place to eat is the Food Court, lower level of the Gateway on the Mall shopping complex, cnr Burelli & Keira Streets. They have tables in the centre and you can choose from Chinese, Italian, Austrian, Mexican, crepes, chicken, pies, kebabs, hamburgers, and so on.

There are several McDonald's in the city and all other Wollongong localities as well.

Pizza Hut and KFC also have outlets in localities surrrounding Wollongong.

Visitor Information

The Wollongong Visitor Information Centre, 93 Crown Street (corner of Kembla Street), ✆1800 240 737 (free call), is open seven days a week 9am-5pm Mon-Fri, 9am-4pm Sat and 10am-4pm Sun. They can be emailed at tourism @wollongong .nsw.gov.au and the website to explore is www.wollongong.nsw.gov.au

Entertainment

For those who want to boogie the night away, there are many night clubs and discos, as well as the licensed clubs. The clubs in Wollongong itself are:

Collegians RLFC, 3A Charlotte Street, ✆4229 7711.
Illawarra Master Builders, 61 Church Street, ✆4229 6466.
Illawarra Leagues Club, 87 Church Street, ✆4229 4611.
Wollongong Ex-Services, 82 Church Street, ✆4228 8522.

For movie goers, Wollongong has two cinema complexes:

Regent Theatre, 197 Keira Street, ✆4228 9238.
Town Cinemas, Burelli Street, ✆4228 4888.

The ***Illawarra Performing Arts Centre***, Burelli Street, ✆4226 3366, has live theatre and musical presentations.

Lighthouse on Flagstaff Hill

Points of Interest

Most historic buildings can be visited on a **walking tour** commencing at Flagstaff Hill (parking available). The sights visited are: Wollongong Head Lighthouse; Breakwater Lighthouse; Belmore Basin; Drill Hall; Throsby's stockman's hut monument; Market Square; Illawarra Historical Mu-seum; Congregational Church; Wollongong Courthouse; St Michael's Provisional Cathedral; Wollongong Uniting Church; The Town Hall; Wollongong East Post Office; Tour-ist Information office; St Francis Xavier's Provisional Cathedral; and Andrew Lysaght Park.

Mount Kembla Historic Village, 7km (4 miles) from Wollongong was the site of the 1902 mining disaster, but it is full of art and craft centres today.

Wollongong Botanic Garden, in Keiraville, is a pleasant spot for picnics and quiet walks, and offers many areas of interest - Sir Joseph Banks Plant Houses, where plants from the wet tropics, deserts and temperate regions are displayed; The Rose Garden; Woodland Garden; Flowering Trees and Shrub Garden; Succulent Plants from South Africa and Central America; Australian Plant Habitats; and The Herb Garden. The Garden is open daily 7am-4.45pm Mon-Fri and 10am-4.45pm Sat-Sun. During

Port Kembla Grain Terminal

winter the gardens close at 6.45pm.

The **Wollongong City Art Gallery**, 85 Burelli Street, ✆4228 7500, has a fine collection of modern and traditional paintings, with changing exhibitions. It is open Tue-Fri 10am-5pm, Sat-Sun noon-4pm.

Magnificent views of the coastline can be obtained from **Mount Kembla Lookout**, **Sublime Point** and **Bulli Lookout**, all of which are only about 15 to 20 minutes' drive from the centre of town.

Kelly's Falls, 2km off the Princes Highway at Stanwell Tops, has a picnic area and easy walking tracks to the falls. Flannel flowers are abundant in spring and early summer.

Nearby is **Symbio Wildlife Gardens**, 7 Lawrence Hargrave Drive, ✆4294 1088, which has native and exotic animals, free barbecues, swimming and wading pools and lunchtime demonstrations of activities from milking a cow to handling reptiles. The gardens are hopen daily from 9.30am, and they advertise that feeding time is 'all the time'. To get to these attractions, take the old Princes Highway from Wollongong, not the F6.

While you are in the area, drive north for half an hour to **Bald Hill Lookout**, where there is a memorial to Lawrence Hargraves, and if the wind is favourable you will see many brightly coloured hang-gliders floating by.

Stanwell Park is in the valley below, and you can call in and browse through Articles Fine Arts Gallery, 111 Lawrence Hargrave Drive, ✆4294 2491, and have a Devonshire tea on the outdoor terrace. The hang-gliders land in the part next to the sea.

South of Wollongong is **Lake Illawarra**, renowned for fishing and prawning, and often ablaze with colourful sailing boats and sail boards. The lake is actually a lagoon covering an area of 35 sq km (14 sq miles), with its entrance at the foreshore suburb of Windang.

The **Illawarra Escarpment State Recreation Area** has many fine walking trails through the rainforest, ✆9585 6444 for details.

Australia's largest steel mill is located around the foreshores of **Port Kembla Harbour**. The harbour sees millions of tons of coal exported each year from the surrounding mines, as well as steel from the steelworks.

Wollongong has two **bicycle tracks**. The one to the north starts at North Beach and goes to Corrimal, 14km (9 miles) away. The southern one starts near the Windang bridge and skirts the shores of Lake Illawarra.

Festivals

The Festival of Wollongong is held each year in November.

Facilities

Ten-pin bowling (8 Commerce Drive, Warilla), car rental depots (Auto Rentals, ✆4229 7766; Avis, ✆4228 4111; Budget, ✆13 2727; Thrifty, ✆4227 3000), catamaran and sailboard hire (Lake Illawarra & Belmore Basin), tennis, squash, horse riding (Otford Valley Farm, ✆4294 2442), golf, joy flights (Albion Park Aerodrome), fishing, leisure centre with heated pools (Beaton Park, ✆4229 6004), horse racing (Kembla Grange, ✆4261 7211), greyhound racing (Bulli, ✆4267 1467 and Dapto, ✆4261 2449), harness racing (Bulli, ✆4267 4224) and indoor cricket (Albion Park Rail, ✆4256 6138 and Unanderra, ✆4271 6685). Deep sea charter boats leave from Belmore Basin. Roller skating is available at Dapto, ✆4261 6333.

WIN Entertainment Centre is a 6,000 capacity, mulit-purpose venue, on the edge of the ocean. It is the home of the Wollongong Hawks, and hosts a variety of events throughout the year. The centre can be contacted on ✆(02) 4230 2800

Outlying Attractions

Shellharbour

The town of Shellharbour is around twenty minutes' drive south of Wollongong on the coastal road. There are caravan and camping areas, modern motels, one of the state's largest licensed clubs, an attractive corner pub, golf, bowls, great restaurants and beautiful beaches.

The name Shellharbour is derived from the many Aboriginal shell middens found here and at nearby Bass Point. The location is listed on the Heritage Commission Register, and is regarded as one of the two most important archaeological sites on the NSW coast.

Bass Point is a popular diving area, as part of its waters form a marine reserve. There is an airport at nearby Albion Park, and joy flights are offered. Nearby is the turnoff to Jamberoo Recreation Park, where you can play mini golf, go bobsledding, grass ski, or take the chairlift to the mountain top. There is also a maze, a licensed family restaurant, children's play area and a barbecue hut.

For more information contact the Shellharbour Visitor Information Centre, ✆4221 6169. They are located in Lamerton House, Lamerton Crescent, and are open 8.30am-4.40pm Mon-Fri, closed weekends and public holidays.

They can be emailed at tourism @shellharbour.nsw.gov.au and the web address is www.shellharbour .nsw.gov.au

Nowra

Population 11,600
Nowra is situated on the banks of the Shoalhaven River, on the south coast of New South Wales.

Climate

Average temperatures: January max 26C (79F) - min 18C (64F); July max 17C (63F) - min 9C (48F). Average annual rainfall: 1275mm (50 ins).

How to Get There

By Rail

Bomaderry is the terminus of the South Coast Railway, and there are train services daily from and to Sydney, ✆13 2232. Pioneer Motor Service operates a daily bus service which connects with the train, ✆13 3410.

By Bus

Greyhound Pioneer, ✆13 2030, have daily services from Sydney/Melbourne/Sydney.

By Road

From Sydney, via the Princes Highway - 162km (100 miles).

Characteristics

Nowra is the hub of the City of Shoalhaven, which has a population of around 83,000. The city area stretches from Berry to Durras North, and has 109 ocean, bay and lakeside beaches, lush rolling pastures, craggy mountain haunts and bush trails. The town has produced two Melbourne Cup winners - Archer and Arwon.

Visitor Information

The Shoalhaven Visitor Information Centre, cnr Princess Highway & Pleasant Way, ✆4421 0778 or ✆1800 024 261, is open 9am-4.30pm daily. Their internet details are www.shoalhaven.nsw.gov.au for tourist information and for email contact beverlyc@shoalhaven.nsw.gov.au.

Nowra

Accommodation

Here is a selection of accommodation with prices for a double room per night, which should be used as a guide only. The phone area code is 02.

Pleasant Way Motor Inn, Pleasant Way, ✆4421 5544. 22 units, pool, spa, bbq - ✪$95.

Parkhaven Motor Lodge, cnr Kinghorn & Douglas Streets, ✆4421 6444. 30 units, licensed restaurant, swimming pool - ✪$95-160.

Marriott Park, cnr Princes Highway & Douglas Street, ✆4421 6999. 16 units - ✪$70-85.

George Bass Motor Inn, 65 Bridge Road, ✆4421 6388. 10 units, comfortable- ✪$80-100.

Cross Country Motel, 242 Kinghorn Street, ✆4421 7777. 18 units, pool, bbq - ✪$70-80.

Nowra Motor Inn, 202 Kinghorn Street, ✆4421 0555. 30 units, licensed restaurant, pool - ✪$70-80.

Riverhaven Motel, Scenic Drive, ✆4421 2044. 22 units, licensed restaurant, indoor heated pool, barbecue - ✪$60-75.

Caravan Parks

Shoalhaven Caravan Village, Terara Road, ✆4423 0770. (Pets allowed under control) - powered sites ✪$17 for two, cabins $30-70.

Rest Point Caravan Park, Browns Road, ✆4421 6856. (No pets allowed) 80 sites, playground, barbecue - powered sites ✪$20-24, cabins $55-100.

Eating Out

Nowra has a wide selection of restaurants, coffee shops, and four licensed clubs. Many of the motels also have restaurants. Some of the choices are:

Nowra Steak House, 16 Kinghorne Street, ✆4423 4193.

Captain's Table, 202 Kinghorne Street, ✆4421 0555.

Boatshed, Wharf Road, ✆4421 2419.

Trevi Fountain, 223 Kinghorne Road, ✆4423 0285. Italian cuisine.

Riverhaven, Riverhaven Motel, 1 Scenic Drive, ✆4421 2044.

Shoreline, Parkhaven Motel, cnr Kinghorn & Douglas Streets, ✆4421 5444.

Nowra Palace, 54 Berry Street, ✆4421 4902. Malayasian and Chinese selection.

Theodore's Brasserie, 116 King-horne Street, ✆4421 0300.

Leong's Chinese Restaurant, 83 North Street, ✆4421 2131.

McDonald's is on the corner of Cambawarra Road, Bomaderry, and the Princes Highway & Browns Road, South Nowra, ✆4421 1099. KFC is in Lot 22, Princes Highway, South Nowra. Pizza Hut is on the corner of McLean Street and the Princes Highway in Nowra, ✆4421 4199.

Points of Interest

Cruises of the Shoalhaven River are available from Shoalhaven River Tours, 49 Greenwell Point Road, Greenwell Point, ✆4447 1978.

The old **Shoalhaven River bridge** was erected in 1881. To cope with the heavy volume of traffic across the River, a second bridge was erected in 1980.

In **Moorhouse Park**, Bridge Road, there is an old flood rescue boat from Terara.

Nowra Olympic Pool and **Nowra Waterways** are in Scenic Drive and are open from September to Easter, ✆4421 2093.

The Showground, in West Street, is the venue for the two-day agricultural show held in February each year.

On the corner of West and Worrigee Streets, is **Meroogal**, an historic house built by Robert Taylor-Thorburn in 1886. It is now owned by the Historic Houses Trust of New South Wales, and is ⏲open Sat 1pm-5pm and Sun 10am-5pm. For further information, ✆4421 8150.

Shoalhaven Historical Museum, cnr Kinghorn & Plunkett Streets, is ⏲open Sat-Sun 1-4pm, and on Mon, Wed and Fri during school

holidays 1pm-4pm, ✆4421 2021.

Werninck Craft Cottage, 102 Plunkett Street, is open Mon-Fri 9.30am-3.30pm, Sat-Sun 10am-4pm, ✆4423 2419.

Situated on the corner of Kinghorn & Kalandar Streets is a **Sea Venom Jet**, which has been donated by HMAS Albatross. A short history of the aircraft and type of service is on a plaque at the site.

HMAS Albatross

Travel south from Nowra along the Princes Highway to the Kalandar Street intersection, turn right at the traffic lights and follow the signs.

The **Royal Australian Naval Air Station**, HMAS Albatross, 9km (6 miles) south-west of Nowra, is the home of the Fleet Air Arm. Educational tours can be arranged, ✆4421 1211 for more information.

The **Naval Aviation Museum** at the Air Station has the finest collection of historic military aircraft in Australia, and a good collection of engines, aviation equipment, models, uniforms and memorabilia. Picnic, barbecue and toilet facilities are provided, and it is open daily 10am-4pm, ✆4421 1920.

Near the base is the **Nowra Hill Lookout**, with panoramic views of the Shoalhaven and Jervis Bay area.

Festivals

February - Nowra Agricultural Show.
November - The Shoalhaven Spring Festival.

Facilities

Lawn bowls, canoeing, fishing, golf, sailing, scenic drives, squash, swimming, tennis, water skiing, 4WD escapes and bushwalking tours. Check with the information centre.

Boats can be hired from the following outlets:

Aquatique, 125 Junction Street, ✆4421 8159 - canoes, scuba and diving gear, surf skis and wave skis.

Shoalhaven Caravan Village, Terrara Road, ✆4423 0770 - canoes.

Outlying Attractions

Kiama

Kiama is a seaside town 36km (22 miles) south of Wollongong.

The Blowhole is the main attraction, but nowadays it only seems to 'blow' in nasty weather. In any case, it is floodlit until 9.30pm.

The best way to explore Kiama is on foot, strolling around the foreshore area.

The Terraces, a row of historic timber cottages, are now gift and specialty stores, and a good place to pick up a bargain. Most of the stores are open daily 10am-5pm.

The **Family History Centre**, 7 Railway Parade, ✆4233 1122, has comprehensive in-house microform and data inventory to enable people to trace their family trees. The Centre is open daily 9.30am-4.30pm.

The **Quarry Leisure Centre**, Havilah Place, ✆4232 1877, has a 25m heated swimming pool, a wading pool, sauna, spa, aerobics, and facilities for indoor sports.

Minnamurra Falls. The Falls are 15km (9 miles) west of Kiama, in a dense subtropical rainforest, and plunge some 50m (164 ft) into a deep gorge. There is a delightful walk from the parking area through the rainforest to the Falls, and the round trip takes about an hour.

Barren Grounds Nature Reserve. The Reserve is 25km (16 miles) west of Kiama on the Jamberoo Mountain Road, and affords magnificent views from the lookout.

The Kiama Visitors Centre is on Blowhole Point Road, ✆4232 3322 or ✆1300 654 262 (free call). Open 9am-5pm daily, visit www.kiama.com.au or send an email to: kiamatourism@ozemail.com.au

Berry

Called the Town of Trees, Berry more than lives up to its name, and is 16km (10 miles) north of Nowra. The town has a population of around 1600, with shopping facilities, motel and hotel accommodation, restaurants, and many antique and craft shops.

The **Berry Historical Museum**, Queen Street, is open Sat 11am-2pm, Sun 11am-3pm and public holidays 11am-2pm, ✆4464 1551, and they can point out the other buildings in the town classified by the National Trust, such as the Court House and National Bank.

Berry Country Fair, featuring local crafts and second- hand goods, is held at Apex Park, cnr Princes Highway & Prince Alfred Street, on the first Sunday of the month.

Local information can be obtained from *Pottering Around*, on the corner of Queen and Alexandra Streets, ✆4464 2177.

Shoalhaven Heads

The township of Shoalhaven Heads is at the southern end of Seven Mile Beach, about 13km (8 miles) east of Bomaderry. It is a popular holiday spot near Seven Mile Beach National Park.

The town offers a bowling club, fishing facilities and a swimming pool. You can hire bicycles at Shoalhaven Heads Hardware Store, ✆4448 7707.

Nearby is **Coolangatta Estate Historic Village Resort**, 1335 Bolong Road, ✆4448 7131, the site of the first settlement in the Shoalhaven district. The complex comprises buildings erected by the district's founder, Alexander Berry, that have been restored as motel units. There is also a 9-hole golf course, a winery, and picnic areas and barbecues.

The **Coolangatta Craft Centre**, 1180 Bolong Road, is housed in the original school house, established in 1861. It is open Wed-Mon 9am-5pm, and daily during school holidays, ✆4448 7205.

Cambewarra Mountain Lookout. The lookout is on Tourist Road, Beamont, north of Bomaderry, and offers panoramic views of the Shoalhaven River Valley and the coastline. Picnic, barbecue and toilet facilities are provided. There is also a kiosk which is open Fri-Wed 9am-5pm and daily during the Christmas school holidays, ✆4465 1321.

Bomaderry/North Nowra

The town of Bomaderry is really a northern suburb of Nowra, separated from it by the river. Bomaderry Railway Station is the terminus of the South Coast Railway Line, ✆4423 6416.

Nowra Golf Club is situated under bush-covered escarpment, near the river in North Nowra, Greys Beach. The clubhouse has first class facilities, and the scenic 18-hole course offers a challenge. Visitors are welcome, ✆4421 3900 (pro-shop ✆4421 2249).

The **Grotto Walk**, west of the golf course, is an easy walk following the River, and beginning off Yurunga Drive.

From **Rockhill Lookout**, off McMahons Road, you can get a spectacular view of the river.

Nowra Wildlife Park is set in 6ha (16 acres) off Rockhill Road, North Nowra, overlooking the river. You can walk amongst the animals,

and have your photo taken with the resident koalas. The park has a well appointed picnic and barbecue area, a kiosk and a camping area, and is open daily 8am-5pm, 4421 3949. Admission is $6 adults, $3 children.

Huskisson

The town of Huskisson, on the shores of Jervis Bay, 24km (15 miles) south-east of Nowra is a real holiday spot. Reputedly, Jervis Bay has the whitest sands in the world, and each Easter Huskisson hosts the White Sands Carnival.

The **Lady Denman Heritage Complex** in Dent Street is worth a visit. The *Lady Denman* is an old Sydney ferry which was originally built at Huskisson, and saw many years of service on Sydney Harbour. After she retired she was sailed back to Huskisson, placed in the park at the Heritage Complex, and now contains the **Museum of Jervis Bay, Science and The Sea**. The park is open daily 9am-5pm, and the museum is open Tues-Fri 1-5pm, Sat-Sun and school holidays 10am-5pm. Nearby is **Lady Timbery's Aboriginal Arts and Crafts Centre**, 4441 5999.

Vincentia

Across the Moona-Moona Creek Bridge from Huskisson is the town of Vincentia, 30km (19 miles) south-east of Nowra. This is another holiday town, with shops, and a 9-hole golf course with superb views of Jervis Bay and the Pigeon House Mountain.

Plantation Point offers sweeping views of Jervis Bay to Bowen Island and Point Perpendicular. There are barbecue and toilet facilities.

Jervis Bay Territory

This area is part of the Australian Capital Territory, and is 35km (22 miles) from Nowra. It contains the Royal Australian Naval College, HMAS Cresswell, the Jervis Bay Nature Reserve and Botanic Gardens Annex.

At Jervis Bay Village you will find a public telephone, police station, supermarket, general store and petrol station. The Administrative Office of Jervis Bay Territory is situated in the grounds of the village, 4442 1217.

Booderee National Park is managed by Jervis Bay Administration, and there is a Visitors Centre on the left near the entrance, 4443 0977. In keeping with the protection of the environment, spear guns, handspears, dogs and other domestic animals are not permitted in the reserve, and fires can only be lit in defined barbecue areas. For enquiries about camping in the park, call into the Visitor Centre, which is open 8.30am-5pm in the Christmas-Easter period, and 9am-4pm during the off-peak season. Entry into the park is $5 per car weekly.

Green Patch is a camping and picnic area within the National Park, and has a sheltered beach, toilets, hot showers, wood barbecues and picnic tables. There is prolific birdlife, many interesting bush walks, and a camping ground that allows a maximum of three weeks' stay.

Murrays Beach, Summer Cloud Bay and Cave Beach are other popular spots in the Reserve.

HMAS Cresswell was established as an officer training college in 1915, and visits to the grounds of the college are permitted on a limited basis (20 minutes on weekends and most public holidays), 4429 7985 for details.

In the college is the **Royal Australian Naval College Historical Collection**, with a display of artefacts specifically related to the college and the Jervis Bay area, and Peter Webber's collection of model sailing ships. It is open on the last Sunday of each month, or by appointment, 4429 7845.

The **Jervis Bay Annex** to the Australian National Botanic Gardens is 2km along the Cave Beach Road, and has a large variety of native plants collected from all parts of Australia. Facilities include nature walks, toilets and picnic area, but no barbecues are permitted. The annex is open Mon-Fri 8am-4pm, and the first Sunday of the month 10am-5pm. Hours may be extended during public and school holidays, 4442 1122.

St Georges Basin

Sanctuary Point and St Georges Basin have a combined estimated population of 6000. There are some lovely spots in and around both places for picnics and all water sports. Catamarans, sailboards and small canoes can be hired from **Sanctuary Point Sail Centre**, 272 Grenville Avenue, ✆4443 0205 (only available during the Summer months).

Lake Conjola

The town of Lake Conjola, is on the shores of the lake of the same name, about 55km (34 miles) south of Nowra.

Boats can be hired at the Post Office and General Store, Carrol Avenue, ✆4456 1163, and at Conjola Boat Hire, ✆4456 1563 (school holidays only). There are tennis courts, a bowling club, fishing and water skiing.

The Craft Corner in the General Store specialises in needlework and tapestry supplies and books, ✆4456 1163.

Milton

Milton is 7km (4 miles) north of Ulladulla, and 61km (38 miles) south of Nowra. It was established in 1860, has many historic buildings, and in the Mick Ryan Park there is a giant fig tree that is estimated to be over 110 years old.

A flea market, featuring local crafts and second-hand goods, is held at the **Settlement Courtyard** on the first Saturday of the month.

Over the long weekend in October every year Milton celebrates the **Milton Settlers' Fair**, which consists of markets, art and craft exhibitions, music and dancing.

Mollymook

Mollymook is less than 5km (2 miles) south east of Milton, situated by the sea.

Beach near Ulladulla

The surfing beach at Mollymook is patrolled daily, and surf skis are available for hire during the Christmas school holidays from the Surf Life Saving Club. Next to the Club is an 'Exersite' outdoor exercise area with equipment and instructions for strengthening and stretching exercises.

Mollymook Golf Club's picturesque 9-hole beachside course has superb sea views from the clubhouse and restaurant. Visitors are welcome, ✆4455 1911. In addition, an 18-hole championship hilltop course is located in Maisie Williams Memorial Drive, with a pro-shop and snack bar facilities. Visitors are welcome here also, ✆4455 2055.

The **Bogey Hole**, a circular natural rock pool, and Collers Beach are reached via Golf Avenue and Riversdale Avenue.

Ulladulla

Ulladulla is 68km (42 miles) south of Nowra, on the Princes Highway, and there is much to see around the harbour and wharf. Trawlers of the fishing fleet are anchored in the harbour behind the safety of the breakwater. Various small craft and the activity associated with fishing are fascinating. Each Easter Sunday, the traditional Blessing of the Fleet Ceremony is conducted on the harbour breakwater. Trawlers are decorated for the event and there is a carnival atmosphere.

The Royal Volunteer Coastal Patrol maintains full sea search and rescue facilities at Ulladulla, for the area from Jervis Bay to Batemans Bay. Radio cover is provided on 2182KHz, 2524KHz and VHF Channel 16 during weekends and holidays periods, and at any other time of day or night by arrangement. However, a continuous watch is maintained 7 days a week on 27880KHz. Pleasure craft owners are urged to lodge sailing plans with the Coastal Patrol Ulladulla either by telephone, ✆4455 3403, or by radio, to ensure they have an adequate radio cover while at sea, and then to advise the base of their safe arrival at their destination.

Pedal boats can be hired on the beach surrounding the harbour during holiday periods.

On **Wardens Head**, the southern point of Ulladulla Harbour, is the lighthouse, and from there you can get an uninterrupted view of the coast. A track leads from the lighthouse to the beach where there is good fishing and surfing.

South Pacific Heathland Reserve stretches from Dowling Street to Pitman Avenue, and features the Chris Humphries Nature Walk covering 12ha (30 acres).

Funland, 93 Princes Highway, ✆4455 3053, is one of the largest indoor fun parks in New South Wales. There are three floors of attractions, including dodgems, the 'sizzler' thrill ride, controlla boats, air hockey, slot cars, kiddy rides, and more. ⏲Open daily from 10am, closes 10pm Sat and school holidays, 5pm Sun-Fri.

The Ulladulla Visitors Centre, Civic Centre, Princes Highway, ✆4455 1269, is ⏲open Mon-Fri 10am-5pm, Sat-Sun 9am-5pm, and should be your first port of call. There is no shortage of accommodation or restaurants in the town, and the Visitor Centre has all the details.

Batemans Bay

Population 9600
Batemans Bay is situated on the Clyde River Estuary, at the foot of Clyde Mountain, 306 km (190 miles) south of Sydney.

Climate

Average temperatures: January max 23C (73F) - min 16C (61F); July max 16C (61F) - min 6C (43F). The average annual rainfall: 916mm (36 in). The hours of sunshine per day are 7 in summer and 6 in autumn, winter and spring.

Characteristics

Batemans Bay is a weekend and holiday retreat for people from Canberra. The beaches of the area are clear and clean with superb fishing. It has all the facilities of a beach resort but it is all very understated. It is the only place where the commercial fishing trawlers are permitted to sell their catch direct to the public. The general atmosphere is very friendly; strangers smile and say hello in the street.

How to Get There

By Air

Hazelton Airlines, ✆13 1713, fly to Moruya and Merimbula from Sydney, Melbourne, Brisbane and Adelaide, with at least two flights daily.

By Bus

Priors Scenic Express operates between Sydney and the Eurobodalla Coast, with a focus on sightseeing opportunities, ✆1800 816 234.
Murrays offer daily services from Canberra, ✆132 251. V-Line have a combined road/rail service between Melbourne and Batemans Bay, ✆132 232.

By Rail

The trains from Sydney, ✆13 2232, terminate at Bombaderry, on the northern side of the

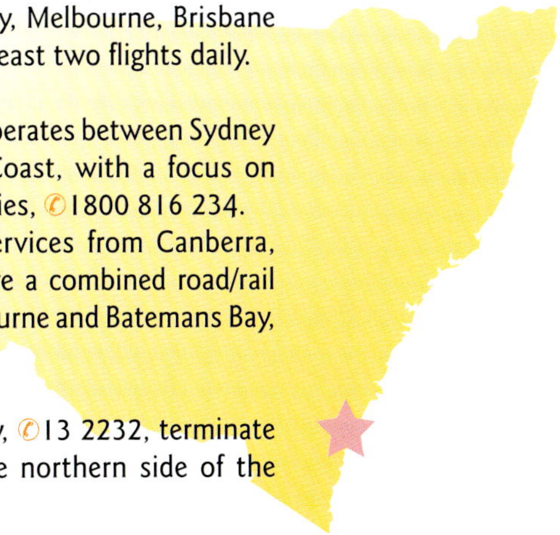

Shoalhaven River, so you will have to organise an alternative form of transport to complete the trip south, be it a hire car or one of the coach services listed above.

By Car

From Sydney and Melbourne, via the Princes Highway - 279km (173 miles) from Sydney and 769km (478 miles) from Melbourne.

From Canberra it is 150km (93 miles) along the Kings Highway.

Batemans Bay

Eating Out

The area boasts fine restaurants with particularly good fish dishes. Most of the larger motels have licensed restaurants which can be recommended. There are also a good number of Clubs - Bowling (✆4472 4502), Golf (✆4472 4967), Returned Servicemen (✆4472 4847) - that also contain restaurants. Here are some additional venues.

Briars, Lincoln Downs, Princess Highway, ✆4472 6388. Licensed, seafood and meat dishes, open daily.

Trappers Seafood Restaurant, 26 Princes Highway, ✆4472 5888. Licensed, a la carte but seafood specialty, open daily.

Gallery, Catalina Country Club, part of the golf club, ✆4472 4967. Licensed, a la carte, open daily. Also has the Garden Bistro, light snacks to grills with a kids' playground.

Innes' Boatshed, Clyde Street, ✆4472 4052. BYO, family restaurant, seafood caught by the chef, open daily.

Rafters, 28 Beach Road, ✆4472 4288. BYO, a la carte, open daily.

Mexican Munchies, Annetts Arcade, Orient Street, ✆4472 8746. Authentic Mexican dishes.

Raymond's, 19 Clyde Street, ✆4472 5700. Chinese cuisine, open daily.

Pinky's Pizza, 3 Clyde Street, ✆4472 3073.

Vietnamese, Thai & Malaysian, Shop 7, Bay Plaza Centre, Orient Street, ✆4472 7274.

McDonalds is on the corner of Hill and Vesper Streets and KFC is on the Princes Highway.

Accommodation

Batemans Bay, as with most towns on the south coast of New South Wales, is well endowed with a variety of accommodation from the usual motels and holiday units to cottages in the area at reasonable prices, outside school holidays. Contact Estate Agents in the area or the local Visitor Centre.

Prices vary considerably depending on the standard and the season. Here we have a selection, with prices for a double room per night, which should be used as a guide only. The telephone area code is 02.

Reef Motor Inn, 27 Clyde Street, ✆4472 6000. 33 units, licensed restaurant, pool, spa, bbq - ✪$105-195.

Lincoln Downs Country Resort, Princes Highway, Surfside, ✆4472 6388. 33 units, 7 suites, restaurant, pool, tennis , bbq - ✪$100-160.

Argyle Terrace Motor Inn, 32 Beach Road, ✆4472 5022. 9 units, pool, bbq - ✪$155-160.

Hanging Rock Golf Club Family, Beach Road, ✆4472 4466. 27 units, playground, barbecue, swimming pool - ✪$55-60.

Holiday Units

Del Costa Holiday Villas, 54 Beach Road, ✆4472 6260. 15 units - ✪$65-130.

The Beach House, 22 Myamba Parade, ✆4472 4086. 1 cottage - ✪$95-130.

Caravan Parks

Easts Riverside Holiday Park, Wharf Road, ✆4472 4048. (No dogs allowed) 47 sites - powered sites ✪$22-36, cabins $60-210.

Coachhouse Marina Resort, Beach Road, ✆4472 4392. (No dogs allowed) - powered sites ✪$25-35 for two, on-site vans $40-100.

Shady Willows Tourist Park, Old Princes Highway, ✆4472 4972. (Dogs may be permitted on application) - powered sites ✪$15-25 for two, on-site vans $35-70 for two, cabins $40-100.

There is a **Youth Hostel** on the corner of Old Princes Highway and South Street, ✆4472 4972. It has 11 rooms at ✪$18 per person twin share.

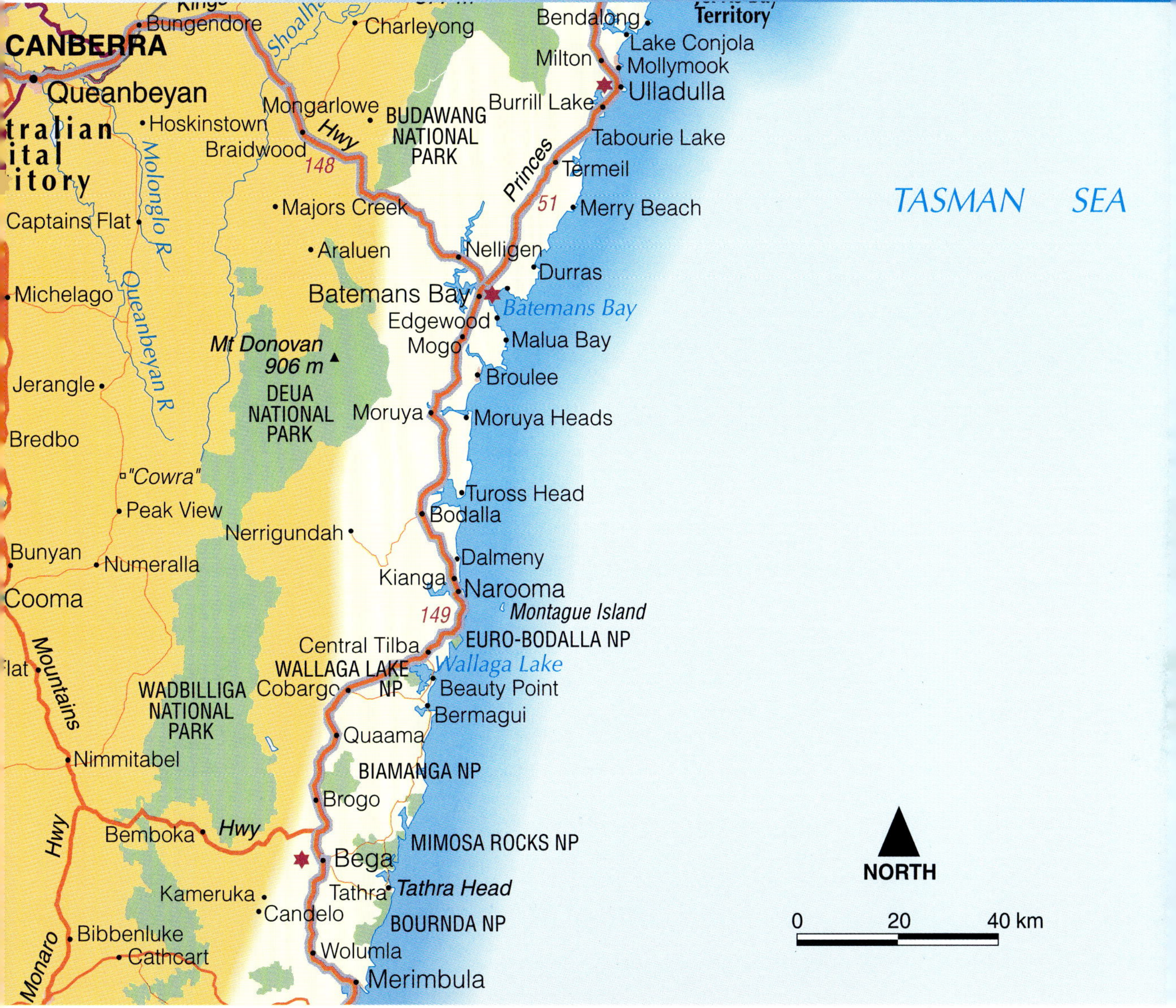

Visitor Information

The Eurobodalla Visitor Information Centre, cnr Princes Highway and Beach Road, Batemans Bay, ✆(02) 4472 6900 or ✆1800 802 528, is open daily 9am-5pm (closed Christmas Day). Email them at info@naturecoast-tourism.com.au or visit their website located at www.naturecoast-tourism. com.au

Points of Interest

The population increases to approximately 90,000 during the peak holiday season (from about mid December to early February). Batemans Bay has **16 golden beaches**, with some sheltered calm waters. McKenzie's Beach is a small beach that has consistent small to medium waves, with the best area at Malua Bay, south of the Surf Club. To the north, there are several good beaches including South Durras near Wasp Head, and Depot, Pebbly and Merry beaches accessible through **Murramarang National Park**.

The **Clyde River**, which is quite a spectacular waterway, is navigable for 51km (32 miles) from Batemans Bay up into the hills. Regular cruises are available up to **Nelligen**, which boasts a number of historically significant buildings.

The MV ***Merinda*** offers a great time out on the Clyde River (✆4472 4052), or you can hire a boat in the town for your own 'explore and see', combined with a little fishing.

The area is well known for its **fishing**. Durras Lake, to the north of Batemans Bay, has flathead, whiting and bream, and various points and bays between there and North Head offer other good spots. Up from the town near the oyster beds and the mangrove flats on the Clyde River, many people catch whiting, mulloway and bream. There is also quite a deal of fishing from the bank around the town. To the south, Malua Bay and Pretty Point are perhaps the most popular spots.

There are many **National Parks** and **forests** in the region, and maps are available from the Visitors Centre. The nearest one to Batemans Bay is Murramarang, which lies between South Durras and North Head.

The Birdland Animal Park at 55 Beach Road is open 9.30am-4pm daily. It includes 'Wombat World', snake demonstrations, an animal nursery, a koala exhibit, and a scale model train. Admission is $8 adults, $5 children and $7 for families, ✆4472 5364.

The **Historical Society Museum** is in the old court house, cnr Beach Road and Orient Street, and is open Thu-Sat 1pm-4pm, ✆4472 8993.

The **Mogo Goldfields**, on the Tomakin Road near Mogo Village 15km (9 miles) from town, are open weekend and school holidays, 10am-4pm. There is a guided tour of the old underground gold mine. You can camp here with all the amenities, ✆4471 7381. The Village is open most of the time and depicts a bygone era. It is well-known for its art and craft shops.

Festivals

The Neptune Festival is held each November.

Facilities

Boat, catamaran and sailboard hire, golf, tennis, lawn bowls and ten-pin bowling are all provided for in the area.

Outlying Attractions

Burrill Lake

Situated 5km (3 miles) south of Ulladulla, Burrill Lake is crossed by the Princes Highway at its eastern arm, but the main expanse reaches inland almost to the township of Milton. The inlet and beach are to the east of the Highway, and if you take the road to Dolphin Point and follow Seaside Parade you will come to the picnic area, rock platforms and popular fishing spots. Accommodation is available in caravan parks, motels and holiday units close to the lake and beach.

Burrill Lake offers boating, sailing, lake and beach fishing, surfing, swimming, windsurfing and prawning in season. Boats can be hired, and there are three launching ramps. A boat hire service, ✆4454 0951 operates from the reserve on the foreshores in Moore Street.

At **Bungalow Park**, you can feed the lorikeets, which arrive at 8am and 3pm (during daylight saving 9am and 4pm), or play mini-golf on a course which is a replica of the Mollymook Hilltop Golf Course. There are also boats available for hire, ✆4455 1621.

Moruya

The town of Moruya is 27km (17 miles) south of Batemans Bay on the Princes Highway. It has some fine old buildings, including the Wesleyan Church built in 1864 with local granite. The airport, which caters for the area, is on the north headland of the river entrance. South Moruya has a fine surf beach.

Accommodation is not plentiful in the area, since Batemans Bay to the north and Narooma in the south provide such facilities.

The area has excellent **fishing** in the Deua River with its mangrove swamps, and along the various coastal headlands. **Surfing** is great from Moruya Heads to Congo, North Head, Broulee South, North Broulee, Pink Rocks (off the north face of Broulee Island - experienced riders only, 6m waves) and Mossy Point near the mouth of the Tomago River.

Behind Moruya, along the Araluen Road, is the 81,158 ha (200,460 acres) **Deua National Park** which extends up the coastal ranges to Batemans Bay. You can try hiking - good luck and be sure to let the ranger know your plans.

Moruya has an **Historical Museum** in 85 Campbell Street, open Mon & Fri 11am-3pm and on Saturdays 11am-1pm (during peak Christmas and Easter seasons it open daily). Admission is $2 adults and 50 cents for children.

Each Saturday from 9am the **Moruya Country Markets** are held in Shore Street, and the **Congo Crafts Gallery**, 4474 2931, is open Wed-Mon 11am-5pm during school holidays, but it's best to phone beforehand.

Moruya boasts a speedway, and a horse racing complex together with golf courses, tennis and bowling clubs.

Bodalla

24km (15 miles) south along the Princes Highway is the town of Bodalla, made famous by Bega cheese which uses it as a brand name. The **All Saints Church** is one of several photogenic buildings in this attractive little town. Just before Bodalla is the turnoff to **Tuross Head**, where you can hire boats for fishing and boating on the lake of the same name.

Narooma

This town is 44km (27 miles) south of Moruya, on the estuary of the Wagonga River. It is another popular fishing resort with excellent beaches for surfing (Mystery Bay, Handkerchief Beach, Narooma Main Beach, Bar Beach, Dalmeny Point, Potato Point, Blackfellows Point and Tuross Head). It has a narrow channel that leads to a small harbour. As with the other towns on the south coast, it offers excellent bushwalks and is a family holiday area.

Montague Island, 8km (5 miles) offshore, is a flora and fauna reserve, and the area around there is well known for its game fishing. The island is the halfway point in the Sydney to Hobart Yacht Race.

Contact the Narooma Visitors Centre, Princes Highway, open every day except Christmas Day 9am-5pm, (02) 4476 2881 or 1800 802 528, with any queries, or to assist in booking accommodation, restaurants or tours. Alternatively, you can email them at the address: eurovcn@acr.net.au or visit the website at www.naturecoast-tourism.com.au

Central Tilba

21km (13 miles) south is Central Tilba, which neighbors Tilba Tilba. Both of these tiny settlements are in the shadow of an ancient volcano, Mount Dromedary. Situated in rather pleasant hilly country at the base of **Mt Dromedary**, Central Tilba has become a tourist spot with art and craft shops, an old wooden general store, a cobblers cottage, a pub, and a quaint restaurant with displays of the traditional crafts. A pleasant day excursion from Narooma.

Cobargo

This village is 19km from Central Tilba. It has various cottage industries of pottery and leather, art and craft galleries, and a pub. You can turn off here for Bermagui, or it can be reached by turning off at Tilba Tilba and going along the coast road and crossing Wallaga Lake.

Bermagui

Located on the coast 18km (11 miles) from Cobargo, Bermagui is the mecca for big game fishing in New South Wales, and was made famous in the 1930s by the novelist Zane Grey. Today a large fishing fleet operates out of Bermagui, and game fishermen from all over come for the sport between November and May.

Charter boats are available (for example, Blue Water Charters, Endevour Drive, 6493 4540) for pleasure cruising or game fishing, and the harbour has a boat ramp and provision for trailer parking. Swimming and surfing are again the other main diversions - at Blue Pool, Horseshoe Bay and Wallaga Lake. Water skiing is the go on Wallaga Lake.

Bega

The town of Bega is 170km (106 miles) south of Batemans Bay, and 80km (50 miles) south of Narooma. It is the commercial centre of the district with a population above 4000. The district is famous for its dairy industry and cheeses.

The **Bega Cheese Heritage Centre** on the northern side of the Bega River, Lagoon Street, 6491 7777, is open for inspection and tasting daily 9am-5pm.

The Bega Family Museum, cnr Auckland and Bega Streets, is open Mon-Fri 10.30am-4pm, Sat 10am-12pm, 6492 1453.

Brogo Valley's Rotolactor is 23km (14 miles) north of Bega on Baldwin Road, Brogo, and is open to the public Mon & Wed 2-5pm, with milking at 3pm, 6493 8330.

The **Grevillea Estate** winery and vineyards is on the Buckajo Road, 6492 3006.

Mumbulla Falls Picnic Area, 20km (12 miles) north of Bega off the Princes Highway along a gravel road, is a very pleasant spot for picnics and a swim. Because of the gravel road, only try it in dry weather.

The largest farm in the Bega Valley is **Kameruka Estate** which is classified by the National Trust. The homestead is set in extensive gardens, with its own church and clocktower. It is open daily, 6492 0509.

Candelo Village, situated 20km (12 miles) south-west, still retains its old world charm with galleries and restaurants. It is a pleasant place for afternoon tea after a short drive.

Mimosa Rocks National Park, sprawls across its 17km coastal stretch north of Tathra and east of Mt Gearge Mountain. It is a perfect site for a picnic, and for enjoying the natural wonders of landscape and wildlife. Camping areas are also available, and it is best to discuss plans and ideas with the Tourist Information Centre, 6492 3313.

Green Dairy Country, Bega

The Sapphire Coast Tourist Information Centre, Office 2, 163 Auckland Street, Bega, ✆(02) 6492 3313 or ✆1800 663 012, tends to be the arrival and departure point for coaches. info@ sapphirecoast.com.au, or www. sapphirecoast. com.au

Tathra

Tathra is a quiet seaside village 18km (11 miles) east of Bega, with a beautiful beach and great fishing spots. Tathra offers the best of both worlds: beautiful beaches with ocean activities as well as the opportunity to explore the wildlife of nearby **Mimosa and Bournda National Parks**. There is a ***campground*** at Bournda National Park with very basic facilities for $10-15 a night for two, ✆6495 4130. Tathra Tourist Centre on Tathra Wharf, Wharf Road, ✆6494 4062, is the best place to find out what you wish to know. The local people are very friendly and helpful.

Merimbula

This flourishing resort town on Lake Merimbula is 26km (16 miles) south of Bega. Merimbula is an activity-based centre, with surfing on Main Beach, Short Point and Tura Beach, sailboarding and water skiing on Lake Merimbula, golf at the 27-hole Pambula-Merimbula golf course, lawn bowls at the ubiquitous bowling clubs and a variety of other activities - tennis, canoeing, horseriding and cycling. It has an RSL club with 'pokies' and live entertainment.

The **Magic Mountain Family Recreation Park**, with its water slides, mini Grand Prix race track and mountain toboggan slide, is just north

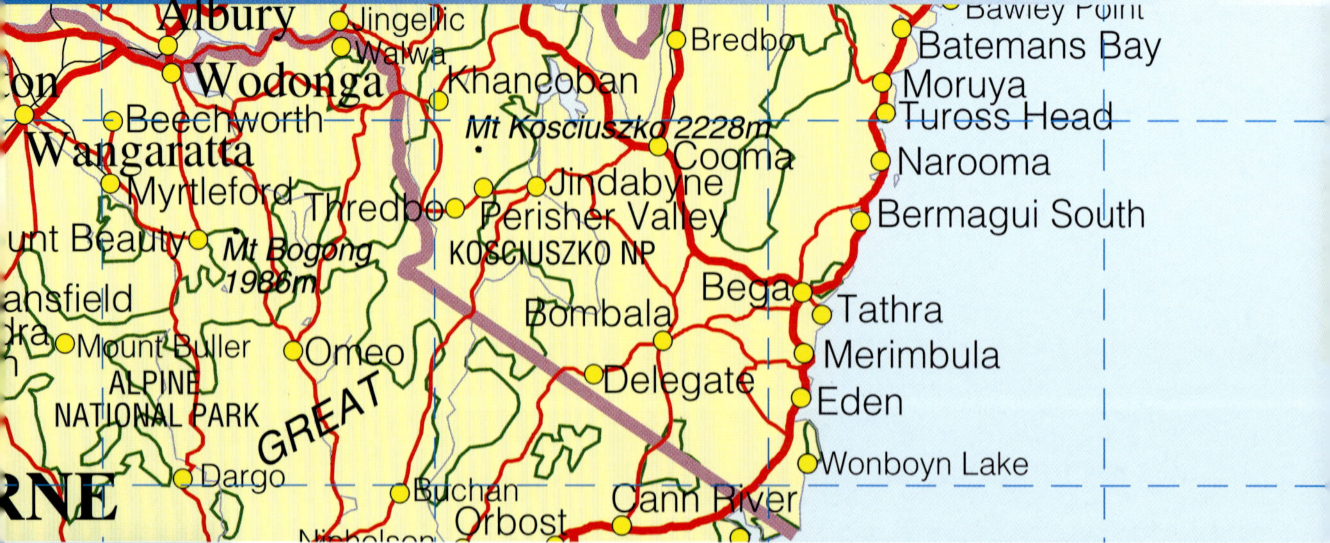

of the town on Coast Drive, ✆6495 2299. The park ⌚opens at 10am and admission is ✪$22 adults, $14 children 5-7 years old and $18 children aged 8-11.

The area also boasts an **Aquarium** (Lake Street, ✆6495 4446), **Yellow Pinch Wildlife Park** (Princes Highway, ✆6494 9225), **Milingandi Leisure Farm** (✆6495 6125) and a **Museum** in Main Street.

Contact the Tourist Information Centre on Beach Street, ✆6495 1129, ⌚open Mon-Fri 9am-5pm, Sat-Sun 9am-1pm, for information on available accommodation.

Eden

Eden is situated some 61km (38 miles) south of Bega, on Twofold Bay. A former whaling station, it is now a deep water fishing port, and the fishing and timber industries are of utmost importance to the survival of the town.

The town's **Killer Whale Museum**, 94 Imlay Street, ✆6496 2094, gives an overview of Eden's history, and houses the skeleton of 'Old Tom' a legendary whale from the area. Also featured is the **Seaman's Memorial Wall**, commemorating those lost at sea. The museum has limited opening times daily.

The **Ben Boyd National Park** flanks Twofold Bay to the north, with its famous Red Cliffs, and borders historic Boyd's Tower to the south. You can camp in the park, and at East Boyd Bay the Forestry Commission runs the Edrom Lodge for students.

For more information on accommodation and things to do, contact the Eden Tourist Information Office, Princes Highway (at the roundabout), ✆6496 1953. It is ⌚open Mon-Fri 10am-4pm, Sat-Sun 10am-noon.

Wonboyn Lake

The locals are proud of Wonboyn Lake, some 30km (19 miles) south of Eden, and surrounded by Ben Boyd National Park and Nadgee Nature Reserve. In addition to the stunning scenery of **Ben Boyd** and **Nadgee**, Wonboyn has a reputation for the finest lake fishing on the Sapphire Coast.

New South Wales: An Overview

Australia is an island continent in the South Pacific Ocean. It is the smallest conti nent and the largest island in the world with a coastline of 19,650km. Its nearest neighbours are New Zealand and Papua New Guinea, while East Timor and Indonesia are a little further away, off the north-western coast.

The country has an area of 7,682,300 square kilometres and is divided into six states - New South Wales, Queensland, Victoria, Tasmania, South Australia and Western Australia - and two territories - Northern Territory and Australian Capital Territory.

The capital of Australia is Canberra in the Australian Capital Territory (ACT). The capital cities of the states are as follows:
New South Wales - Sydney
Victoria - Melbourne
Queensland - Brisbane
Tasmania - Hobart
South Australia - Adelaide
Western Australia - Perth
Northern Territory - Darwin.

History of New South Wales

In the 1640s Australia's east coast was chartered by the Dutch and dubbed New Holland then 130 years later an englishman Captain Cook sailed into what is now called Sydney Harbour. He called the area 'New South Wales' and claimed Australia for the British. It's colonisation some 18 years later was hastened by America's Declaration of Independence ending two decades of British rule there. Britain was no longer able to transport convicts to North America, so the decision was made to found a colony in New South Wales.

The First Fleet, commissioned by Thomas Townshend, Baron Sydney, set sail for Botany Bay on May 13, 1787, led by Captain Arthur Phillip. The fleet assembled at Mother Bank, the Isle of Wright, later arriving at Cape Town to take aboard plants, fruit trees and animals. The HMS Supply, along with the ships Scarborough, Friendship and Alexander sailed ahead of the fleet, first sighting the NSW coast on the 3rd of January, 1788.

They arrived at Botany Bay on the 18th of January, where upon anchoring, it was discovered there was no fresh water locally available. When the rest of the fleet arrived on the 19th, much to Phillip's surprise, it was decided to go further north, to Port Jackson (now also known as Sydney Harbour).

There they were to find a lush, pristine forest in a cove fed by a stream (now called the Tank Stream), where it was decided they would settle. A formal flag raising ceremony was held by Arthur Phillip on the shore to proclaim the Colony of New South Wales, in the name of the King of England on the 26th of January, 1788.

Captain Arthur Phillip was later to name the cove they landed at Sydney Cove (now Circular Quay), in honor of Thomas Townshend, Baron Sydney (1733-1800), the minister responsible for the Colony. Later usage of the name dropped 'Cove' and the area became known as Sydney.

Sydney began its life as a penal colony, with

a total of 568 male and 191 female convicts with 13 children, 206 marines with 26 wives and 13 children, and 20 officials having made the voyage.

Their earliest huts were composed of cabbage-tree palm, while the convicts were housed in huts made of boards wattled with slender twigs and plastered with clay. By 1790, however, there were 40 convicts employed making bricks and tiles, 50 brickie labourers, and 4 stonemasons. The total convict population that year was 730 persons, with 413 having some medical treatment. In fact free settlers did not begin arriving until 1793.

There was a shortage of coinage in NSW, and rum, an easily produced spirit from sugar cane, began to be used as currency. Needless to say, this was to slow Sydney's development considerably, as it is all too easy, for soldiers and convicts, to drink compared to trading it for food, clothes and supplies. The colony, not making money, could not pay its bills nor buy the many things it needed from elsewhere.

The soldiers of the NSW corps, whose officers had the monopoly on this endless supply of rum, dominated the early governers of the colony. Originally formed to protect the fledging colony from perceived threats of other European powers, they also served as police.

With the arrival of Governor Lachlan Macquarie in 1810 (along with the 87th Regiment) the NSW Rum Corps were sent packing back to England.

The colony, with the population of Sydney being about 10,000 metamorphosed. Much of what you see in Sydney today is a result of Macquarie's leadership and vision.

The coins that the original settlers had, were the George III twopence, called the Cartwheel penny because of its size. In 1812, in order to relieve the problems caused by the lack of coins, Governor Macquarie bought Spanish dollars from India.

He then had holes cut in them to discourage exportation. These well known Australian coins were called the Holey Dollar for the larger part of the coin, while the piece cut from the middle was called the Dump. Declared legal tender September 30th, 1813, the Dump was worth about 15 pence, while the Holey Dollar was valued at 5 shillings sterling.

With the crossing of the Blue Mountains in 1813 and the subsequent discovery of the prosperous hinterland, the way was finally clear for the growth and development of modern Sydney.

Transportation of convicts to New South Wales (NSW) was finally abolished in 1840 and shortly afterwards, in 1842, Sydney was declared a city. The population grew rapidly during this period, helped by the discovery of gold and the gold rush of 1850 - one year after the Californian gold rush of 1849. Australia received many American and Chinese immigrants at the same time.

In 1901 the six British colonies in Australia formed a federation to become the Commonwealth of Australia. This marks the period of the modern country. Sydney continued to grow and by 1925 became a metropolis of 1 million people. This grew to 2 million by 1963.

Today Sydney has diverse demographics with people from over one hundred countries contributing to its population of nearly 4 million.

Australian Population

During the 1950s and 1960s, people wishing to migrate from Europe and the United States were provided with assisted passage by the Australian government. However, it was not until the late 1960s that restricted entry to Australia from Asia was eased. In the last 40 years Australian society has undergone a tremendous change with now one in four people being a migrant or the child of a migrant.

Australia since the 1970s has become aware of its presence in South-east Asia. The countries of the region are starting to have more of an impact on Australian life. Many new migrants are Asian, and society reflects this blend of European and Asian cultures.

Approximately 85 per cent of the 18,783,600 inhabitants live in urban areas. The east coast of Australia is the most populous because of the fertile plain east of the Great Dividing Range of mountains. The major cities are the state capitals, and the most populous state is New South Wales with 6,173,000 people, followed by Victoria with 4,533,300 people.

The social environment is heavily influenced by the US media and movies. California has a lot in common with Australia's east coast.

Australian Holidays

Christmas, New Year and Anzac Day (April 25) are the only holidays that are held at the same time throughout the country. Easter is a moveable feast that can fall in either March or April. Australia Day is accepted by all as January 26, but some states have their public holiday on the exact day, and others choose the closest Monday, so as to have a long weekend break.

The whole of Australia stops for five minutes on the first Tuesday in November for the running of the Melbourne Cup horse race, but only people living in Melbourne have the day off work.

In addition, school holidays are different in each state, although the long Christmas break is the most popular holiday time, and runs roughly from the end of the second week in December to the end of January.

It is a good idea to check with the Visitor Information Centres in the cities and towns before or upon arrival, as prices and availability of services will be affected on public holidays.

Australian Language

Australians speak English, although due to the many people from other countries that have come to live in the country, it is not unusual to hear conversations in other languages when travelling by public transport. Melbourne, for instance, has the second largest Greek population of any city in the world, surpassed only by Athens.

Like the English, Australians call 'gas' petrol and 'fries' chips; but you will find links to the US are perhaps stronger, with McDonalds, Pizza Hut and KFC firmly established in every suburb. There are a few words and phrases that are unique to Australia and in common usage, and dictionaries of Australian slang are available at local bookshops. Australians do say "G'Day", and if stressing authenticity or the truth of a statement, they might say that something is "fair dinkum" or "dinky-di".

Australian Religion

The vast majority of Australians belong to the Christian Churches. There is only a slight margin between Roman Catholics and Anglicans, whose numbers hover around 26% each, reflecting the influence of migrating Irish and Italian Catholics, and the steady flow of English Anglicans into the country. All other religions and sects are present in Australia. Jews, Hindus and Buddhists are all represented strongly on account of the post World War II influx and other political developments since, which opened access to Australian shores. By and large there is peaceful coexistence, and the multicultural composition of society is typically celebrated and embraced.

Australia: General Info

Appendices

Entry Regulations

All travellers to Australia need a valid passport, and visitors of all nationalities, except New Zealand, must obtain a visa before arrival. These are available at Australian Embassies, High Commissions and Consular offices listed in local telephone directories. No vaccinations are required.

Before you land you will be given immigration forms as well as Customs and Agriculture declarations. As a general rule you must declare all goods of plant or animal origin. Quarantine officers will inspect these items and return them to you if no disease or pest risk is involved. Even if they are not prohibited, some may need to be treated before being allowed entry.

Each incoming traveller over the age of 18 years is allowed duty free goods to the value of $400, plus 1125mL of liquor and 250g of tobacco products. These items must not be intended for commercial purposes and you must carry them with you through customs.

Exit Regulations

There is a Passenger Movement Charge or Departure Tax of $30 for everyone over the age of 12 years, but this is generally prepaid with inclusion in the price of an airline ticket. People taking money out of the country, above the value of A$10,000 in Australian and/or foreign currency, must file a report with Customs. For more information on Customs or Quarantine Regulations, visit the following web sites:

www.aqis.gov.au for Quarantine
www.customs.gov.au for Customs

GST Refund

Overseas visitors qualify for a part refund of any GST they pay for items bought in Australia, if the total purchases made at any one business exceeds $300, and the purchases were made no more than 30 days before the date of departure. Present the goods, a tax invoice, your passport and a boarding pass at the TRS (Tax Refund Scheme) booth in the international airport you are leaving from. The items on which you are allowed to claim back GST are only the hand-held items you intend to carry with you onto the plane. Present your documents for verification and you will be given the refund to which you are entitled. If the total is less than $200 you can ask for the refund to be made in cash, otherwise it will be in the form of a mailed cheque or a credit arrangement. Foreign currency will also be accommodated in this transaction. Note that any general consumption purchases made within Australia (for example, hotel accommodation or meals) do not qualify for a refund claim.

Be aware that there is no GST imposed on duty-free items sold in duty-free stores.

For further details and enquiries, phone the Australian Customs Information Line on 1300 363 263.

Embassies

Nearly seventy countries have diplomatic representation in Canberra. Some missions are called Embassies, and others who represent countries belonging to the Commonwealth, are called High Commissions. There are also Consuls in the State capitals, and their addresses can be found in the local White Pages telephone directory.

Money

The Australian Currency is decimal, with the dollar as the basic unit. Notes come in a colourful array of $100, $50, $20, $10 and $5 denominations, with minted coins for lesser amounts - gold $1 and $2 coins, and silver 50c, 20c, 10c and 5c.

Currency exchange facilities are available at international airports, and most banks and large hotels.

The Australian dollar tends to fluctuate quite frequently. For the most accurate and up-to-date currency conversions, it is recommended that you use the simple and easy facility at www. xe.com/ucc

Travellers cheques are one of the most convenient ways of carrying money when travelling, and these can be exchanged at any bank, large hotels, and in large department stores.

Automatic Teller Machines are another possibility. These machines are widely available in Australia, both in the cities and in country towns, and most are open 24 hours a day. Some banks allow access to overseas savings accounts via networks such as Cirrus and Plus, but it's best to check with your bank before departure to see if this is available.

If you are intending to stay for any great length of time, you might consider opening a local bank account. Different banks have different withdrawal limits, but it is generally about $1000 per day. All Australian banks operate this type of account.

Eating Out

In every town and city in this guide we have included a selection of restaurants, and have stated whether they are licensed or unlicensed (BYO). Just to confuse everyone, some restaurants are both, so if you are unsure, check when reserving your table. Without going into the licensing laws of why this is so, here is a short explanation of how it will affect patrons.

A licensed restaurant has a wine list, and can provide beer, mixed drinks, ports, liqueurs, etc. Patrons are not allowed to provide their own drinks.

A BYO restaurant does not have a licence, so you Bring Your Own wine or beer or whatever. Glasses are provided, and a corkage fee (for opening the bottles!) may be charged, which is usually around $1.50 per bottle. The restaurant usually has a selection of soft drinks, mineral water and fruit juices.

A restaurant that is licensed and BYO can provide alcohol, but you have the choice of bringing your own wine (which is often cheaper), but you are not allowed to bring your own beer or mixed drinks.

Liquor stores in Australia are called 'bottle shops'. Many hotels have one, usually with its own street entrance, and there's one in every shopping centre.

Miscellaneous

Telephones

If you are calling any Australian number from overseas, dial 61 for the country code and then a single number for the area code (for example, when calling Sydney, in New South Wales, you would dial 2), then the eight digit number. Area codes refer to states rather than districts. If calling from interstate, use the following prefix before any number you dial to: New South Wales- (02), Australian Capital Territory- (02), Victoria- (03), Tasmania- (03), Queensland- (07), South Australia- (08), Western Australia- (08), Northern Territory- (08)

Public telephones are easy to find in the cities and suburbs on street corners, in hotels, shops, cafes, and so on. A local call costs 40c from a phone box, but may be dearer from the privately leased phones outside shops. Emergency calls are free.

For international calls, you can dial direct to nearly 20 countries from almost any hotel, home, office or public phone in Australia. Simply dial 0011 + country code + area code + local number. Country Direct is the easiest

Appendices

way of making international telephone card and reverse charge (collect) calls. Upon dialling your Country Direct number, you are immediately put in touch with your own country's operator who will then connect the call. To find out your country's number ✆1800 801 800 (free call).

Newspapers

Morning and afternoon newspapers are available everywhere, with each state having their own press, as well as selling the national paper *The Australian*.

Radio and Television

There is a national radio station and a national television channel, both of which are run by the Australian Broadcasting Commission (ABC). The capital cities have many AM and FM radio stations, and several free-to-air television channels. The television channels are: 2 (the national channel), 7 (commercial), 9 (commercial), 10 (commercial) and 0 (SBS, which is government sponsored.

Post

Australia has an efficient postal service, and postcards sent by airmail to overseas countries cost $1. To send a letter by Air Mail (weighing up to 50g) to the Asia Pacific Zone costs $1 and to the Rest of the World, $1.50.

Time Zones

Australia is divided into three time zones: **Australian Eastern Standard Time, which covers Queensland, NSW, Victoria and Tasmania, is GMT plus 10 hours;** Australian Central Standard Time, which covers South Australia and the Northern Territory, is GMT plus 9.5 hours; and Australian Western Standard Time, which covers Western Australia, is GMT plus 8 hours.

During summer, some of the states operate on daylight saving putting their clocks ahead one hour on a designated Sunday morning in October, and back one hour on a Sunday in March. For NSW, Victoria and South Australia, it is the last Sunday in October and the first Sunday in March, but Tasmania remains on Summer Time until the end of March. Western Australia, Queensland and the Northern Territory do not have daylight saving, so at those times there are five different time zones in the country.

Credit Cards

American Express, Diners Club, Visa, Bank Card and MasterCard are widely accepted and usually signposted at participating retail outlets.

Beaches

Australian beaches are famous throughout the world, and they certainly live up to their reputation. All have white sandy shores, and rolling surf. Some offer better waves than others, and the bigger beaches are usually divided into sections for swimmers and for board riders.

The Surf Lifesaving Clubs which patrol the beaches during summer are often staffed by voluntary workers, young people who give up their weekends and holidays to keep a watchful eye out for others. They put up flags to show which part of the beach is safest for swimmers, and there are usually signs requesting people to swim between the flags. This is good advice - don't ignore it.

Electricity

Domestic electricity supply throughout Australia is 230-250 volts, AC 50 cycles. Standard three pin plugs are fitted to domestic appliances. 110v appliances, such as hairdryers and contact lens sterilisers, cannot be used without a transformer.

Videos

Australia uses the PAL system of videos. For the US market, tapes must be the NTSC system.

Internet General Information Sources

For general information on Australia, the best site to explore is
www.australia.com,
which is the official web page of the Australian Tourist Commission.

For phone numbers nationwide, go to:
www.whitepages.com.au
www.yellowpages.com.au
www.colourpages.com.au

Travel Information

How To Get to New South Wales

To reach New South Wales and Australia from overseas, visitors must come either by air or sea.

Before booking a flight, it is best to shop around for any cheaper fares that may be available. Your travel agent will be able to advise. You may also be able to find a Package Tour that meets all your requirements. These save you money because the companies that organise them can obtain cheaper fares and accommodation prices, as they are booking for groups. Again, your travel agent is the best person to ask.

Accommodation

Australia has well-developed hotel and motel accommodation in cities, resorts and rural areas. A typical room is usually spotlessly clean and has air-conditioning, a private bathroom, tea and coffee making facilities, a telephone, television, and a small refrigerator. Note that some small hotels may not have a private bathroom for every room, and it is best to enquire when booking. Because of the climate, many hotels and motels have small outdoor swimming pools.

Although the rooms are often the same, there is a difference between a hotel and a motel in Australia. A hotel must have a public bar among its facilities; motels often provide a bar for paying guests and invited friends, although they are not obliged to do this. Most hotels and motels have a dining room or restaurant.

Premier class hotels include names familiar throughout the world - Hilton, Sheraton, Hyatt, Nikko, Holiday Inn, Intercontinental, Marriott, Ibis and Mercure, can all be found in Australia's major cities.

Motels have generally been developed to meet the needs of travelling motorists and are located in cities, towns and resorts, and along the major highways.

The majority of hotels and motels offer accommodation on a room-only basis, but some include one or more meals in their tariff. Enquire about any meals that might be automatically included in the room price and check whether you can pay just for the room, if this suits your travel schedule better. For example, there is no point paying for lunch if you plan on leaving before daybreak, or for a dinner if you know you won't reach your destination until late.

Youth Hostels in most parts of the country offer an inexpensive alternative for budget conscious travellers. Membership of the Youth Hostels Association is required, 9261 1111. They have a comprehensive internet site showing all the hostel locations at www.yha.com.au or you can send an email to the address: yha@yhansw.org.au

Most towns and holiday resorts have caravan parks and camping grounds with shower and toilet facilities, at very reasonable rates. Caravan parks usually have some cabins or on-site vans available for overnight or longer stays. This is a comparatively inexpensive form of accommodation, but it usually means that you have to have your own bed linen, blankets and pillows.

Travelling Within Australia

By Air

The major interstate carrier is Qantas, ✆13 1313. Virgin Blue, ✆13 6789 also offers limited services. Both offer reduced fares and 'specials' from time to time, and it is best to find out what is available when you intend to travel.

At the time of printing, the airlines listed above are in the process of significant changes, so it is best to check with an AFTA travel agent, listed in the phone book, about regional flights at the time of your trip.

By Rail

Train travel is possible between Sydney, Brisbane and Melbourne. Most towns in between are also linked, as well as those in popular outlying areas of each state. Rail Australia offers two rail passes that can only be purchased outside of Australia:

Austrail Flexipass - 8 (✪$550), 15 (✪$800), 22 (✪$110) or 29 (✪$1440) days travel in 6 months with unlimited stopovers, in economy class.

Austrail Pass - unlimited travel for 14 (✪$660), 21 (✪$860) or 30 (✪$1035) days consecutively anywhere in Australia, including metropolitan services, in economy class.

Passes that are available within Australia include:

East Coast Discovery Pass - travel one-way with unlimited stopovers in a six month period: Brisbane to Cairns (✪$160); Sydney to Brisbane/Gold Coast (✪$94); Sydney to Cairns (✪$248); Melbourne to Brisbane/Gold Coast (✪$176); Melbourne to Cairns (✪$228). Note that the above rates apply to travel in the opposite direction.

Countrylink Discovery Pass - unlimited use of Countrylink trains and connecting coaches for 14 (✪$165), 30 (✪$198), 90 (✪$220), or 180 (✪$330) days.

Queensland Road Rail Pass - unlimited use of Queensland Rail services (long-distance) and McCaffertys Coaches for any 10 days over a 60 day period (✪$286) or any 20 days over a 90 day period (✪$374).

To get the latest prices, visit the Rail Australia web site at 👁www.railaustralia .com.au/pass_ rates.htm

By Bus

The major interstate coach companies are Greyhound Pioneer and McCafferty's. Tickets for both companies are now interchangeable.

McCafferty's can be contacted on ✆13 1499, or 👁www.mcaffertys.com.au

Aussie Passes: a pre-selected travel route along which you can stop off at designated points.

All Australian
Validity: 365 days, Cost: ✪$2100 full fare, ✪$1790 concession.

Aussie Highlights
Route: Melbourne - Sydney - Brisbane - Cairns - Uluru (Ayers Rock) - Adelaide - Canberra and many other outback, rural and coastal destinations in between.
Validity: 365 days, Cost: ✪$1255 full fare, ✪$1066 concession.

Sunseeker
Validity: 183 days, Cost: ✪$411 full fare, ✪$349 concession.

Best of the East
Validity: 365 days, Cost: ✪$1026 full fare, ✪$872 concession.

Coast to Coast
Validity: 183 days, Cost: ✪$424 full fare, ✪$360 concession.

Reef & Rock
Validity: 183 days, Cost: ✪$596 full fare, ✪$507 concession.

Outback & Reef
Validity: 183 days, Cost: ✪$726 full fare, ✪$617 concession.

An Aussie Kilometre Pass, valid for 12 months, allows you to 'bulk buy' the distance you think you will need to cover for your holiday, at a rate designed to increase your value for money with every kilometre purchased. Prices range from ✪$281 for 2000km to ✪$1077 for 10,000km to ✪$1975 for 20,000km.

By Road

Australians drive on the left-hand side of the road, and the speed limit in built-up areas is 50km/h or 60km/h, and on the open road up to 110km/h.

In an effort to cut the number of road fatalities, Australia has random breath testing which is carried out by police officers either from a standard police car or from what are known locally as 'booze buses'. The allowable blood alcohol level varies from state to state, but is generally around 0.05, or two standard drinks in the first hour and only one during every subsequent hour. But since body tolerance levels differ, it is best simply not to drink if you expect to drive soon after.

Travelling to and around New South Wales

By Air

By Air

As Mentioned Above, the major interstate carrier is Qantas, 13 13 13. Virgin Blue, 13 6789 also offers services to New South Wales. Flight times and prices vary throughout the year, so it is best to examine them ahead of time.

By Rail

State Rail, (02) 8202 2000, operates a train service that links destinations around the State. City Rail(13 1500) covers suburban Sydney and extends to the Hunter, Central Coast, Blue Mountains, Southern Highlands and South Coast regions.

From Brisbane, Countrylink XPT trains run directly to Sydney daily. Alternatively, you can take the Coach to Murwillumbah and change to a connecting XPT to complete the journey From Melbourne, Countrylink XPT trains run direct to Sydney twice a day.

By Bus

Greyhound Pioneer, 13 2030, and McCaffertys 13 1499, have the following Return Services: Sydney/Thredbo, Sydney/Toowoomba, Sydney/Brisbane, Sydney/Canberra, Sydney/Adelaide and Sydney/Melbourne.

By Road

To get to Sydney, take the following route:

From Melbourne, via the Hume Highway (867km), via the Princess Highway (1032km).

From Brisbane, via the Pacific Highway (975km), or via the New England and Cunningham Highways (1008km).

From Adelaide, via the Sturt Highway (1427km), or via the Princess Highway (1936km).

From Darwin, via Tennant Creek, Mount Isa, Toowoomba, then New England Highway (4262km).

From Perth, via Great Eastern Highway, Eyre Highway, Sturt Highway and Hume Highway (3128km).

General Index

A

B

L

M

N

Maps Index

Bamaga
Weipa
Groote Eylandt
Gulf of Carpentaria
Cape York Peninsula
Great Barrier Reef
Laura
Cooktown
Daintree
Mossman
Port Douglas
Cairns
Mornington Island
Karumba
Burketown
Normanton
Atherton
Ravenshoe
Barkly Tableland
Great Dividing Ranges
Magnetic Island
Townsville
Threeways
Tennant Creek
Mt Isa
Cloncurry
Bowen
Airlie Beach
Whitsunday Islands
Wauchope
Mackay
Barrow Creek
Winton
QUEENSLAND
Longreach
Alice Springs
Emerald
Rockhampton
Blackwater
Gladstone
Blackall
Simpson Desert
Bundaberg
Hervey Bay
Fraser Island
Maryborough
Gympie
Noosa Heads
Charleville
Roma
Maroochydore
Caloundra
Toowoomba
BRISBANE
Lake Eyre
Warwick
Coolangatta
Maree
AUSTRALIA
Lightning Ridge
Lismore
Andamooka
Leigh Creek
Bourke
Moree
Grafton
Woomera
Armidale
Coffs Harbour
NEW SOUTH WALES
Hawker
Tamworth
Port Augusta
Quorn
Broken Hill
Port Macquarie
Whyalla
Dubbo
Taree
Peterborough
Port Pirie
Parkes
Lithgow
Newcastle
Forbes
Bathurst
Wyong
Clare
Burra
Mildura
Blue Mts
SYDNEY
Gosford
Maitland
Renmark
Berri
Griffith
Mittagong
Wollongong
Gawler
ADELAIDE
Murray Bridge
Wagga Wagga
Goulburn
Nowra
CANBERRA
Kangaroo Island
Barossa Valley
Echuca
Albury
A.C.T.
Ulladulla
Shepparton
Wodonga
Batemans Bay
Bendigo
Cooma
Ararat
Ballarat
Bright
Bega
PACIFIC OCEAN
Mt Gambier
MELBOURNE
Eden
Warragul
Snowy Mts
Portland
Geelong
Moe
Lakes Entrance
Warrnambool
Forster
VICTORIA
King Island
Bass Strait
Flinders Island
Burnie
Devonport
Launceston
Queenstown
TASMANIA
HOBART
Southport
Port Arthur